ANNE DUDEN
A REVOLUTION OF WORDS

GERMAN MONITOR No. 56
General Editor: Ian Wallace

International Advisory Board

Anna Chiarloni	Università di Torino
Geoffrey V. Davis	TU Aachen
Gert-Joachim Glaeßner	Humboldt-Universität, Berlin
Gerd Labroisse	Vrije Universiteit, Amsterdam

ANNE DUDEN
A REVOLUTION OF WORDS

Approaches to her Fiction, Poetry and Essays

Edited by
Heike Bartel and Elizabeth Boa

Amsterdam - New York, NY 2003

The paper on which this book is printed meets the requirements of "ISO 9706:1994, Information and documentation - Paper for documents - Requirements for permanence".

ISBN: 90-420-1134-3 (bound)
©Editions Rodopi B.V., Amsterdam - New York, NY 2003
Printed in The Netherlands

Acknowledgements

The editors and publisher wish to thank Anne Duden for her kind permission to publish the poem 'Herzgänge'.

The editors and publisher wish also to thank Cambridge University Press for permission to print material in the essay by Stephanie Bird adapted from her forthcoming book, *National Identity: Ingeborg Bachmann, Anne Duden, Emine Sevgi Özdamar*, which is due to appear with Cambridge University Press in 2003.

Most of the essays in this volume originated as papers for a symposium on the work of Anne Duden held in May 2001 at the University of Nottingham. The editors would like to thank the GOETHE-INSTITUT INTER NATIONES and the University of Nottingham for generous financial assistance both for the symposium and this volume.

On behalf of the contributors and everyone else who attended the symposium, we wish also to extend our warmest thanks to Anne Duden whose active engagement in discussion and readiness to enter into dialogue with those giving papers made the symposium such a memorable event. Thanks are due too for Anne Duden's generosity with her time and for her patience and good humour in answering questions, which have greatly helped in the preparation of this volume.

University of Nottingham

Heike Bartel and Elizabeth Boa

Table of Contents

'Herzgänge'
Anne Duden   i

List of Abbreviations   ix

Introduction: notes from a symposium - notes towards *Hingegend*
Elizabeth Boa   1

‚Gestalt aus Bewegung'
Beobachtungen zu Anne Dudens Kurzprosa und Essayistik
Dirk Göttsche   19

Trauma and Terrorism:
the problem of violence in the work of Anne Duden
Margaret Littler   43

Considering Ethics in the Short Prose of Anne Duden
Stephanie Bird   62

Material Movements in Texts by Anne Duden
Teresa Ludden   72

Visions of Nature in Texts by Anne Duden
Metaphor, Metonym, Morphology
Juliet Wigmore   88

Grenzen der Übersetzung
Anne Dudens *Übergang* in englischer und französischer Sprache
Wiebke Sievers   102

An Easter of words
Steps towards a reading of Anne Duden's *Steinschlag*
Georgina Paul   123

‚Bilder […] / aus einem Deutschland / das nie existiert hat'
Ein Lektürevorschlag zum Anfang von Anne Dudens *Steinschlag*
Claudia Roth   **149**

‚Steinatem'
Zur Metaphorik des Atmens in Anne Dudens ‚Steinschlag'
Heike Bartel   **159**

Bibliography   **182**

Index   **187**

Notes on Contributors   **190**

Herzgänge

In Northumberland schon
war es das Ende.
Alles lag außer sich
in der Vergangenheit
zuckend aufschluchzend und winselnd.
Nur Stücke englischer Landschaft
und das auch nur tagsüber
waren erhaben
und die ausgetretenen Stufen der Nachttreppe
in Hexham Priory
sowie die azurne Turmuhr
diese leicht gewölbte aus der ausgezählten Ewigkeit
herausgetrennte Scheibe
scharf geschnittene Linse des Himmels
die auf allen Fotos an der Stunde
festhielt
die die Verlassende
verließ.

IHRE   letzten Tage
verbrachte ich in Northumberland
und es sollte mir bloß kein Ende
dazwischenkommen
und überhaupt keiner die Worte stören
an denen die Welt hängt
wie am seidenen Faden.

- AN DIE GÖTTER AN DIE SCHATTEN -
an alles hier Gewesene
das gehügelte Meer aus Moor und Heide
an das lichternde Grün und Rostrot
den Purpur und Zimtstaub ganzer Farnhänge
an das lange verblühte Wut- und Vernunftkraut

das Kuckucksheil
das auf nackten Äckern wächst
selbst an das Grabmal des Römers
der hier
zum Zeichen seines Ablebens
über einen Barbaren am Boden noch hinwegreitet.

IN THE BEGINNING THE WORD ALREADY WAS
wie nebenbei gesagt und doch vor allem.
Aber Wahrheit und Wirklichkeit
lassen sich nur halbherzig erzählen
und halbfertig in Worte fassen
damit es weitergehen kann.

Seit fünfzig Jahren war sie gestorben
stehend liegend sitzend sich krümmend.
ich hatte teil an ihr und
starb stück- und streckenweise mit
aus der Nähe aus der Ferne
und manchmal ganz unbesehen
und es gab nicht die geringste gute Aussicht
obwohl Nachbarn Freunde Verwandte
und einer der Söhne
ständig das Gegenteil behaupteten.
Immer gehetzt und abgewrackt
auf dem vorletzten Atemzug
ging es noch gerade irgendwohin
bisweilen sogar
wider besseres Wissen freudig erregt
ins englische Jenseits
mit Erbrechen Durchfall und schwacher Blase.
Bei einem bestimmten Lichteinfall klebt am Bett noch
nach Jahren
das unausgesetzt Klägliche
und der Nachhall der wüstesten und wütendsten Nacht.
Und weder das Bett noch das Urteil
das ich über mich spreche
bei so viel Unauflösbarem
lassen sich löschen. Und die Gefühle

lassen sich nur ablegen wie eine brandige Gespinsthaut
ein in die Körperaußenwand schwelend sich einfressendes und
nach innen durchschlagendes Nessushemd
als verbrühte sich dort selbst noch die Hitze
am Fiebersekret.

Ich selbst stand ja
lebenslänglich im Sterben
immer inmitten der Aushaucher Fallsüchtigen und Vergifteten
der in Stücke gehenden und
zugleich eingeschmolzenen Weltteile und
konnte nur noch eine einzige Verbindung herstellen
nach England nämlich wo gleich zu Beginn
hoch über der Themse in Richmond
die Fleischlampions der Eiben
so glühen
sogar dann noch wenn
sie aus dem Dunkel auf die Trottoirs gefallen sind und
die Kehlchen ihre Stimmen ausschicken
in die Nacht hinein oder
so früh schon daß noch keiner es hören kann
was sowieso keiner hört.
Ich brauche den ganzen Tag
um mich zum Leben hin
anzuziehen
und nachts ist kaum Schlaf
denn ich weiß noch nicht ob mir einer die Hals- und Fußkette
öffnen könnte.

Nie lassen sich die Gefühle verschieben
noch die Beunruhigungen die Rettungsversuche
die letzte Kraftanstrengung. Bis die Worte
wieder in Frage kommen und
die Sterbenden sich umbetten
und aus dem Gesichtsfeld gelegt haben.
WORD OF ALL WORLDS.

Oft ist es zu grell hier für die wegfallende Zeit
während sie

steintot eingesunken unter dünner Decke
reliefartig
wie unter der nachgebildeten Haut
eines anderen
nur noch abwarten kann
immer noch einmal die nächste Zeit mit dem großen Hunger
eines ganz klein und leicht gewordenen
Leibes
des nackten Körpers eines nicht mehr flügge werdenden
Vögelchens
heißhungrig auf Schneenarzissen
die sich mittlerweile durch gedämpften Zuruf
unterirdisch vermehren.

Man lehnt sich ins Auge zurück um diese Zeit
die nicht mehr zu retten ist
kalt auffangen zu können und
man überläßt sich unstet
den Blicken
um vielleicht die einst
abgetrennten Ekstasen wieder
heranzuziehen und sich nun in die
Wiege der Erscheinungen zu legen.

Perlwehen gingen durch die Wiese
am Grobsloch
und heute über den Bahndamm in Willesden
drei vier Wochen lang.
Und unter dem Laub eines nicht einmal sehr
großen Baumes
in Maresfield Gardens
wattierte ein ganz leichter Wind im Vorübergehen
plötzlich die Ohren
und etwas weiter noch hielten
die Hortensien ihre Verfärbungen den Blicken
entgegen.
Nachts stürzte aus dem schon herbstlich frostigen Weltraum
mit der Deichsel voran
der Große Wagen auf eines der Glashäuser zu. Es war

sein Ziel und
er würde es treffen aber weich nachfedernd
nicht zerschlagen.

Während ich
einen großen Schreibtisch in der Form eines Schachtes
leerräumte
und dabei noch auf einen Brief
von ihr an mich
stieß wie auf einen Schatz
lag sie
weder lebend noch gestorben
am anderen Ende desselben Raumes in einem ausladenden
Bett auf dem Rücken.
Mit geschlossenen Augen.
Und ihr Mund ging plötzlich
lautlos auf
und blieb nun weit geöffnet so daß
die ganze Mundhöhle bis zum Zäpfchen
sichtbar wurde wie ein offenstehendes
Mansardenzimmer
auf der Höhe von Birkenkronen.
Von der Sonne im Raum
und der Helle
war die Mundhöhle selbst hell und milde durchsonnt.
Ja die Wangen waren durchscheinend rötlich und
man sah deutlich
daß sie wie feines Tuch abwechselnd leicht
sich blähten und wieder erschlafften.
Die ganze Höhle bis hin zur
Schlundenge
und zum
Zungengrund
und auch die Lippen und Gaumensegel und –zäpfchen
flatterten und bebten leise.

Sie war also zum Atmen
aufgebahrt
in der südlichsten der vierten Kammer.

Eine Schlafbegrabene im
angestammten Luftzelt über der
Rautengrube.
Und unter Hinter- und Nachhirn
verschlug
sich nichts mehr.

Es begann die lange Traumzeit
in der sie
müde auferstanden
herumlag
in der sie verschwand und abgerissen verstört und abgekämpft
eine alte bag-lady
wieder auftauchte oder auch
um dreißig Jahre verjüngt
an der Haustür klingelte und vieles
erzählen und unternehmen wollte.
Immer blieb im Dunkeln wo sie
seit ihrem Sterben gewesen war.
Es war aber auch nicht wichtig.
Oft mußte ich mit ihr
die völlig geschwächt und hinfällig war und die
innerhalb weniger Tage
wieder sterben würde
bei Nacht über einen Fluß
eine Schlucht einen rasenden Gebirgsbach oder über schon
überlaufende Talsperren
über die nur schwankende und schlingernde
Hänge- und Notbrücken oder
schmale und geländerlose Betondämme führten.
Ein schwerer Koffer mußte
mitgenommen werden
auch ein kleines Mädchen das ich zuerst
hinübertrug
während aus dem steinigen Flußbett
Schreie heraufschallten.
Es waren ja Überführungen zwischen
unwirtlichen und unhaltbaren
Zonen.

Einmal
im Wasser eines stillen Sees oder Teichs
aber schwamm sie die am Ufer
verdämmernd bewegungslos gelegen hatte
robbenähnlich
mit glänzenden Augen
umher.
Manchmal mußte die ganze Umgebung
nach ihr weil sie in verlassenem Gelände
verloren gegangen war
abgesucht werden. Und
ich wußte einfach nicht ob man gehalten war sie bei
den Behörden
und sei es nur für die wenigen Tage
wieder für lebendig
erklären zu lassen
oder zumindest Bescheid zu sagen
daß sie doch nicht tot war.

Bis sie dann doch noch einmal im Nachthemd
nach England kommt
wo es
in Gloucestershire ein Hotel gibt
in dem die verschiedenen Jahres- und Tageszeiten
auf verschiedene Räume und Bereiche
verteilt sind
und wo die immer offene Lounge
in der Frühjahr ist und später Vormittag
auf einen alten englischen
Grabgarten geht
zwischen dessen vielen auch
schrägstehenden Gedenksteinen anhaltend
Sommer und Abend
wird. Dort
finde ich sie
das Stimmengewirr aus der Lounge im Ohr
hilflos
durchnäßt und
von Speiseresten befleckt auf

der Erde liegend und
sie sagt sie wolle
heim
obwohl sie ihr Lebtag
dieses Wort nicht in den Mund genommen hätte.

Abbreviations

References for Anne Duden's works are given in the text as indicated in this list.

A = *Der wunde Punkt im Alphabet*, Rotbuch: Hamburg, 1995, second edition 1996 = A^2.

D = 'A mon seul désir', in: Heinz Ludwig Arnold, ed., Lutz Seiler, Anne Duden, Farhad Showgi, *Heimaten*, Wallstein: Göttingen, (Göttinger Sudelblätter), 2001, 29-37.

H = *Hingegend. Gedichte*. Zu Klampen: Lüneburg, 1999, second edition 2001 = H^2.

J = *Das Judasschaf*, Rotbuch Verlag: Hamburg, 1985, second edition 1997 = J^2.

S = *Steinschlag*, Kiepenheuer & Witsch: Cologne, 1993.

Ü = *Übergang*, Rotbuch Verlag: Hamburg, 1982, second edition 1996 = $Ü^2$.

V = 'Vom Versprechen des Schreibens und vom Schreiben des Versprechens', in: Heinz Ludwig Arnold, ed., Robert Gernhardt, Peter Waterhouse, Anne Duden, *Lobreden auf den poetischen Satz*, Wallstein Verlag: Göttingen, (Göttinger Sudelblätter), 1998, 37-45.

W = *Wimpertier*, Kiepenheuer & Witsch: Cologne, 1995, second edition 1997 = W^2.

Z = *Zungengewahrsam*, Kiepenheuer & Witsch: Cologne, 1999.

Elizabeth Boa

Introduction:
notes from a symposium - notes towards *Hingegend*

The first part of this Introduction offers a brief chronology of Anne Duden's life and publications and surveys topics in her poetological essay, 'Vom Versprechen des Schreibens und vom Schreiben des Versprechens' and in the critical essays gathered in this volume, most of which were first delivered as papers at a symposium on the work of Anne Duden held at the University of Nottingham in May, 2001. The second part explores places and spaces as poetic motifs in a recent essay by Anne Duden on the topic of *Heimat*, 'A mon seul désir', and in her volume of poems, *Hingegend*.

Authorial Poetics and Readers' Responses

Anne Duden had the nomadic childhood of many Germans of her generation. She was born in 1942 in Oldenburg where her mother had come from Berlin to be with her war-wounded husband who was in hospital there. The family returned to Berlin towards the end of that long first year - Anne Duden was born on 1 January - but as the city came under increased bombardment, the mother with her two young children moved in 1944 to Ilsenburg in the Harz region where Duden's father, who had relatives in Ilsenburg, joined them later in the year after their house in Berlin had been bombed. Following the foundation of the two German states in 1949, a pass was needed to enter or leave the militarily sensitive no-go area along the border with West Germany where Ilsenburg was situated. In 1953, Anne Duden's mother, by then separated from her husband, applied for a pass, ostensibly to visit East Berlin. Once there, the family then sought refuge in West Berlin. After some months in refugee camps in West Berlin, they were flown to a reception camp in Uelzen near Hanover, moving later in the year to Anne Duden's birthplace of Oldenburg where she lived from 1953 to 1962 and went to school. Writing in the essay 'Zungengewahrsam' of this childhood of sudden disruptive departures and border-crossings, Duden stresses not the external facts but their traumatic internal impact on the child's imagination: 'das Trauma ist nicht der Zonenwechsel, Wechsel vom Osten in den Westen, von denen ja ohnehin nur der Osten die Zone war. Das Trauma ist/war eine Verschiebung der Herzen, des Herzens.' (Z 22) Such early memories along with later painful knowledge of the history of the Third Reich would feed into Duden's writing both thematically and in pervasive metaphors of physical and psychic border-crossings. Moving in 1962 to West Berlin following her school years, Duden trained initially as a bookseller and studied literature and sociology. She lived through the turbulent years of student unrest in the late 1960s and early 1970s, when she had various jobs, then joined the publishing house Wagenbach in 1972 and became co-founder of the left-wing publishing house Rotbuch which broke away from Wagenbach in 1973. There followed a time of intense collaborative work to build up Rotbuch, years marked also by a sequence of personal and public crises which ultimately led to Duden's decision to move from Berlin to London. In 1975, Duden suffered a terrible injury to the lower part of her face when the car she was in was attacked by a group of drunken American soldiers and an iron pole was thrust through the windscreen. This proved to be the beginning of a turning point in her life, setting in train with growing urgency the wish to devote more time to writing, for Duden had been writing since her teens. In 1977, Duden took three-month leave from Rotbuch to visit London and to find the time to reflect on her life, returning in September to Germany for the Frankfurt book fair. It was just at this time that the events of the so-called German Autumn were unfolding. The assassinations of Siegfried Buback, the Chief Prosecutor, in April and of the banker Jürgen Ponto in July, and the abduction in September and subsequent murder in October of Hanns Martin Schleyer, chairman of the West German Confederation of Employers, led to hugely increased police activity. The day before Schleyer's dead body was found in the boot of a car, the deaths in obscure circumstances in Stammheim prison of Andreas Baader, Gudrun Ensslin and Jan-Carl Raspe of the Baader-Meinhof terrorist group and the violent storming of the hijacked Luthansa plane in Mogadishu added fuel to the mood of public hysteria, intensifying calls for political and security measures which seemed to many liberal and leftist intellectuals to threaten the survival of democratic rights and freedoms in West Germany. For a mix of reasons, then, Duden decided to move to London to find the distance from Germany and the time for reflection which the hectic life in the Rotbuch publishing collective scarcely allowed. With help from friends in London and with generous encouragement especially from the poet Erich Fried, who also lived in London and who urged her to publish, Anne Duden gradually found her way into life as a writer.

Since 1978 Anne Duden has lived in London, but returning frequently to Berlin and other German cities. Her literary reputation was immediately established in 1982 with the publication of *Übergang*, a

Introduction: notes towards *Hingegend*

generically ambiguous text readable as an almost-novel or else as an experimental sequence of loosely related short stories, to be followed in 1985 by her novel *Das Judasschaf*. These remain still the most discussed and controversial of Duden's works, as witness the contrasting approaches in three essays in this volume by Margaret Littler, Teresa Ludden, and Stephanie Bird. After some years of poetic gestation, *Steinschlag* a sequence of poems in free rhythms, was published in 1993 to great critical acclaim, establishing Duden's literary reputation anew, this time as a poet. As Georgina Paul suggests *Steinschlag* has required time for critical gestation and the three essays here by Georgina Paul, Heike Bartel and Claudia Roth, are the first more extensive commentaries on this striking poem cycle. Since 1993, Duden has continued to publish in a variety of forms. In 1995, *Wimpertier*, a mixed collection of prose pieces and poems, came out and in the same year *Der wunde Punkt im Alphabet*, a collection of essays, sketches, and commentaries on paintings which, like *Das Judasschaf*, display the writer's intense engagement with visual art, as does 'Ausgehend von Liegenden', a later essay of 2000, which revisits some of the paintings, notably by Carpaccio, which figured in *Das Judasschaf*.[1] Duden's language is marked by a tension between hallucinatory evocation of extreme states of mind and of physical anguish and cool precision in conveying sensory detail. In her narrative works, subjective bodily and psychic states, painful acts of remembering and of telling, take on metaphoric expansion of meaning to bear testimony to the history of the twentieth century and to the dark side of European culture. Autobiographical raw material such as the emotional shock of a dislocated childhood or the injury suffered in 1975 is subject to the complex transformative processes of writing as Duden's texts perform a paradoxical double movement towards recovering the immediate, not-yet-rationalised psychosomatic force of extreme experiences yet at the same time bringing such material to resonate with recent and with more remote historical and cultural meanings. Such resonances are set in motion by a whole range of poetic devices. As Dirk Göttsche suggests, Anne Duden's work belongs in a modernist tradition, with roots in Romantic aesthetics. Her work is never naively naturalistic but always marked by ironic reflection upon representation and the poetic medium. Ekphrasis, in the sense of literary writing about visual art, is a frequent feature of her work. Nature is often refracted through ekphrastic correspondences between literature and painting in Duden's prose works, whether it be the German Renaissance painter Altdorfer, as Juliet Wigmore shows, or the contemporary artist Clea Wallis, as Teresa Ludden discusses, while Heike Bartel sets the stony metaphors in *Steinschlag* in relation to Cézanne's stony paintings. The expressive intensity of hyper- or surrealist images is combined with an analytic and essayistic vein. The essay of 1998, 'Vom Versprechen des Schreibens und vom Schreiben des Versprechens', which appeared along with contributions by two other writers in the volume *Lobreden auf den poetischen Satz*, reflects on the nature of poetry and of the act of writing. This self-reflexive strain continues in *Zungengewahrsam*, a volume of short pieces on poetics and art which came out in 1999, the same year in which the volume of poems, *Hingegend*, appeared. The most recent publication, an essay with the title of 'A mon seul désir' on the topic of *Heimat*, or rather on *Heimaten* in the plural from this German author who lives in London, came out in 2001 and shows secret connections with the poems of *Hingegend* in the evocative conjuring up of remembered places and landscapes imbued with the sense of times past and present, but infused also with darker tensions and anxieties, signalled in the contradictions embedded in the title *Hingegend*: 'Hin' along with 'Gegend' suggests a place towards which the poet is drawn by longing; 'gegen' suggests rejection and opposition; 'hingegen' denotes the contradiction between opposing movements of attraction and repulsion. Much of Duden's work is characterised by such tensions, which can reach the extremes of horror juxtaposed with mystic exaltation or, as in *Hingegend*, with grotesque comedy.

The essay 'Vom Versprechen des Schreibens und vom Schreiben des Versprechens', offers a fascinating reflection on the author's self-understanding of her writerly practice. Towards the end, Duden recalls how returning from looking at pictures, her ear and eye were inhabited by two lines of poetry which seemed to have sprung over from a painting into language. Such a hearing eye or seeing ear is reminiscent of the synaesthetic perception in Goethe's Fifth Roman Elegy: 'Sehe mit fühlendem Aug', fühle mit sehender Hand'.[2] Duden's lines run:

> Ein Dämmerungsvogel im Tiefflug
> rettet sein kurzes unverdrossenes Leben. (V 44)

The visual work from which the lines have transgressed into another medium is not the classical sculpture which Goethe's seeing hand was remembering in the contours of his sleeping mistress's body, but a painted Annunciation: thus Mary becomes a figure for receptivity to the poetic sentence and the angel a figure for its unexpected and potentially terrifying arrival. In the iconography of the Annunciation the Holy Spirit appears as a bird, just as the angel Gabriel's wings convey his status as messenger between heaven and earth. (The 'Dämmerungsvogel' will reappear as a figure poetic inspiration in *Hingegend* and in the Heimat essay.) An Annunciation is, as Duden puts it 'ein Sprach-, Spruch- und Sprechgeschehen' (V 44): the words Gabriel and Mary exchange are often written on a scroll, and Mary often holds an open book in her hand, on her lap, or else it lies behind her on a lectern as she turns to receive the messenger.[3] Earlier on in the essay Duden writes of ordinary language ('der gemeine Satz') as a post-lapsarian arena of power struggles, violence, and fear because of the secret knowledge that 'jeder *Be-* eine *Ent*hauptung folgen kann' (V 40-41). By contrast, 'der ungemeine Satz' is not assertive or death dealing. But the poetic sentence does engage with human history, just as the Annunciation heralds redemption from the Fall through the Word made flesh by being born from a woman's body into the historical world of power, violence and injustice. Poetic language is, then, not a pre-lapsarian edenic discourse. It *is* an opening towards the Utopian, but from here and now, an opening which may indeed intensify the horror of the actual and historical ground from which it springs. *Das Judasschaf* memorably conveys such a crossing over from the historical world into the stillness of a religious painting, which paradoxically transmutes horror into harmony.

This insight touches on one of the most troubling aspects of Duden's work both to the author and her readers, namely the intense pleasure of literature, even, or perhaps especially, the literature of horror or the abject which Margaret Littler discusses, just as the paintings Duden writes of frequently depict - with great beauty - scenes of great horror. The Annunciation as theme has inspired many of the most supremely beautiful paintings in the whole Western canon of religious art, yet it initiates a story which will culminate in horror and which is already inscribed in the Book Mary has just been reading.[4] Echoes of Christian iconography, which Georgina Paul notes in *Steinschlag*, for example, are a frequent feature of Duden's work; the dissolution of boundaries which Teresa Ludden explores in *Übergang* and *Das Judasschaf* recalls the writings of Christian mystics; the images of a force which bites and ruptures the physical fabric of the female body, which Stephanie Bird examines in *Übergang* and *Wimpertier*, are reminiscent of the gouging of stigmata in the body of Catherine of Sienna. Such recourse to Christian motifs by a writer concerned with twentieth-century Germany could seem to assimilate recent history to a religious myth which purports to find meaning in horror, a move which would be troubling to many readers. A similar strategy would be the reduction of historical disasters to the status of natural catastrophes, which come and go in the cycle of the seasons, but as Claudia Roth argues, Duden rejects such naturalisation right at the beginning of *Steinschlag*. Likewise, rather than a religious reading of contemporary history, Duden's poetics essay and many of the other allusions to Christian art in her work may be seen as poetological reflection on the dilemma of writing in the knowledge of recent history, of poetry after Auschwitz as Theodor Adorno famously put it, which has affinities to the paradoxical pleasure we take in the beauty of religious art depicting the anguished body yet the martyr's bliss.[5] The extreme receptivity, the imaginative opening, the pleasure in words which (almost) express with immeasurable beauty the immeasurably horrific make the author guilty, a guilt Duden embodies in the figure of the *Judasschaf*. (Such guilty pleasure in the literature of horror is reminiscent of Kafka as is the animal metaphor.) The essays by Margaret Littler, Teresa Ludden, and Stephanie Bird offer three responses to this dilemma: Littler is troubled by the implications for the female subject of such opening to pleasure-in-pain and by what might seem like an ahistorical, masochistic fascination with suffering; Ludden, by contrast, welcomes a radical dismantling of the dualisms of Western Philosophy which split sovereign mind from inert body and under which women especially have suffered; Bird's reading in the framework of the ethics of Levinas might in part answer Littler's concerns but might also, in the irrationalism of the encounter with the absolute other, reinforce them. Dirk Göttsche places Duden in a tradition ultimately stretching back to the Romantic critique of the Enlightenment and echoes of that old quarrel still perhaps sound here in the concern that a too radical 'feminine' blurring of boundaries between self and world perhaps threatens women's autonomy as the sex only recently emancipated to a condition of subjecthood.

Duden's poetics essay suggests that she aspires to what Barthes called the 'scriptible' or writerly pole of literature in contrast to the readerly or 'lisible'.[6] As the essays gathered in this volume show, her work leaves ample space for readers to (re-)write or re-frame her texts - Bird's framing in the ethics of Levinas, Ludden's in post-structural theory, Littler's feminist or Roth's political frame, Göttsche's post-Romantic modernist context. Such framing helps us to read texts, which address the difficult question of how to write in the knowledge of recent history from the position of a female German writer of her generation. The purely writerly text, Barthes suggests, is nowhere to be found, at most fleetingly in certain works-at-the-limit. Such works of radical linguistic experiment are not products to be consumed, but transform the reader from consumer into producer or writer of texts which demand to be (re-)written. Potentially the most productive encounter with texts is surely that of the re-writer-as-translator, and as Wiebke Sievers argues in her essay on English and French translations of *Übergang* Duden's work-at-the-limit demands to be written anew in the new language rather than being narrowed down into a readable product. According to Barthes, such narrowing down is what interpretation does and is, it must be confessed, the aim of the essays in this volume - such is the nature of the academic encounter with the poet, though Georgina Paul charts a least reductive process of intensive reading over time. In the *Heimat* essay, Duden suggests that even the author is not immune from this melancholy fate: the very act of writing about *Heimat*, of turning the imagined place into script, memorialises it for others perhaps, but consigns it to oblivion for the writer: 'Ja, das Aufschreiben besiegelt das Verschwinden.' (D 37)

Besides the reflections on such writerly dilemmas, Duden's poetics essay gives pointers towards her craft, for although she evokes the mystic arrival of the poetic sentence which comes to the writer as the angel comes to Mary, she also writes of the years of gestation that may precede and the sheer hard work that follows that blessed arrival. Just as the Word which comes to Mary is already written in the Book she has just been reading, so words are trans-historical: they bring with them past (if not divine) usage and the potential for future use. But the words that constitute poetic sentences must be renewed - Duden uses the comical conceit of mummified words unwrapping themselves with woody fingers and breaking out leafily from their bandages. Words have the quality of fabric which can be unpicked or reknitted, broken down or restructured both in themselves and as elements of discourse. (The metaphor of words as fabric returns in the ekphrastic conjuring up of the angel's and Mary's garments, which just touch at the hem in clothy conversation.) Thus Claudia Roth suggests how Duden unpicks the meteorological terms in which political upheavals are regularly clothed. Words bring with them intertextual echoes of poetic forebears. Georgina Paul finds echoes of Celan and Eliot. Heike Bartel and Claudia Roth trace both the poetic legacy and the physical presence of Hölderlin as silenced, suffering body: in Duden's texts history is inscribed in stigmatised bodies. Duden often breaks down words into their constituent parts or, as the German language generously allows, knits semantic fragments together into neologisms woven into larger metaphoric patterns such as Heike Bartel explores in her analysis of *Steinschlag* or as the title *Hingegend* exemplifies. Wiebke Sievers excavates the wealth of metaphoric meaning in the title *Übergang* and the depth of cultural allusion which makes Duden's work so hard to translate. Georgina Paul illuminates the metaphoric blending of space and music in the *Klangräume* which she discerns in *Steinschlag* and which exemplify in practice Duden's modernist aesthetic of musical simultaneity which Dirk Göttsche analyses in *Zungengewahrsam* and Margaret Littler finds in 'Übergang'. Duden's poetry may stretch and strain the fabric of German grammar, but the underlying 'Satz-Corpus' (V 38) remains, as Claudia Roth shows on the example of the opening of *Steinschlag*.

A post-modern turn? Global vistas and local scenes in *Hingegend*
Metaphorical spaces, but also places and localities imbued with memory, are another key element in Duden's poetics, as the motif of 'Gegend' or region embedded in the title *Hingegend* implies and as the essay on *Heimat*, 'A mon seul désir', makes explicit. To be sure, the essay begins by leaving the past and its places behind - 'Alle Orte meines vergangenen Lebens liegen wie Krankheiten hinter mir' (D 29) - but like the return of the repressed, so too the past places return and impinge on the present. The present is London, where the author arrives and leaves as a traveller through the air-ways so that she sees the city from above, stretched out below, and divided by the yoyo line of the river. But there is the one place, like a dowry from the past, 'an dem ich immer Boden unter den Füßen gehabt habe...' (D 30) Where London is named, unnamed and identified only negatively as not her birthplace (the traditional location of the remembered *Heimat*), Duden's dowry, her 'Mitgift' (D 30), from a nomadic past characteristic of hers, the 'second generation' of those who born during the Third Reich, is the third stopping place on a zigzagging journey in war-torn, then post-war Germany, a place near the Brocken - the pedantic seeker after facts will guess Ilsenburg - with gravel and granite paving stones underfoot and redolent of leaves, twigs, pine-needles, meadow grass and coltsfoot.[7] The essay continues, however, with a sequence of evocations of London, of cloudy English skies, of a moment of mystic intensity in the evening light near Hall Junior School, of walking home with her dead mother in a dream. London and insular Britain appear as places of mourning for the author's dead mother and of

remembrance of that other place of childhood. In the end the essay evokes not so much *Heimat* as *one* fixed place, *a* maternal ground, *the* foundation of personal identity, but rather a mystic experience of connections and correspondences signalled in twilight birdsong in a London street. Duden borrows Bachelard's term '*Unermeßlichkeit auf der Stelle*' (D 32) for this receptiveness to an opening out of something immeasurable from somewhere specific. *Heimat* is not the place in itself, but its remembrance from somewhere else. An imagined other place set in correspondence to the place of remembrance, as Duden's essay does with Ilsenburg remembered in London, Heimat becomes here a figure also for poetic enchantment. Duden's spatial metaphor of 'Horizontal-, Vertikal- und Total-Intensität' (D 32), rather like Baudelaire's nature as a temple of living pillars in his sonnet 'Correspondances', evokes a poetic condition of heightened synaesthetic perception of correspondences and analogies, conveyed also, perhaps, in the title of the *Heimat* essay.[8] 'A mon seul désir' is the motto on the tent in the sixth tapestry in the sequence known as 'La Dame à la licorne' which is housed in the museum l'Hotel de Cluny in Paris. The lady is standing at the entrance to the tent on a flowery ground with her heraldic beasts, the lion and the unicorn, and a little dog on a cushion. The preceding five tapestries are dedicated to the five senses of taste, sight, touch, smell, and hearing. The sixth title, 'A mon seul désir', thus evokes a utopian longing beyond the sensual yet to be reached only through the senses or through a synaesthetic mingling and mutual heightening of sense experience. This essay by a German writer who lives in London and commutes between cities began by evoking a nomadic existence of air travel with a cartoon-like post-modern view of the city seen from above, then moves through the remembrance of an earth-bound childhood *Heimat,* to reach the immeasurable realm of literature which always opens out, however, from somewhere specific. The bird's-eye view from an aeroplane gives way to the poet on the pavement listening, for a moment like the lady in the fifth tapestry dedicated to hearing, to the 'Gesang der Dämmerungsvögel, der ja selbst die lautesten Weltgegenden zu übertönen, berauschen und verlocken unternimmt.' (D 33) The twilight song of 'Dämmerungsvögel', signals a moment of ambiguity between day and night, light and darkness, waking and sleeping, a moment of passage between past and present and between the prosaic and the poetic realm.

In Duden's poetics essay discussed above, the 'Dämmerungsvogel' (V 44) crossed over out of a painting where the Dove, entering from above through a stained glass window into the hazy interior of a church, signifies how the eternal Word, the Logos, will becomes flesh. In transgressing from the painting into Duden's text, the bird becomes an ephemeral, mortal creature which just saves 'sein kurzes unverdrossenes Leben' (V 44). Yet the song of 'Dämmerungsvögel' (D 33) heard in a London street transports the imagination in an opposite movement out of a specific place into immeasurable poetic space. The same motif, extended by a further line, appears also in 'Hibernaculum', one of the poems in the volume *Hingegend*. The poet recalls that it is only two hours ago,

> daß ein Dämmerungsvogel im Tiefflug
> zwischen Rushhour-Schüben sein kurzes
> unverdrossenes Leben rettete. (V 44)

An overdetermined symbol of memory, music, poetry and spirit, of mortality yet vitality, of threat and of salvation, the bird is here firmly located in a contemporary setting by the term 'Rushhour', borrowed from the global language of a post-modern age. The collection juxtaposes themes familiar from Duden's earlier work - historical and cultural memories and personal recollection prompted by a sequence of places, real and imagined - with contemporary environmental concerns.

The title of the first poem 'Kammerherz' reverses the elements in 'Herzkammer', the German term for ventricle, to create the ever-present imaginary place of empathetic opening to, but also of fearful retreat from, the world. The poem begins with an image suggesting, that like the sun which 'also ariseth',[9] the heart rises ever anew as if always for the first time, like the first springtime of the world: 'Herzaufgänge / als stünde die Welt / nur einmal im Laub / pro Leben.' (H^2 7) The lines 'Dunstvergötterte / Silberschrift / englisch' (H^2 7) gesture towards religious painting, whether of paradise or the angelic greeting, 'der englische Gruß', in an Annunciation. But the scene which follows mixes idyllic springtime motifs of meadow, flowers, and the delicate tracery of dew drops on foliage with a deathblow, then skulls and caverns (readers of *Das Judasschaf* might think of Carpaccio's paintings). Following this mythic opening image of a world of beauty yet horror - not paradise but a postlapsarian Spring and Cain's deathblow to Abel perhaps - the next two verses conjure up the din of modern urban life, and the shock and fear evoked in the householder peering out from behind curtains by the human detritus of cities in a world of poverty policed by violence. In the last verse, the rest is an almost-silence, which the poem itself breaks, however: the heart still, just, rises. Modes of death-dealing violence shift in the course of the poem from a 'Totschlag' (H^2 7) suggesting a club, through

Introduction: notes towards *Hingegend*

the 'Genickfänger' (H^2 7), the metal knife of the hunter or assassin, to the forces of order, themselves violent, looking for the 'Schmauchspuren' (H^2 8) of guns, a weapon of our times. The next poem, 'Verkommnis', laments in four sections threats to the environment and to human survival. First comes the theme of ecological degradation and industrial depredation: plant species and wild places destroyed, food poisoned, arms manufacturers whose products threaten global catastrophe. Ours is an age of unparalleled extremes of first-world wealth and third-world poverty and of violence on an obscene scale, which is giving rise to the movements of refugees so troubling to wealthy western societies. This Duden evokes in the next section in images of the poor in burgeoning cities bereft of all traces of nature, of children fending for themselves, of dead, staked-out victims of social conflicts and wars who are the only ones to see what is happening: 'Die Kontinente wachsen / ruckhaft zusammen / erbrechen Flüchtende ineinander.' (H^2 10). First and Third Worlds are mingling, as the abject poor move from continent to continent. The third very short section touches on global warming in images of baked, hardened surfaces and dead fledgling birds on yellowing grass. The uncanny noise of sun-induced rustling in the closing lines seems to eerily herald some cosmic apocalypse: 'Es rauscht aber lauthals vor Sonne.' (H^2 11) The ancient Biblical motif of the sun which also rises now signifies not just the mortality of successive generation in contrast to the earth that abides forever, but a threat to the succession of the generations itself. But the last section allows for no apocalyptic religious meaning: 'Kein Würgeengel fällt in den Blick...' (H^2 12) The machinery of destruction, once set in motion, proceeds monotonously and seemingly ever more remote from human agency. Set against dead fledglings there is only 'der schlagende Sturmvogel im Rippenkäfig' (H^2 12).

Following these two opening poems, the one a mythic evocation of perennial violence, the second a global vision of modernity in crisis as the 'Kammerherz' becomes the 'Rippenkäfig', the title poem 'Hingegend' pans in from the global to the local in a poem of historically-infused personal memories prompted by named German places. The poem continues the theme of 'Flüchtende', in recalling the poet's own childhood experience as a refugee. Like the opening of 'Kammerherz' which mixed the idyllic and the deadly, the first verse of 'Hingegend' interweaves images of bones, an enraged brain and bleeding body, of compulsion and anxiety, with a bucolic landscape of dog-roses and cobwebs trailing across a child's eyes, of silvery-ripe rye fields, poplars, hops and the sweet decay of lagoons in the buzzing summer heat, cut off from the main current of the river Regen. The verse resists rational reading, but does powerfully convey a mood of contradiction between idyllic landscape and mental and physical anguish. As the poem develops, the opening view of a river landscape in South Germany - the Regen is a tributary of the Danube, the confluence located in Regensburg - , is juxtaposed with a different scene when the poet re-visits Hanover and the nearby small town of Nienburg, both places explicitly named. The short second verse builds a bridge between two regions, then, in a self-deprecating, comic picture of the poet as traveller, on a sentimental journey, visiting cathedrals like the Regensburg Dom and weeping into her breakfast scrambled eggs over memories of a past journey as refugee.[10] (The reception camp for refugees from the GDR to which Anne Duden and her family were transported by in 1953 was near Hanover.) Her sense of disorientation and loss comes out in the scrambled word 'Ichausweser' (H^2 13). 'Ichausweser' echoes 'ausweisen' (exile), contrasts with 'anwesend' (present), and picks up on 'zwangseingewiesen' (forcibly admitted) in the first verse, so suggesting the status of a refugee in a camp, a subject who has lost that ground under her feet associated in the *Heimat* essay with Ilsenburg. But whether the weeping into the scrambled eggs is for the loss of *Heimat*, or for the anguish infiltrating a lush summer day on the river Regen is unclear. From the pastoral, the poem now moves in the next two sections to the urban, to the railway station in Hanover, which has been tunnelled through and built over the heaped-up rubble of a bombed-out city. The high-rise buildings rise ever higher, the cars proliferate, trees are destroyed. In a further amalgam of bodily and natural imagery as in the first verse, the poet feels in her nerves the exhaustion now afflicting trees which flourished in past summers. An anonymous grown-up voice urges the poet-become-child to pull herself together and the next section moves out of the city again to the 'Hingegend um Nienburg' (H^2 15). There is still beauty, but under threat, as the wild animals who once co-inhabited our landscapes are threatened with extinction in a myriad of ways. The penultimate verse evokes the river bird, the 'Eisvogel' or kingfisher, the mythic Halcyon spirit of nature at peace with itself. The kingfisher builds its nest to float on water in the Halcyon days of magically calm winter weather so signalling hope for renewal through love and comfort for the homeless. The poem ends with two evocations of falling asleep after a day of memories and of empathy between the natural creatures and the figure of a weeping king, the king emerging from a cross-linguistic pun on the English 'king-fisher'.[11] The closing at once calm yet sinister exhortation to the poet from the anonymous voice speaking in the formal second-person of address, 'Nun entschlafen Sie endlich.' (H^2 16), mixes the idyllic with the threatening, so returning to the opening mood of a poem in which adult admonition fails to silence childhood memory.

Read in the context of the collection *Hingegend*, the title poem marks a shift from the global to specific localities and remembered places. 'Vor Ort', moves to more intimate spaces still, first a bed and domestic details dimly perceived as by someone half asleep, perhaps ill, then a garden, insects, bird-call and flowers, the title being suggestive of somewhere provincial or on the outskirts of the city, or, like a garden, a place across the threshold from a house. The placing of this poem immediately following the admonition at the end of 'Hingegend', 'Nun entschlafen Sie endlich' (H^2 16), has the reassuring feel not of passing over into death, but of waking from sleep. Duden here re-visits, in the charm of banal detail brought to new life through the poet's eye, a tradition of small-scale, domestic poetry of house and garden stretching back to Droste and Mörike, even to Goethe's provincial epic *Hermann und Dorothea* or to garden motifs in some of his late lyrics. Like 'Hingegend', this poem too resists easy reading, but a sequence of sense impressions is clear enough: crumpled bed clothes; the caress of damp air on the skin; moonlight through the slits of the blinds; the bluish light of a television screen; a sore throat (?) felt as the scratchy sensation of having swallowed a lump of clay or holly leaves. Then the garden, shrubs, flowers with impressive Latin names, and pests squashed between a gardener's fingers (a faint echo perhaps of the busy housewife in Goethe's small town idyll who never lets the chance pass to remove the caterpillars from her cabbages).[12] The poem closes with two further motifs: the call of a bird on the roof top, perhaps a cockerel or the golden oriole mentioned in verse three, which starts as strangulated sounds in the throat; at once the image and the sound of boldness, the bird contrasts with the silent fuchsias who hang their lute-shaped goblet heads earthwards:

> Stattdessen
> Kelchlaute hängend
> eingeschwiegen ins Nordbeet
> fuchsienrot
> versessen auf Ende. (H^2 19)

In the neologism 'Kelchlaute', '-laute' could be the plural of 'Laut' meaning sounds, but 'Kelchlaute' also catches the goblet shape of the flower and the stamens which hang from it like the strings of a lute; either way the flower becomes emblematic of the lyric mood. The closing line 'versessen auf Ende', evoking the brilliant fuchsias with their hanging heads, has a comic ring in contrast to deathly images earlier in the collection. Such garden imagery with a religious undertone - the term 'Kelch' is that used both of flowers and of the communion cup - could be compared with a late garden poem by Goethe from his *Chinesisch-Deutsche Jahres- und Tageszeiten*:

> Weiß wie Lilien, reine Kerzen
> Sternen gleich, bescheidner Beugung
> Leuchtet aus dem Mittelherzen,
> Rot gesäumt, die Glut der Neigung.
>
> So frühzeitige Narzissen
> blühen reihenweis im Garten.
> Mögen wohl die guten wissen
> Wen sie so spaliert erwarten.[13]

Goethe's star-shaped flowers on stiffly upright stems yet with modestly bowing, prayerful heads mix the pure white of lilies or candles with the red of passion. Like Duden's late-summer fuchsias, Goethe's early-spring narcissi too are silent yet expectant. In both poems, the neat garden setting, whether Goethe's rows or Duden's 'Nordbeet' in her *Englisch-Deutsche Jahres- und Tageszeiten*, is comically incongruous with the mystic intensity of colour and the beauty of form of the single flower.

Following spring, then high and late summer moments, - sometimes idyllic, sometimes desperate in mood - , the volume closes with two winter poems. The first, 'Winter-Reise', is in three parts headed 'Aufbruch', 'Aufenthalt' and 'Einbruch': first a departure by aeroplane which conveys an absurdly incongruous sense of the organic human body, 'das Empfindungsbündel' (H^2 22), transported through the aeons in a vibrating machine, the sustenance it needs slithering around on little plastic pop-up tables; then the defiant song of a single bird standing out against general undifferentiated local and global noise of our age (this time the *Dämmerungsvogel* appears in the early morning); the third section is in memorium for Morris Moss, a bricklayer whose naked foot, as his dead body is borne home, looks like the foot from a Pietà disappearing into the house. The McGonigallesque specific name and the fragmentary image of the foot appear as the last in a puzzling montage of disconnected and sometimes incomprehensible elements in this poem which lacks the linear narrative the title seems to promise, the last section bringing not arrival from a journey but the shocking break-in of sudden, unexpected death.[14] Such a form, juxtaposing images of a vulnerable human body high above the earth enclosed in a machine, with the tiny voice of a bird in flight set against man-made destruction of nature, with a dead man's foot as a fragment from an old story, enacts the loss of meaning-giving narrative which has been associated with the post-modern condition, post-modernist too the comic-grotesque mood of the first and third sections. By contrast, the last poem, 'Hibernaculum', does tell a story of sorts in the course of its eleven sections. The preface locates the place of inspiration as a railway platform in Dulwich for trains to France, and the time of writing as months later when the poet begins in the South of England to tell her retrospective narrative of a winter visit to a skiing resort somewhere in Europe.[15] Like the recollection of Ilsenburg in London in the *Heimat* essay or the juxtaposing of different landscapes and times in 'Hingegend', here too recollection from somewhere else, this time in true Wordsworthian fashion of emotion recollected in tranquillity, awakens the poetic mood which in this poem is predominantly comic. First comes an invocation to Walburga (ca. 710-777), the patron saint of travellers. Appropriately enough in the work of a poet-commuter between England and Germany, Walburga was an woman from Wessex who did her good work in Heidenheim, near Ingolstadt; her insignium, a phial of curative oil, would still come in handy for a skier's aches and pains.[16] Motifs in the course of the poem include a winter landscape of mountains and forest, ski-lifts and canons fired off to induce snow-fall, avalanches of cars instead of snow, hotel-dinners of green mange-tout tastefully arranged around chicken drumsticks draped in cream-sauce. The poet, a woman on her own, eats early at the little 'Katzentisch' (H^2 29) which is normally reserved for children or serves later as a buffet for the serving dishes and wine-bottles of important male diners at big tables. She has catastrophes (breaking crockery, spilled wine, problems with her guidebook), visits nearby towns and villages, and dines in a top-hotel which serves food under cloches shaped like the severed breasts of Agatha, a third-century Christian martyr, who presides along with Walburga as a further patron saint of travelling women. The poetic spirit, the 'Dämmerungsvogel' (who elsewhere transgressed from an Annunciation) appears here between bursts of rush-hour traffic and just before the canons are fired off - a lyric moment of song in the noisy age of mass tourism. The poem closes with a further moment of post-modern sublime, as the red of the setting sun, so much more intense than the poet's cinnamon-coloured hair, lights up the drivers in their cars and the poet at her bus stop. In contrast to the sinister mood at the end of 'Verkommnis' with its images of dead birds and dead grasses killed by the sun - 'Es rauscht aber lauthals vor Sonne.' (H^2 11) - , hope for the future returns in the closing lines of 'Hibernaculum' in the image of the setting sun,

> die den Vorbeifahrenden nachleuchtet
> die Zimthaarstränge stumpf erscheinen läßt
> und der Reisenden nachgeht
> vielleicht bis zum nächsten Mal
> oder noch darüber hinaus. (H^2 39)

Her readers too hope for the next publication from the traveller-poet Anne Duden.

Notes

[1] 'Ausgehend von Liegenden', in: Wolfgang Kemp et al., eds, *Vorträge aus dem Warburg-Haus*, Band 4, Akademie Verlag: Berlin, 2000, 37-64.

[2] J. W. von Goethe, 'Römische Elegien V', in: Erich Trunz, ed., *Goethes Werke. Gedichte und Epen*, Erster Band, Hamburger Ausgabe, 7. Aufl., Christian Wegener: Hamburg, 1964, p. 160.

[3] My thanks to Anne Duden who in conversation identified the work as the Annunciation (1425-30) attributed to Jan van Eyck in the National Gallery in Washington. Mary is depicted in a Romanesque basilica as the angel bows before her. Unparalleled in his realism of detail, van Eyck has printed the message emerging from Mary's mouth in reverse to be legible to the Holy Ghost, depicted as a Dove flying obliquely down towards Mary's head along a beam of light from a stained-glass window on high.

[4] In van Eyck's painting Mary holds up her open hands to display her palms in a gesture anticipating Christ's wounds.

[5] On debate over the decades on Adorno's famous tag see Günter Bonheim, *Versuch zu zeigen, daß Adorno mit seiner Behauptung, nach Auschwitz lasse sich kein Gedicht mehr schreiben, recht hatte*. Königshausen & Neumann: Würzburg, 2002.

[6] Roland Barthes, *S/Z*, Éditions du Seuil: Paris, 1970, pp. 9-12.

Introduction: notes towards *Hingegend* 17

[7] Ilsenburg is a small town with a medieval castle, set in the Ilsetal, near Wernigerode, at the beginning of the Heinrich-Heine-Wanderweg down from the Brocken, the *Weltberg* as Duden terms it in her essay. Heine celebrated the region in his *Harzreise*. There is perhaps a concealed allusion to Heine in *Hingegend* which contains two wintry poems, 'Winter-Reise' (more Schubert than Heine?) and 'Hibernaculum', and evokes in the title-poem, 'Hingegend', the region around Hanover which figures in Heine's *Deutschland. Ein Wintermärchen*. Heinesque too is the comic element in *Hingegend*.

[8] 'La Nature est un temple où de vivants piliers / Laissent parfois sortir de confuses paroles' and further down, 'Les parfums, les couleurs et les sons se répondent,': Charles Baudelaire, 'Correspondances', from 'Les Fleurs du Mal', in: Baudelaire, *Poèmes*, André Ferran, ed., Hachette: Paris, 1959, pp. 32-3.

[9] Ecclesiastes, 1, 5.

[10] Thanks again to Anne Duden for information on the biographical background to this poem which juxtaposes, without explanatory links, recent memories of visiting Regensburg during a poetry-reading tour with a compacted evocation of Hanover now and in 1953. Regensburg's Gothic cathedral and bombed-out Hanover exemplify the extremes of human creativity and destruction, just as the riverene landscapes of the Regen and the Weser convey the poignant beauty of nature and the horror of its threatened destruction.

[11] Anne Duden has indicated that the figure of the 'ausgeweinter König' also relates to the medieval statues of meditative kings and prophets in the Regensburg Dom.

[12] Moving through her garden Hermann's mother 'Nahm gleich einige Raupen vom kräftig strotzenden Kohl weg:/ Denn ein geschäftiges Weib tut keine Schritte vergebens.' J. W. von Goethe, 'Hermann und Dorothea', in: Erich Trunz, ed., *Goethes Werke. Gedichte und Epen*, Zweiter Band, Hamburger Ausgabe, 7. Aufl., Christian Wegener: Hamburg, 1965, 437-514 (here: p. 460).

[13] J. W. von Goethe, 'Weiß wie Lilien', in: Erich Trunz, ed., *Goethes Werke. Gedichte und Epen*, Erster Band, Hamburger Ausgabe, 7. Aufl., Christian Wegener: Hamburg, 1964, p. 387.

[14] William McGonigall (1825-1902) is a Scottish poet renowned for poetry so bad it is almost good. His ballad on the Tay Bridge Disaster includes the names of the engineers who built the bridge.

[15] Anne Duden was invited to participate along with other writers and artists in a project which involved writing on or painting a winter theme after visiting the

Sauerland in Nordrhein-Westfalen, which has the biggest skiing area in Germany North of the Alps.

[16] Walburga has also given her name to *Walpurgisnacht*, the night of May 1 when the witches gather on the Brocken near Ilsenburg, Duden's childhood *Heimat*, although the historical Walburga had no such connection.

Dirk Göttsche

‚Gestalt aus Bewegung'
Beobachtungen zu Anne Dudens Kurzprosa und Essayistik

This essay places Anne Duden's short prose in her volumes *Wimpertier*, *Der wunde Punkt im Alphabet*, and *Zungengewahrsam* in the tradition of modern German short prose transcending and transforming traditional genres (prose poem, prose sketch, 'Denkbild'). Recurring themes, motifs and textual structures in Duden's short prose writing are analysed in the light of her modernist adaptation of Romantic poetics ('Gestalt aus Bewegung'), while the exploration of aesthetic experience in her essays is discussed with reference to Adorno's concept of the essay as literary form.

Während die deutschsprachige Belletristik seit den 1980er Jahren das epische Erzählen und die große Form des Romans wiederentdeckt hat, gehört Anne Duden zu jenen AutorInnen, die die ästhetische Tradition der Moderne fortschreiben, indem sie herkömmliche Darstellungsverfahren wie die des epischen Erzählens dekonstruieren und kleine Formen der Literatur zur intensiven Erprobung neuer Ausdrucksmöglichkeiten nutzen. Zwar ist die Autorin mit einem größeren Prosatext – *Das Judasschaf* (1985) – bekannt geworden, doch schon dieses Werk, das bezeichnenderweise nicht den Gattungstitel ‚Roman' führt, steht in der modernen Tradition der quasi-experimentellen Dekonstruktion des Erzählens, die immer auch neue ästhetische Strukturen hervorbringt. In den seither publizierten Bänden Kleiner Prosa sind immer deutlicher jene zwei Traditionslinien hervorgetreten, die hier in ihrer grundlegenden Bedeutung für Anne Dudens Werk betrachtet werden sollen: zum einen die Tradition des Essays in seiner namentlich von Theodor W. Adorno theoretisch formulierten Bedeutung als offene Ausdrucksform eines literarischen ‚Prozesses geistiger Erfahrung'[1]; zum anderen das für die Entwicklung der literarischen Moderne exemplarische, jedoch noch keineswegs hinreichend erforschte Gebiet der Kurzprosa (Prosagedicht, Prosaskizze, ‚Denkbild') mit seinen programmatischen Grenzüberschreitungen zwischen Lyrik und Prosa, Erzählen und Reflexion, diaristischen und deskriptiven Momenten, Philosophie und Literatur.

Nicht zufällig überkreuzen sich beide Traditionslinien bereits in der klassischen Moderne im Werk von Autoren wie Robert Walser, Robert Musil und Walter Benjamin und besitzen zudem mediengeschichtlich im Feuilleton eine gemeinsame Schnittmenge. Anne Dudens kurze Prosa kennt nicht nur in ihren faszinierenden Bildbeschreibungen immer wieder die Form des Essays, ihre zuletzt in *Zungengewahrsam* (1999) in überraschendem Wiederanschluß an die Romantik formulierte Poetik des Schreibens als einer auf vielschichtige Texträume zielenden ‚Schriftbewegung', die ausschießlich ihren eigenen ‚Bewegungsgesetze[n]' folgt (Z 42, 55), entspricht zugleich der gattungsüberschreitenden Tradition moderner Kurzprosa, die durch den Entwurf innovativer ästhetischer Reflexionsräume moderner Wirklichkeitserfahrung gekennzeichnet ist und seit den 1970er Jahren eine breite Renaissance erlebt hat. (Zu nennen wären Marie Luise Kaschnitz, Thomas Bernhard, Botho Strauß, Walter Helmut Fritz, Johanna Walser, Christoph Wilhelm Aigner, Hans-Jürgen Heise, Klaus Merz und viele andere mehr.) Auch wenn Anne Duden die prägnante Kleinstform des nur wenige Zeilen umfassenden Denkbildes bislang nicht erprobt hat, so verbindet ihre Prosa doch auf andere Weise Momente moderner Essayistik mit Aspekten des Prosagedichts und solcher Kurzprosaformen, wie sie von Robert Walser, Robert Musil, Walter Benjamin und anderen entwickelt worden sind. Es entsteht ein Formenspektrum vom klassischen Essay über die Prosaskizze bis zum Prosagedicht, das thematisch und ästhetisch an die genannten Traditionslinien der literarischen Moderne anschließt und durch die fast regelmäßige Erstpublikation in Zeitungen und Zeitschriften zugleich deren mediengeschichtliche Verflechtung mit dem Feuilleton fortschreibt. Nach einigen Vorüberlegungen zu Anne Dudens poetologischem Selbstverständnis sollen im folgenden Spielarten ihrer Kurzprosa und Essayistik in exemplarischen Textanalysen beleuchtet werden.

‚Schriftbewegung' und ‚Komposition' – Poetologische Voraussetzungen

Die aus Paderborner und Züricher Poetikvorlesungen der Wintersemester 1995/96 und 1996/97 hervorgegangenen ‚Erkundungen einer Schreibexistenz', die Anne Duden unter dem Titel *Zungengewahrsam* veröffentlicht hat, verbinden den theoretisierenden Rückblick auf die autobiographische Geschichte ihres eigenen Weges zum Schreiben und eine dezidierte Geste der Überschreitung jener Ästhetik weiblicher Schmerzerfahrungen, mit denen die Autorin ursprünglich bekannt geworden ist (Z 46f.), mit dem vielschichtigen Entwurf einer Poetologie, die zentrale Momente der europäischen Moderne des 20. Jahrhunderts im Spiegel einer Relektüre deutscher Frühromantik neu interpretiert. Es geht offensichtlich darum, literarisches Schreiben einerseits gegen außerästhetische Anforderungen als genuines Medium ästhetischer Erfahrung neuerlich zu begründen und andererseits gegen die Fallstricke traditioneller Autonomieästhetik fest im geistigen und sinnlichen Prozeß des Lebens zu verankern. Der Schlüsselbegriff der ‚Schriftbewegung' (Z 42, 43 u.ö.), in dem Leben und Werk, Schreiben und Text ähnlich wie im ‚écriture'-Begriff des französischen Poststrukturalismus und Feminismus (Derrida, Cixous, Kristeva) miteinander vermittelt werden,[2] befreit die Literatur vom ‚Paßgang gemächlicher Gattungen' (Z 42) und zielt in der gemeinsamen Tradition der Romantik und der Moderne auf die Entstehung ‚immer neuer, immer anderer Arten' von Literatur (Z 47).

Diese auch für die Entstehung und Entwicklung der modernen Kurzprosa seit dem ausgehenden 19. Jahrhundert grundlegende Überschreitung tradierter Gattungsgrenzen in einem kontinuierlichen Prozeß ästhetischer Innovation erhält ihre spezifische Bestimmung bei Duden durch eine Ästhetik des Textes als Raum, und eben diese Textraumästhetik führt noch näher an die charakteristische Verräumlichung der Textstrukturen in der modernen Kurzprosa heran. Gegen die herkömmliche Auffassung der Literatur als ‚Kunst des Nacheinander' (die sich traditionell von der Opposition zwischen Poesie und Malerei in Lessings *Laokoon* herleitet) stellt Duden das Modell eines Schreibens, in dem ‚alle Schichten, über/unter/ineinander, Stimme werden', in dem ‚Alles und alles [...] einander [berührt]', in dem ‚aus gegenstrebigen Teilen und sich immerzu verlagernden Elementen' ‚die Möglichkeit unendlich sich staffelnder Berührungspunkte' entsteht (Z 42, 44). Dieses Modell – gewissermaßen eine romantisierende moderne Überbietung von Goethes bekanntem Konzept der wechselseitigen bzw. ‚wiederholten Spiegelungen'[3] – wird nicht nur mit der für Dudens Werk zentralen poetologischen Metapher ‚unendlicher Übergänge' belegt, sondern auch mit der temporalen Metapher der ‚Simultaneität' und vor allem mit der musikalischen Metapher der ‚Vielstimmigkeit' bzw. ‚Polyphonie' (Z 42, 44).[4] Die Anklänge an die (früh-) romantischen Grundgedanken der ‚ewige[n] Berührung in allem' (Arnim),[5] an Friedrich Schlegels Konzept der unendlichen ästhetischen Progression im ständigen Wechselverhältnis von Leben und Kunst oder an Novalis' Auffassung der Sprache als ‚ein musikalisches IdeenInstrument' und an sein Diktum ‚Man muß schriftstellern wie komponieren' sind unverkennbar.[6] Die Ästhetik der Romantik fungiert in *Zungengewahrsam* mithin als Reflexionsmodell einer Poetologie aus der Tradition der literarischen Moderne, die auf ein Höchstmaß an Intensivierung von Wahrnehmung und Bewußtsein zielt, auf eine geradezu absolute ästhetische Strukturierung, deren allseitige innere Bezüglichkeit ihr semantisches Potential als Prozeß realisiert, wobei der Gleichzeitigkeit und Gleichgewichtigkeit des Unterschiedlichen und Gegensätzlichen besondere Aufmerksamkeit gilt.

Der musikalischen Metaphorik romantischer Ästhetik verdankt sich in diesem Zusammenhang insbesondere Dudens ergänzender Begriff der ‚Komposition' (Z 52, 45). Er stellt der produktionsästhetischen Linearität der ‚Schriftbewegung' (und der unvermeidlichen Linearität der Lektüre) die Sinnräumlichkeit der Werkstruktur gegenüber, wie Dudens ästhetische Begrifflichkeit überhaupt immer aufs neue aus unterschiedlichen Blickwinkeln die fundamentale Dialektik von Raum und Zeit im literarischen Werk ausschreitet. Der tschechische Strukturalist Kvetoslav Chvatík hat für die Gegenstände ästhetischer Betrachtung den Begriff einer ‚Struktur als Prozeß' entwickelt,[7] und in eben diesem Sinne begreifen Dudens dialektische poetologische Metaphern der allseitigen Berührung, des Übergangs, der Simultaneität, der Polyphonie, der ‚Schrift- [und] Raumbewegungen' (Z 42, 52) das Ergebnis der literarischen Arbeit als ‚Gestalt aus Bewegung, die sich an nichts hält als an ihre eigenen Bewegungsgesetze' (Z 55). Als ‚Gestalt aus Bewegung' ist der literarische Text das Medium eines ästhetischen Sinnraumes, der sich gleichwohl nur in seinem Vollzug erschließt, auf der Spur der ‚Schriftbewegung', und dies zielt natürlich in erster Linie auf ‚nicht-schematisierte' Formen der Literatur, deren Produktion und Rezeption geläufige Konventionen des Schreibens und Lesens durchbrechen. Analoges meint die Abgrenzung, daß sich im literarischen Kunstwerk nicht etwa eine vorgefertigte ‚Methode', sondern ‚ein Rhythmus des Erkennens, der Wahrnehmung, des Denkens' ‚ins Werk' setze (Z 50) – ein Gedanke, auf dessen Rückbindung an Ingeborg Bachmann und Friedrich Hölderlin die Forschung schon hingewiesen hat.[8]

Gefährdet ist die spezifische Erkenntnis- und Wahrnehmungsleistung dieser ästhetischen ‚Bewegungsgesetze', die die Literarizität des Textes verbürgen, in dieser Denktradition nicht nur durch äußere (gesellschaftliche und berufliche bzw. mediale) Zwecksetzungen, die der ‚Schriftbewegung' ihre Freiheit nehmen – hier stellt sich etwa das Problem des Feuilletons als literarischer Publikationsform –, bedroht ist sie auch durch Konventionalisierung, beispielsweise durch den kritisierten ‚Paßgang gemächlicher Gattungen'. (Die poetische Form des theoretischen Diskurses in *Zungengewahrsam* ist selbst ein Beispiel für die literarische Subversion vorgängiger Gattungen, hier jener der Poetikvorlesung, die seit ihren Anfängen in Ingeborg Bachmanns *Frankfurter*

Vorlesungen 1959/60 längst eigene Konventionen entwickelt hat.) Und doch bilden sich in der Schnittfläche thematischer Interessen und stilbildender literarischer Verfahren natürlich auch bei Anne Duden rekurrente Formen aus, Spielarten der Kurzprosa, die in autorspezifischer Weise bestimmte Traditionslinien der Moderne aufgreifen und fortschreiben. Und da *Zungengewahrsam* in werkgeschichtlicher Hinsicht ausschließlich im Umkreis von Kurzprosa entstanden ist, dürfen diese ‚Erkundungen einer Schreibexistenz' (obwohl sie sich auch auf *Das Judasschaf* beziehen lassen) zumindest *auch* als eine Poetik der Kurzprosa gelesen werden. In diesem Sinne ist nun zu fragen, wie sich Anne Dudens anspruchsvolle Poetologie im Feld der Kleinen Prosa und des Essays literarisch umsetzt.

Spielarten moderner Kurzprosa bei Anne Duden

Die von Anne Duden in der Tradition der ästhetischen Moderne reaktualisierten poetologischen Konzepte der ‚wiederholten Spiegelungen' und der ästhetischen Polyphonie sind im historischen Kontext ihrer Entstehung um 1800 vor allem in der Großform des Romans produktiv geworden – man denke an Wielands *Aristipp*, Arnims *Gräfin Dolores* oder Goethes *Wilhelm Meisters Wanderjahre*. Anne Dudens poetologische Dialektik von ‚Schriftbewegung' und ‚Komposition' schließt zugleich aber an die Geschichte der modernen Lyrik (und ihre Vorgeschichte um 1800) an, in deren komplexen Texträumen die eigenen ‚Bewegungsgesetze' literarischen Schreibens tradierte Gattungskonventionen auf ganz andere Weise in multidimensionale ästhetische Sinnräumlichkeit transformieren. Dies gilt in besonderer Weise für das Prosagedicht, in dem sich der Grenzübertritt von freien lyrischen Formen zur Prosa überkreuzt mit der komplementär-entgegengesetzten Bewegung einer Lyrisierung der Prosa. Nach Vorläufern um 1800 – insbesondere in Novalis' *Hymnen an die Nacht* – ist das Prosagedicht im Gefolge des französischen *poème en prose* in der Jahrhundertwende 1900 zu einer eigenständigen Spielart moderner Kurzprosa geworden, die sich von Max Dauthendey und Georg Trakl über Johannes Poethen, Walter Helmut Fritz und andere bis in die Gegenwart verfolgen läßt. Die ‚polyphone' Intensivierung der motivisch-thematischen und ästhetischen Wechselbezüge in Teilen von Anne Dudens Kurzprosa läßt sich durchaus in dieser Tradition der Grenzüberschreitung zwischen Lyrik und Prosa lesen, auch wenn die Texte nicht die Kürze typischer moderner Prosagedichte besitzen.

Offenbar hat die Autorin selbst – abweichend von der hier vorgeschlagenen Begrifflichkeit – anläßlich von Lesungen 1995/96 ihre Gedichte (nicht ihre Kurzprosa) als ‚Prosagedichte' bezeichnet.[9] Nun lassen sich in ihren Gedichten (in *Steinschlag*, 1993, und den entsprechenden Teilen von *Wimpertier*, 1995) zwar (etwa in der Syntax und im narrativen Grundzug) durchaus Moment einer Prosanähe ausmachen, die in den thematisch-motivischen und stilistischen Gemeinsamkeiten der Lyrik und Prosa von Anne Duden begründet sind. Dennoch ist diese Begriffsverwendung wenig hilfreich, denn so kontrovers die Bestimmung und Abgrenzung des Prosagedichts diskutiert wird[10] – der Verzicht auf das Erbe des Verses, den Zeilenbruch des modernen Gedichts, gilt neben der Kürze und der Intensität ästhetischer Strukturierung doch als eines der Minimalkriterien des Prosagedichts. So hat etwa Marie Luise Kaschnitz, in deren Werk sich auf ganz andere Weise ein Nebeneinander thematisch-motivisch verwandter Gedichte und Kurzprosatexte findet, ‚Gedichte in Prosaform' als eine Möglichkeit gesehen, im Vergleich zu ihren Kurzgeschichten und literarischen Tagebüchern ‚alles noch dichter [zu] fügen und [zu] fassen'[11] – ganz im Sinne von Anne Dudens polyphoner ‚Gestalt aus Bewegung', die autobiographische Erfahrung ästhetisch multidimensional transformiert.

Ein Beispiel für die Nähe von Anne Dudens Kurzprosa zum Prosagedicht ist in diesem Sinne der Text ‚Im verlorenen Ton' aus dem Band *Der wunde Punkt im Alphabet* (1995). Vor dem angedeuteten Hintergrund einer Fahrt ins ländliche Wales im Frühling – heraus aus dem Alltag der städtisch-industriellen Zivilisation – thematisiert der Text ein überwältigendes Klangerlebnis, das sich von seinem Ausgangspunkt – dem Gesang einer menschlichen ‚Stimme' (A^2 95) – löst und den Aufenthalt ästhetisch verwandelt: Ohne daß ein Sänger, ein bestimmter Gesangstext oder ein Vortragsort sichtbar würden, also von vornherein im rein ästhetischen Raum musikalischer Erfahrung, ist diese Stimme ‚frühmorgens, mittags und auch noch spätabends' zu hören (A^2 95). Anknüpfend an eine Motivtradition, die von den Sirenen der *Odyssee* bis beispielsweise zu Kafkas Texte *Josefine, die Sängerin* reicht, löst der ‚Sog' dieser Stimme ‚Gegenstände', ‚Orte' und ‚Richtungen' auf (A^2 96) und transformiert so Raum und Zeit in die eigenen, autonomen ‚Bewegungsgesetze' eines ästhetischen Zeit-Raums, dessen ganz andere Welt mit synästhetischen und Naturmetaphern inszeniert wird:

> Nichts als jene eine einzige Stimme, kühn und bänglich zugleich, und diese Tonfolgen, die nichts versprechen, nichts beklagen, sich auf nichts berufen als

auf die eigene Befindlichkeit und einen zwischen Gedächtnis und rasch verfallender Vergangenheit aufgespannten Zeitraum, einen unsichtbaren und nicht zu begreifenden Aufenthaltsort, ein Nest aus Hauch und Dunkelheit, das einem aus Luftwurzeln entwachsenen Ast- und Blattwerk aufliegt. (A^2 97)

Als Ausdruck ‚der vollkommenen Verlorenheit, der grenzenlosen Einsamkeit, des überwältigenden Mangels' (A^2 95) vermittelt dieser auf sich gestellte Gesang eine ‚Grenzenlosigkeit', die die kontrastierend erinnerte Vielstimmigkeit des Alltags vorübergehend auslöscht (A^2 96f.). Im U-topos der ästhetischen Erfahrung vermittelt die Stimme paradoxerweise dennoch Geborgenheit (‚Nest') und Unzugehörigkeit in einem – in einer Schwebe, die in dem Bild des ‚aus Luftwurzeln entwachsenen Ast- und Blattwerk[s]' symbolisch zur Anschauung gelangt. Trotz der Unterschiede in der motivischen Einbettung erinnert dieser Gesang – in seiner Opposition zur sozialen Welt, im Ausbleiben jeglicher Antwort, in seiner magischen Kraft als ein ‚Sog', dem die Hörer ‚verfallen' (A^2 96), in seiner Fähigkeit zur Aufhebung konventionellen Zeitempfindens – an die Ekstatik der romantischen Zauberberg/Venusberg-Topik, auch wenn das Thema hier ein anderes ist. Denn es geht nicht um die sozialen oder psychologischen Probleme der ausgedrückten ‚Befindlichkeit' (diese werden gar nicht angesprochen), sondern um das ästhetische Erlebnis selbst in seiner zeit- und raumsprengenden, die gesamte Wahrnehmungswelt verwandelnden Wirkung. Nicht das (im Dämonischen symbolisierte) Unverfügbare der menschlichen Natur (wie in der romantischen Topik), sondern das Rätsel der ungeheuren Kraft ästhetischer (Hör-) Erfahrung ist das Thema, und dieses Thema ist (wie so oft bei Anne Duden) zweidimensional: Es verbindet die im engeren Sinne ästhetische Frage nach der Natur des Gesangs mit der anthropologischen nach der Natur unserer Empfindungswelt, deren Komplexität sich erst in der ästhetischen Erfahrung erschließt.

Trotz seiner zeiträumlichen ‚Grenzenlosigkeit' ist das Klangerlebnis aber doch als eines auf Zeit gestaltet. Der letzte Abschnitt des Prosastücks läßt mit dem Übergang der Hörenden in den Schlaf auch den Spannungsraum des Gesangs abklingen, wenn auch nicht vollständig aufhören. Wie zunehmend unklar wird, ob der Text tatsächlich ein unmittelbares Hörerlebnis oder nicht vielmehr dessen fortdauernde Resonanz im Hörenden darstellt, so endet er in einer Schwebe zwischen Ende und Übergang: ‚Schwer zu sagen, ob sie [die Silben der gesungenen Worte, D.G.] vergehen oder entstehen wollen, sich sammeln oder zerstreuen. Es muß ihnen überlassen bleiben, einstweilen.' (A^2 98) Schon im zweiten Absatz, der bereits das Motiv der schlaflosen Nacht einführt, verweist die Wendung, daß die Stimme ‚manchmal' durch die Nacht ‚irrlichtert' (A² 95), auf die Möglichkeit ‚endloser' Wiederholung von Tag zu Tag. Schien die musikalische Transzendierung von Raum und Zeit von ihrem Anfang her in diesem Sinne auf Dauer zu zielen, so liest sich der Text von seinem Ende her gleichwohl als ein ‚Aufenthalt' ‚im verlorenen Ton' (so der Titel), dessen ekstatische Qualität in der Kürze des Textes ein formales Korrelat findet. Daß der Rückblick auf die vielstimmige gesellschaftliche Welt nicht chronologisch vorangestellt, sondern kontrapunktisch in der Textmitte in das Stimmerlebnis eingebettet wird, unterstreicht die künstlerische Verdichtung der Darstellung.

Der Text ‚Im verlorenen Ton' (A 95-98) zeigt die für moderne Kurzprosa insgesamt charakteristische Verwendung lyrischer Strukturierungsmittel wie Motiventwicklung, Variation, Kontrapunktik und Rahmenbildung. Stilbildend ist neben der für Anne Dudens Schreiben typischen Metaphorik der Übergänge und Raum-Zeit-Metamorphosen aber vor allem der prägnante Verzicht auf ein lyrisches oder autobiographisches Ich als Brennpunkt des dargestellten ästhetischen Erlebnisses. Wie zwar der ästhetische Ausdruck einer ‚Befindlichkeit' im Gesang betrachtet, nicht aber nach dieser selbst gefragt wird, das Erlebnissubstrat der ‚Stimme' also vollkommen abstrakt bleibt, so arbeitet die Darstellung mit der scharfen Spannung zwischen der (traditionell lyrischen) Intensität subjektiver ästhetischer Erfahrung (dem Hörerlebnis und seiner verwandelnden Kraft) und der Distanzierung dieser Erfahrung vom Subjekt des Textes in ein Objekt literarischer Betrachtung, das allgemeingültigen Gesetzen ästhetischer Wahrnehmung gehorcht: ‚Wen jetzt diese Stimme erreicht [...], der ist ihr schon verfallen [...].' (A² 96) Diese Darstellungstechnik stattet den Text mit einer Verbindlichkeit und Selbstreflexivität aus, die sich auch in der argumentativen Rhetorik der Sprache niederschlägt: ‚Unvorstellbar, daß', ‚Ihr zufolge', ‚Schwer zu sagen, ob' usw. (A² 95-98). Es geht nicht um den Ausdruck von Gefühlen, sondern um eine hellwache Intensität gleichzeitig sinnlicher und intellektueller Wahrnehmung und ihrer Versprachlichung. Dabei spiegelt sich das Thema in der Form: Wie die Stimme sich ihre eigene Welt schafft und die soziale Wirklichkeit vollkommen übersteigt, so trägt dieses Kurzprosastück sich gewissermaßen selbst, abstrahiert von allem narrativen oder autobiographischen Kontext und konzentriert sich ganz auf die resonanzreiche Darstellung und Reflexion einer ästhetischen

Erfahrung, die angesichts der Bedeutung von Musik und Gesang (Körper) in Anne Dudens Poetologie paradigmatische Züge besitzt.

Noch deutlichere prosalyrische Qualitäten besitzt das Titelstück des Bandes *Wimpertier* (1995), in dem Duden unterschiedliche Bild- und Motivebenen so übereinander legt bzw. ineinander schiebt, daß eine komplexe ästhetische ‚Gestalt aus Bewegung' entsteht (W^2 27-29). Den Ausgangspunkt bildet hier eine synästhetische Komposition aus unterschiedlichen Elementen (Wasser, Luft, impliziter [Erd-] Boden), Farben (gold, blau, rosig), Sinneswahrnehmungen (Licht, Lärm, Kälte, implizierte Tast- und Geruchsempfindungen) und Kondensatzuständen (Wasser, Nebel, Gas), die im Rahmen einer Motivik des Liquiden (‚Wassermassen', ‚Lichtnebel', ‚Gas verströmt') einen rein ästhetischen Wahrnehmungsraum konstituieren, dessen Multivalenz exemplarisch in der Spannung zwischen Erleichterung – ‚Endlich. Abends' – und Bedrohung steht (‚Gas verströmt sich und findet kein Ende'). Diese Komposition wird dann als ein Augenblick der Wahrnehmung identifiziert – ‚Dies ist, von allen Momenten, immer noch der beste' –, für dessen Freiheit das Auf- und Durchatmen steht und damit zugleich ein wahrnehmendes, empfindendes, atmendes Subjekt. Zugleich führt der zweite Absatz jedoch – in der Tradition von Kafkas berühmter Erzählung *Die Verwandlung* – die phantastische Ambivalenz dieses Subjekts ein, insofern es (einmal ‚sie', einmal ‚ich' genannt) zunächst teils als ein anthropomorphisiertes primitives Wassertier, teils als eine alpträumende (junge) Frau verstanden werden kann, bevor der durch Kapitälchen hervorgehobene Satz ‚EINE FRAU WIRD BESEITIGT' klärt, daß die Tierweltmotive tatsächlich als Metaphern seelisch-körperlicher Befindlichkeit zu lesen sind. Am Schluß greift der Text die Verknüpfung von Tiermetapher und weiblichem Subjekt im Titelmotiv noch einmal auf: ‚Ihr Körper, noch Momente zuvor ein nächtliches geschlossenes Auge, ein großes schlafendes Wimpertier, nun gewaltsam dazu gebracht, das Riesenlid, das ihn ganz bedeckte, zu heben, aufzuschlagen.' (W^2 29) Das Gleiten zwischen Tier- und Menschenwelt und die Verschiebung der gewohnten Proportionen (der Körper als Auge und dieses als kleines Tier) sind in dem dargestellten Prozeß imaginärer Metamorphose also wiederum Ausdruck einer höchsten Intensivierung der Körpererfahrung als (archetypischer) Selbsterfahrung an den Grenzen personaler Identität.

Obwohl dieses Prosagedicht genretypisch die klassische Zeitachse epischer Sukzession unterläuft, deutet sich in der Textbewegung von einer Zeit-‚Schwelle' zur nächsten, von einem Abend zum Wiederaufwachen am Morgen (als dem gewaltsamen Einbruch von ‚Licht' und ‚Wahrheit') doch der rudimentäre narrative Faden einer durchträumten Nacht an, deren Alpträume symbolisch Gewalterfahrungen zur Sprache bringen und Erinnerungsarbeit zur ‚Geschichte *im* Ich' (Bachmann)[12] leisten. Diese poetische Traumsprache erinnert in ihren Nacht-, Gewalt- und Todesmotiven, auch in ihrer Thematisierung von Familienbeziehungen (Mädchen, Bruder, Mutter) an Prosagedichte Georg Trakls wie *Traum und Umnachtung* oder *Offenbarung und Untergang*. Allerdings wird der Themenbereich soziale Gewalt und Geschlechterverhältnis bei Duden aus weiblicher Perspektive entwickelt und viel enger an konkrete Körperempfindungen gebunden als bei Trakl oder Kafka. Zugleich schließen grundlegende Motive des Prosagedichts – die Assoziation von Weiblichkeit und Wasser (auch in den Anspielungen auf die Ophelia-Motivik der Wasserleiche), bzw. allgemeiner von Weiblichem und Elementarem, die Darstellung von Nacht und Traum als Raum einer intensiveren Selbst- und Körper-, insofern auch Naturerfahrung gegenüber der brutalen ‚Wahrheit' des ‚Lichts' am Tage – deutlich an romantische Topoi und ihre Tradierung in der Literatur und Kunst des 19. Jahrhunderts an, wenngleich natürlich die dort mitgedachte geschichts- und naturphilosophische Dimension der Motive nicht mehr adaptierbar ist. Die Radikalität von Anne Dudens Kurzprosa besteht in diesem Zusammenhang – auch im Vergleich mit Autorinnen älterer Generationen wie Marie Luise Kaschnitz und Ingeborg Bachmann – nicht zuletzt darin, daß sie (wenn überhaupt) keine andere Utopie mehr kennt als die Intensivierung körperlich-geistiger Bewußtheit und die Anerkennung von Differenz im Medium ästhetischer Erfahrung, und doch ist gerade diese Auszeichnung ästhetischer Erfahrung in einer von Gewalt und Schmerz geprägten Lebenswelt, wie Duden sie darstellt, ein romantisches Erbe ihres spezifischen Beitrags zur Fortschreibung der literarischen Moderne in der Literatur der Gegenwart.

In ihrem Band *Der wunde Punkt im Alphabet* hat Anne Duden offensichtlich unterschiedliche Formen der Kurzprosa und des Essays erprobt. Schaut man zunächst auf die nicht eindeutig essayistischen Stücke, so treten neben den prosagedichtartigen Text ‚Im verlorenen Ton' feuilletonistische Prosaskizzen, deren oft satirischer oder ironischer Blick auf moderne soziale Realität im Bestand moderner deutschsprachiger Kurzprosa vielfältige Resonanzen hat. Die Skizze ‚Paläontographie oder Liberate my mind' läßt sich – auch in ihrer genretypischen Schlußpointierung – geradezu als ein Benjaminsches Denkbild lesen.[13] Die Körperkultur einer Kurklinik ist hier der motivische Vorwurf für ein groteskes Sittenbild der heutigen Leistungsgesellschaft, in der ‚das ganze Leben [...] im Grunde eine schwere Krankheit' ist, die sich den ‚Gesichtern und Körpern' als Zerstörung eingräbt (A^2 46f., 43). In der Kurklinik kommt prismatisch eine allgemeine Überforderung ans Licht, die die einzelnen körperlich und seelisch gleichermaßen entstellt. Und doch entdeckt der ironische Betrachter – ‚das muß zugegeben werden' – im letzten Absatz in manchen Gesichtern ‚nach vier oder fünf Wochen zum ersten Mal ein Lächeln', das ahnen läßt, ‚wie diese Gesichter einmal gemeint gewesen sein könnten' (A^2 47). So gewinnt die physiognomisch akzentuierte Kulturkritik der Skizze die Doppelfunktion eines ethnologischen Blicks, aus dessen imaginärer (‚paläontographischer') Außenperspektive sich die moderne Gesellschaft grotesk entlarvt, und einer weitergehenden anthropologischen Frage nach dem Schicksal, das die ‚Natur' des Menschen in der kulturellen Konstruktion der heutigen westlichen Welt erfährt. Die Skizze arbeitet zwar mit dem seit Jacques Lacan, Michel Foucault und ihrer feministischen Rezeption grundlegenden Gedanken der ‚Einschreibung' der Kulturgeschichte und ihrer sozialen Normen in das Subjekt und seinen Körper arbeitet, sie rekurriert in ihrem pointierenden Schlußmotiv mithin jedoch noch einmal auf den aus der Anthropologie des 18. Jahrhunderts tradierten Topos der ‚wahren Natur' des Menschen und ihrer kulturellen Entstellung.[14]

Dieser ironischen ‚Paläontographie' moderner Körperkultur steht in der Skizze ‚Das schöne Leben' eine thematisch verwandte Satire der deutschen Wohlstandsgesellschaft zur Seite. Die ‚Unfähigkeit zu trauern' (Mitscherlich), die deutsche Festkultur und Bierseligkeit, das ‚Gerede' kommerzialisierter Jugendkultur werden durch die Motive des ‚Baubooms' und der Autogesellschaft ergänzt und als Zeichen der Oberflächlichkeit einer Wohlstandsgesellschaft dargestellt, die dabei ist, im schönen Schein zu ersticken: ‚Das Leben lebt nicht, aber es ist schön und wird gefeiert.' (A^2 53) Daß diese etwas pauschale Kulturkritik einen Bogen spannt von der Problematik deutscher Vergangenheitsbewältigung im Zeichen des Nationalsozialismus über den Verlust des Naturempfindens bis zu phantastisch pointierten Motiven der Urbanisierung, technologischen Innovation und Beschleunigung, das verbindet Anne Duden hier auf überraschende Weise mit der Kurzprosa von Marie Luise Kaschnitz, und zwar auch darin, daß die Kritik an dem ‚falschen Leben' (Adorno)[15] der westlichen Moderne eine entschieden moralische Schlußwendung nimmt:

> Das Leben lebt nicht, aber es ist schön und wird gefeiert. Und bald kann, wenn der Bauboom so weitergeht, auch noch das letzte Fleckchen Erde luft- und wasserdicht zugedeckt werden, so daß die Autos dann schlußendlich mit der schon lange angestrebten Totalgeschwindigkeit in alle Richtungen über alles – auch die letzten stolpernden Herzen und geöffneten Augen – hinwegflitzen können. (A^2 53)

Ähnliche ‚Denkbilder' der Modernisierungskritik finden sich etwa in Kaschnitz' Kurzprosaband *Steht noch dahin* (1970) – man denke dort an Skizzen wie ‚Es läßt sich leben' und ‚E.Z.' oder an das Prosagedicht ‚Nacktschneckensommer' – oder in ihrer surrealistisch inspirierten Kritik an der Wiederaufbaugesellschaft, deren Mobilität und Technologiebegeisterung in dem literarischen Tagebuch *Tage Tage Jahre* (1968) (insbesondere die Motivreihe um das hypermoderne ‚Pilzhaus' im boomenden NachkriegsFrankfurt).[16] Diese Form der Kulturkritik erinnert zugleich auch an die Phänomenologie modernen Großstadtlebens und ‚postmoderner' Partnerbeziehungen in der Kurzprosa von Botho Strauß, insbesondere in *Paare Passanten* (1981), obwohl Anne Dudens Klage über den Verlust von Naturempfinden, Erfahrungsintensität und Mitmenschlichkeit sich von dem zynischen Blick auf die Verlustbilanz der Funktions- und Mobilitätsgesellschaft bei Strauß deutlich unterscheidet.[17]

Eine andere Möglichkeit des ‚Denkbildes' hatte Anne Duden zuvor bereits in dem Band *Wimpertier* mit der Skizze ‚Fassungskraft mit Herzweh' ausprobiert (W^2 31f.). Während das dort unmittelbar vorangehende Prosagedicht ‚Wimpertier' mithilfe seiner lyrischen Bildkomposition eine komplexe ästhetische ‚Gestalt aus Bewegung' entwirft, arbeitet dieses Kurzprosastück mit einer einfachen, im Motiv der elementaren ‚Wandlung' des Körpers wiederum an Kafka anschließenden Bildidee: ‚Mein Leben ist ganz klein geworden. Eine Winzigkeit, in der ich mich nicht mehr wiedererkenne.' Das Gefühl der Selbstentfremdung wird grotesk als eine Schrumpfung des Körpers dargestellt, die das Ich gewaltsam ‚auf kleinstem Raum' zusammenpfercht und dadurch eine (gefährliche) Intensivierung der Körperempfindungen und Gefühle herbeiführt. Der Schluß des Stückes pointiert die groteske Bildidee in komischer Weise, indem das zu große Herz im zu kleinen Körper nun gemäß langläufiger Gefühlstopik im wörtlichen Sinne der Ort ist, an dem ‚meine Eltern, Brüder und viele andere, als Kinder zusammengekauert und weinend, ja ununterbrochen aufschluchzend' sitzen und durch ihre ‚Tränenflüssigkeit' den Körper der ‚lebende[n] Winzigkeit' von innen heraus verätzen. Die schmerzhaft erhöhte Sensibilität des geschrumpften Subjekts veranschaulicht also grotesk das autodestruktive Potential des

Mitgefühls, dessen Kraft an diesem bildhaften Grenzfall dennoch zugleich nachhaltig anerkannt wird.

Anders als die kulturkritischen Prosaskizzen besitzt ‚Fassungskraft mit Herzweh' in seiner Pointierung als bildhaftes Gedankenspiel aphoristische Qualität. Viele der Kurzprosastücke (wie oben die prosagedichtartigen Texte ‚Im verlorenen Ton' und ‚Wimpertier') haben bei Anne Duden aber auch Züge autobiographischer Prosa, in der Kurzform also solche der Tagebucheintragung. Dabei geht es nicht um eine mögliche (aber nicht notwendige) autobiographische Qualität der dargestellten Erfahrungen und Empfindungen, sondern um die poetische Adaptierung einer literarischen Ausdrucksform für die Reflexion von Problemen moderner Identität und Subjektivität.[18] Anne Dudens Distanzierungstechniken – die Anonymisierung des Ich/sie zum paradigmatischen weiblichen Subjekt in seiner kulturellen und sprachlichen Verfaßtheit, die Abstraktion von allen konkreten sozialen und Alltagskontexten – zeigen als solche bereits die Transformation einer im engeren Sinne autobiographischen ‚Schriftbewegung' (Z 42) in eine literarische Kunstform der Kurzprosa, wobei die Verwandlung und Überformung dieses Diskurses bei Duden entschieden weiter geht als beispielsweise bei Marie Luise Kaschnitz, deren literarische Tagebücher bei aller künstlerischen Gestaltung dennoch den autobiographischen Effekt eines authentischen Ich bewahren.

Als Beispiel dieser ästhetischen Adaptierung autobiographischer Ausdrucksformen in der Form der Kurzprosa kann hier das Prosastück ‚Krebsgang' aus dem Band *Wimpertier* dienen (W^2 57f.). Auf der nurmehr angedeuteten narrativen Folie wiederum einer durchträumten Nacht überkreuzt der Text in der distanzierenden dritten Person (‚sie') mit Hilfe seiner Raummotivik die Disposition eines weiblichen Subjekts mit Kriegs- und Gefangenschaftsbildern, die als Metaphern für eine Welt der Gewalt stehen. Das Subjekt findet sich in einem Raum ultimativer Gefährdung bei völliger Verunsicherung, ‚mitten im Krieg' und auf einem ‚Schlachtfeld, das als solches nicht kenntlich ist', in einer amorphen ‚Gegend', der man nichts ansieht von ihrer tödlichen Qualität. ‚Suchscheinwerfer' und ‚Folterwerkzeuge' weisen dieses alptraumhafte Kriegsszenario als Inbild politischer Gewalt bis hin zu Massenvernichtung und Völkermord (Shoah) aus. Das Titelmotiv des ‚Krebsgangs', mit dessen Seitwärtsbewegung die Träumende vergeblich den ‚Schrecken' zu entkommen trachtet, wird zum Ausgangspunkt einer grotesken Verwandlung auch dieses weiblichen Subjekts in ein Tier, einen Krebs. Die an ‚Wimpertier' erinnernden, damit verbundenen Metaphern des Liquiden (‚hinter ihren Augen eine unter niedriger Decke eingeschlossene Wassermasse', ‚Strom der Grabtücher') münden hier aber in die Vernichtung des Subjekts, das sich ‚in die Kloaken geschleudert und dann der vielfach und amtlich beklagten Zersetzung und endgültigen Auflösung' ausgesetzt sieht. Das Opfer politischer Gewalt wird so zugleich als Abfall der Gesellschaft dargestellt und damit noch in seinem Leiden einer äußersten Entwürdigung und moralischen wie faktischen Vernichtung ausgeliefert.

Der Einbruch dieser tödlichen Schrecken in das träumende weibliche Subjekt als der Reflexe und psychophysischen Einschreibungen historischer und sozialer Gewalt folgt nun einerseits einer kunstgeschichtlich gesättigten Psycho-Logik: Die Träume müssen zu ihrem schrecklichen Ende geträumt werden und – wie es in phantastischer Flug- und Naturmetaphorik heißt – ‚ihre Nistplätze erreichen', sonst hinterlassen sie ‚zerrissene Bilder', die die ‚Foltermächte' im Halbschlaf des Erwachens erneut in Gang setzen, weil die Alpträume ‚verstört und ziellos [...] nirgends landen konnten'. Hier wird dem autobiographischen Substrat der Traumaufzeichnung offenbar eine Reminiszenz an Francisco de Goyas bekanntes Bild *Der Traum der Vernunft erzeugt Ungeheuer* eingeschrieben, die noch einmal die geradezu archetypische Dimension der thematisierten Gewalt veranschaulicht und den Text zugleich in den diskursiven Kontext der für Anne Dudens Werk zentralen Auseinandersetzung mit der ‚Dialektik der Aufklärung' (Adorno/Horkheimer) stellt.[19] Zum anderen aber setzt der Schluß dieses Kurzprosastücks der Bildwelt sozialer und politischer Gewalt in scharfem Kontrast leuchtende Naturmotive entgegen – ‚die Gruppen der geschlossenen Krokusse', ‚der Atem der Amseln' –, die als Zeichen des neuen Tages und der sich wieder öffnenden Sinneswahrnehmungen der Aufwachenden (Blick, Gehör) ganz traditionell naturlyrisch als Symbole des Friedens, des Neubeginns und der Geborgenheit fungieren. Das kulturkritische Motiv des ‚gehörige[n] Abstand[s]' zu den ‚Machenschaften der Stadt' und das Elementarmotiv der ‚ersten Verbindungen' ‚zwischen den niedrigen Luftschichten und der Erde', das den Text als Variante von Dudens poetologischer Motivik der Übergänge und Vernetzungen beschließt – diese Motive rehabilitieren die einfache Naturerfahrung als Gegenpol zur geschichtlichen Welt der Gewalt. In ganz konkreter Bildlichkeit sind die Amseln den geflügelten Alpträumen der Nacht entgegengestellt, ‚Kühle', ‚Nüchternheit' und ‚Milde' lösen das Fieber der Gewaltträume ab. Auf kleinstem Raum stellt diese poetisch transformierte, potentiell autobiographische ‚Aufzeichnung' also ein paradigmatisches weibliches Subjekt in die äußerste Gegensatzspannung moderner Befindlichkeiten zwischen dem Abarbeiten sozialer Gewalt als der Kehrseite moderner Rationalität einerseits und der dennoch augenblickshaft noch einmal als möglich dargestellten Unmittelbarkeit von kathartischer Naturerfahrung als Selbstvergewisserung andererseits.

Vervollständigt wird das Spektrum der Kurzprosaspielarten schließlich von Minimalerzählungen, narrativen Kurzprosatexten unterhalb der Ebene konventioneller narrativer Gattungen wie der Erzählung und der Kurzgeschichte. Ein Beispiel ist der Text ‚Fancy Calling it Good Friday' aus dem Band *Wimpertier* (W^2 33-36), in dem ein normal verlaufender, aber ‚anders' empfundener Flug das weibliche Subjekt in einen veränderten Wahrnehmungs- und Empfindungsmodus versetzt. Für diesen ‚ver-rückten' Zustand erhöhter Sensibilität und Gefährdung, der durch das religiöse Titelzitat (Karfreitag) in eine scharfe Kontrastspannung zu älteren Konzepten metaphysischer Erfahrung gestellt wird, steht hier die Metapher des bedrohlichen ‚flachen Stollens', in dem der (Lebens-) Flug in einer Inversion der Dimensionen (unter/überirdisch) zu zerschellen droht (entsprechende Motive in populären Science-Fiction-Filmen mögen hier Pate gestanden haben). In diesem Empfindungsmodus verändert sich schlagartig die Wahrnehmung; die Welt des Ich stellt sich als ungesichert und bedrohlich dar, und es ist wiederum der (Alp-) Traum, der im Anschluß an den Flug diese vermeintliche ‚Wahrheit' ins Bewußtsein rückt, indem er als ‚Überfall' die Zersprengung des Ichs ‚in alle Richtungen' durchspielt. Erst im Durchgang durch dieses Durchträumen der möglichen Katastrophe kann das Ich in die ‚normale' Wirklichkeit zurückfinden, in der es am Morgen nach dem Flug erwacht. Diese Minimalerzählung mit ihren zwei ineinander verspannten Episoden (Flug und Traumnacht) kreist also wiederum um die plötzliche Verwandlung der vertrauten Welt als Signal einer untergründigen Bedrohung personaler Identität; erzählt wird im wörtlichen Sinne eine ‚innere Geschichte' (Blanckenburg), deren Sujet sich charakteristischerweise in einem Motiv (dem ‚flachen Stollen') verdichtet, in dem sich Zeit- und Raumdimensionen überkreuzen und verschieben.

In einer Schreibweise, die den ‚Paßgang gemächlicher Gattungen' programmatisch unterläuft und die literarische Form gemäß dem jeweiligen Sujet aus den ‚eigenen Bewegungsgesetzen' des entstehenden Textes frei entwickelt, sind die Übergänge zwischen den unterschiedlichen Spielarten der Kurzprosa sowie zwischen diesen und anderen (jeweils verwandten) Prosaformen notwendigerweise fließend. So ließen sich thematisch-motivische und allgemein stilistische Elemente von Anne Dudens Kurzprosa auch in ihren längeren Erzähltexten bis hin zur *Übergang* und *Das Judasschaf* nachweisen. Auch hier bringt die ‚Schriftbewegung' komplexe ästhetische Texträume hervor, die als vieldimensionale ‚Gestalt aus Bewegung' komponiert sind, auch wenn das narrative Element hier stärker ist als in den Kleinen Formen. Ähnlich offen sind die Grenzen zwischen Denkbildern bzw. Prosaskizzen im engeren Sinne und Essays, und der Einschluß von Bildbeschreibungen in *Das Judasschaf* führt exemplarisch vor Augen, wie die Autorin mit der Kombination unterschiedlicher Genres experimentiert.

Der Essay als Feuilleton und als Reflexionsmedium ästhetischer Erfahrung

Schon im Kurzprosawerk von Autoren der klassischen Moderne wie Robert Walser (*Fritz Kochers Aufsätze*), Musil (‚Triëdere' im *Nachlaß zu Lebzeiten*) oder Benjamin (Teile der *Einbahnstraße*) sind die Übergänge zwischen emblematischen Prosaskizzen und kurzen Essays fließend. Insbesondere in der durch Benjamin, Adorno (*Minima Moralia*) und Ernst Bloch (*Spuren*) geprägten Tradition der Grenzüberschreitung zwischen Literatur und Philosophie im Feld der Kleinen Prosa partizipiert der Essay an der Transformation und Innovation tradierter Schreibweisen und Genres durch die moderne Kurzprosa. Den in diesem Sinne anspruchsvollsten Entwurf zu einer Poetik des Essays im Kontext der literarischen Moderne hat zweifellos Adorno in seinem Aufsatz *Der Essay als Form* (1958) vorgelegt. Gegen die Begrenzungen wissenschaftlicher Systematik, gegen den ideologischen Zwang der ‚Meinung' und gegen die unterstellte Beliebigkeit des ‚Feuilleton[s], mit dem die Feinde der Form diese verwechseln',[20] versteht Adorno den Essay programmatisch als ‚Versuch', als ‚die kritische Form par excellence', in der der Geist sich in der ‚Spekulation über spezifische, kulturell bereits vorgeformte Gegenstände' frei entfalten und so ‚das Verhältnis von Natur und Kultur' neu vermessen kann.[21]

Ohne hier auf die Verankerung dieser Poetik des Essays in der Kritischen Theorie eingehen zu können, ist festzuhalten, wie nahe Adornos Verständnis des Essays als ‚Prozeß geistiger Erfahrung' an Anne Dudens poetologische Dialektik von ‚Schriftbewegung' und ‚Komposition' heranführt:

> Weniger nicht, sondern mehr als das definitorische Verfahren urgiert der Essay die Wechselwirkung seiner Begriffe im Prozeß geistiger Erfahrung. In ihr bilden jene kein Kontinuum der Operationen, der Gedanke schreitet nicht einsinnig fort, sondern die Momente verflechten sich teppichhaft. Von der Dichte dieser Verflechtung hängt die Fruchtbarkeit von Gedanken ab. Eigentlich denkt der Denkende gar nicht, sondern macht sich zum Schauplatz geistiger Erfahrung, ohne sie aufzudröseln.[22]

Auffällig ist nicht nur die Zurücknahme des denkenden Subjekts in einen ‚Schauplatz geistiger Erfahrung', die an Anne Dudens Übersetzung autobiographischer Motive in kulturell begründete Erfahrungsmuster paradigmatischer weiblicher Subjekte erinnert; auffällig sind vor allem die Analogien in der poetologischen Topik: Wie die ‚Schriftbewegung' bei Anne Duden bringt der ‚geistige Prozeß' bei Adorno seine eigenen ‚Bewegungsgesetze' hervor; wie das literarische Schreiben bei der Autorin produziert das essayistische bei dem Philosophen komplexe Textstrukturen, die mit der traditionellen Textraummetaphorik der ‚Verflechtung' bzw. Textur (‚Teppich') beschrieben werden. Adornos weitere Ausführungen unterstreichen diese Analogien noch und zeigen zugleich auch seine Verwurzelung in jener romantisch-modernen Tradition der Ästhetik, an die Anne Duden in *Zungengewahrsam* neuerlich angeschlossen hat. Nicht zufällig spielt Adorno in seiner Begründung der Freiheit essayistischen Denkens als der Grundlage der literarischen Form des Essays auf das romantische Fragment an, bestimmt seine ‚Wahrheit' als Produkt seiner Form und erläutert seine ‚Autonomie der Darstellung' im Rekurs auf die Musik.[23] Das essayistische Nachdenken über den ‚Essay als Form' mündet schließlich in eine ganz ähnliche Engführung von musikalischer Ästhetik und poetologischer Raummetaphorik wie bei Duden: Die ‚Übergänge' des Essays ‚desavouieren die bündige Ableitung zugunsten von Querverbindungen der Elemente, für welche die diskursive Logik keinen Raum hat'; stattdessen ‚streift der Essay die musikalische Logik, die stringente und doch begriffslose Kunst des Übergangs'.[24] Die Analogien zu *Zungengewahrsam* sind offensichtlich. Unabhängig von der Frage, ob die Autorin im traditionellen Sinne von Adorno 'beeinflußt' worden ist, veranschaulicht Adornos Poetik des Essays mit ihrem Rückgriff auf die romantische Ästhetik mithin exemplarisch die Stellung und Bedeutung des ‚Essays als Form' im Feld von Anne Dudens Kurzprosa.

Bei aller Nähe der Konzepte sind natürlich auch die Differenzen nicht zu übersehen. Daß die ‚Offenheit' des Essays seine ‚utopische Intention' gewährleistet,[25] ist im gegenwärtigen Umkreis diskursanalytischen

Denkens, wie es auch Anne Dudens Werk eingeschrieben ist, keineswegs mehr so selbstverständlich wie für Adorno. Überhaupt steht Adornos Glauben an die Freiheit des Geistes bei Anne Duden ein viel konkreteres Ansetzen bei Strukturen sinnlich-körperlicher, kultureller und insbesondere ästhetischer Erfahrung gegenüber. Auch in ihren Essays geht es der Autorin nicht in erster Linie (wie Adorno) um die ‚Wechselwirkung der Begriffe', sondern um die quasi-musikalische ‚Verflechtung' von Motiven und Bildern in der Darstellung und Reflexion insbesondere moderner Wirklichkeits- und Kunsterfahrung. Der Essay ist bei ihr keine philosophische, sondern entschiedener als bei Adorno eine literarische Form, die durchaus nicht den Schritt zur Alltagsreflexion im Stil des Feuilletons scheut. Sicherlich wäre es auch eine Überzeichnung, wollte man Anne Dudens emphatische Poetik der literarischen ‚Gestalt aus Bewegung' im gleichen Sinne auf ihre Essays beziehen wie etwa auf ihre Prosagedichte. Bemerkenswert ist gleichwohl, wie regelmäßig Anne Duden den Essay zur Darstellung und Reflexion ästhetischer Erfahrung verwendet und wie die gewählten Sujets (Werke der bildenden Kunst und Architektur) nun ihrerseits als ‚Gestalt aus Bewegung' gelesen werden, so daß die für die Poetologie der Autorin zentralen Konzepte und Metaphern sich in der ästhetischen Reflexion der Essays auf andere Künste transponiert finden. ‚Prozesse geistiger Erfahrung' gestalten diese Essays gerade dort, wo sie den Gesetzen ästhetischer Erfahrung und insbesondere der Transzendierung konventionellen Zeit- und Raumempfindens nachgehen.

So entwickelt beispielsweise der Essay ‚Unter einem Dach' aus dem Band *Zungengewahrsam* für das überwältigende Raumerlebnis englischer Kathedralen ganz ähnliche Kategorien, wie die Autorin sie für die komplexe Sinnräumlichkeit von literarischen Texten verwendet. Indem sie die Dimensionen ihrer modernen städtischen Umwelt sprengen, stellen sich diese Kathedralen als ‚Sanktuarien des Raumes' dar (Z 75), deren ‚Aura der Erhabenheit' beim Betrachter eine ‚Bereitschaft für das Nichtabsehbare' auslöst (Z 76), die sich in der literarischen Form des Essays in einen offenen Prozeß zugleich ästhetischer und geistiger Erfahrung umsetzt. Dieser Prozeß führt nach der initialen Sprengung der alltäglichen Raumdimensionen mit dem Schritt in die (wiederum nicht singuläre, sondern typische) Kathedrale in eine vollständige Verwandlung des Raum- und zugleich des Zeiterlebens. Wird die Linearität der ‚Schriftbewegung' in der ‚Komposition' des Textes verräumlicht, so verzeitlicht hier umgekehrt die Bewegung des Blicks im ‚Sog' der Ferne, Tiefe und Höhe des Kirchenschiffes den Raum: Der ‚Blick' beginnt, ‚der

Zeit gleich, die an den Wänden bis ins Gewölbe hinauf zu fließen, zu rieseln, sich zu kräuseln scheint,' hin- und her-, auf- und abzufließen ‚und so fortzuzirkulieren' (Z 78). Zeit und Raum überkreuzen sich, Architektur und Licht verbinden sich im Blick des Betrachters zu einer dynamischen Einheit des Gegensätzlichen, die den konkreten Ort in einen multidimensionalen ästhetischen Zeit-Raum verwandelt: ‚Alles oszilliert hier zwischen Zustand und Ablauf, Ruhe und Erregung, Statik und Dynamik.' (Z 78) Der Essay konzentriert sich dann im weiteren auf die Kunst der Schlußsteine (‚green man'), die die Inversion der Dimensionen in besonderer Weise symbolisieren, indem ‚das da oben einen hier unten entdeckt' (Z 79), die mehrdimensionale Plastik der Steine eine ästhetische Refiguration der Raumerfahrung konstituierenden Perspektiven und Proportionen erzwingt.

Eine ähnliche Raumästhetik entwickelt Anne Duden in dem Essay ‚Die Dinge sind dem Raum geneigt' über den Besuch einer Skulpturenausstellung im öffentlichen Raum der Stadt Nordhorn (Z 132-140). Mit einem Zitat des französischen Ästhetikers Maurice Merleau-Ponty – ‚Der Schriftsteller als Spezialist der Sprache ist ein Spezialist der Unsicherheit'[26] – expliziert der Essay einleitend die ihn strukturierende Analogisierung von poetologischen Kategorien – der Essay verschreibt sich programmatisch der Offenheit der ‚Horizonte' und der ‚Vernetzung' der Zeit- und Raumdimensionen in der literarischen Bewegung der ‚Schrift' (Z 132) – und solchen der Raumästhetik des Skulpturenwegs in Nordhorn, der seine eigene ‚Raumsprache' hervorbringt (Z 138). In seinem Vollzug vermittelt der ‚Text-Raum' des Essays einen Eindruck von dem ‚Raum-Text' (Z 139) der in die Stadtlandschaft gesetzten Skulpturen, die vermittels ihrer ‚Umgebungsfühligkeit' ein neues ‚Beziehungsgeflecht zwischen den Dingen' entwerfen (Z 136f.). Diese ‚Vernetzung' von Skulptur und Umgebung wirkt laut Beobachterin auf die Skulpturen zurück, läßt sie selbst ‚in Bewegung geraten' (Z 137, 134) und schafft so eine eigenständige ästhetische Welt, die den Betrachter zur Reflexion seines Raumverständnisses und seines (im Alltag instrumentellen) Verhältnisses zu den Dingen zwingt (Z 138). Noch radikaler ist die Verwandlung geläufiger Zeit- und Raumwahrnehmung im Medium ästhetischer Erfahrung in den abstrakten Gemälden von Clea Wallis, denen Anne Duden ihren Essay ‚Vergittert im Gefilde' widmet (Z 114-124). Jenseits ‚aller Raumgrenzen, -muster und –vorstellungen' wird hier ästhetisch ein anderer, 'unsichtbarer' Raum sichtbar, dessen ‚Dynamik' den Blick des Betrachters in eine unabsehbare ‚Bewegung' versetzt (Z

118f., 122f.).²⁷ Wiederum dient die Musik (‚Tanzrhythmus', ‚Komposition', englische Renaissance-Musik; Z 122f.) als Reflexionsmedium der multidimensionalen Komplexität dieser ästhetischen Erfahrung.

Mit dem Essay über Clea Wallis ist zugleich die größte thematische Gruppe in Anne Dudens Essayistik angesprochen, ihre Bildbeschreibungen, vor allem zu Werken der frühen Neuzeit, deren Weltlandschaften und ‚Augen-Blicke' narrativ und deskriptiv als komplexe Zeit-Räume, als optische ‚Gestalt aus Bewegung' vergegenwärtigt werden. Diese poetische Form essayistischer Kunstbetrachtung stellt ein eigenes Thema dar, dem hier nicht mehr nachgegangen werden kann.²⁸ Im Hinblick auf den hier unternommenen Versuch einer Analyse von Anne Dudens Kurzprosa und Essayistik im Licht ihrer in *Zungengewahrsam* entwickelten poetologischen Überlegungen ist gleichwohl festzuhalten, wie erfolgreich die Autorin in ihren Bildbeschreibungen die Fläche der Gemälde in komplexe ästhetische Räume mit vielfältigen ‚Verweisungszusammenhängen'²⁹ übersetzt und zugleich die ästhetischen Zeichen der Zeit bzw. Zeitlichkeit in den Bildern entfaltet, so daß der Verräumlichung der Zeit im Bild die Verzeitlichung des Raumes in der literarischen ‚Schriftbewegung' der Essays antwortet. Es ist eben diese lebendige Lektüre der Gemälde als komplexer ästhetischer ‚Kompositionen', die diesen Essays die literarische Qualität von ‚Prozessen geistiger Erfahrung' verleiht.

Nicht alle Essays von Anne Duden allerdings widmen sich ästhetischen Erfahrungen, nicht alle besitzen die poetische Qualität ihrer Bildbeschreibungen oder lassen sich auf andere Weise auf ihre anspruchsvolle Poetologie des Textes als ‚Gestalt aus Bewegung' bzw. auf Adornos Entwurf des Essays als ‚Prozeß geistiger Erfahrung' beziehen. Manche der Essays sind durchaus einfacher strukturierte, oft humorvoll getönte Feuilletons (potentiell autobiographischen Charakters) über Alltagserfahrungen in thematischer Nähe zu den kulturkritischen Prosaskizzen. Zu nennen wären hier Texte wie ‚Umwege' und ‚I wish you well' aus dem Band *Der wunde Punkt im Alphabet*, beide mit dem Leben in London befaßt. Im ersten Fall handelt es sich um eine narrativ inszenierte Betrachtung über die Widrigkeiten der Benutzung des notorisch unzuverlässigen und veralteten Londoner U-Bahn-Netzes, wobei die Aufmerksamkeit für Ausscheidungen und Abfälle am Rande der Wege, die das Ich des Essays unternimmt, sowie die Zwecklosigkeit der ganzen Fahrt – ein Stromausfall veranlaßt die Schließung der Bibliothek, deren Besuch das

Ziel war – diesem Feuilleton einen leicht skurrilen Anstrich geben (A^2 21-25). Der zweite feuilletonistische Essay (A^2 91-94) beleuchtet mit ironischer Pointierung das Tagesprogramm Londoner Rundfunksender, das im Rhythmus der Hauptverkehrszeiten morgens und nachmittags das Tempo des modernen Geschäftstages spiegele, um ‚am Scheitelpunkt des Tages, mitten auf der Strecke zwischen Arbeitsbeginn und Feierabend' ‚plötzlich' ‚eine atemberaubende Drosselung' zu erfahren, in der sich die Aufmerksamkeit nun den vom konventionellen Arbeitstag Ausgeschlossenen, den ‚zumeist weiblichen Wesen in den Verliesen' ihrer Häuser widmet (A^2 92). Aus der ironischen Distanz dieses gewissermaßen ethnographischen Blicks auf den Medienalltag der britischen Metropole stellen sich die therapeutischen Radiogespräche für Hilfesuchende als eine ‚Geisterstunde', als ein ‚Spuk' dar, der den Schmerz der von ihren Partnern verlassenen oder betrogenen Anrufer entschieden unwirklich (und darin ungerechterweise zugleich komisch) erscheinen läßt. Deren Leiden wird geradezu aus der Normalität, dem öffentlichen Selbstbild der durchrationalisierten Mobilitäts- und Leistungsgesellschaft ausgeschlossen. So verfolgt die Autorin auch in dieser leichteren Spielart der Kleinen Prosa ihr Interesse an der kulturellen Konstruktion sozialer Wirklichkeit aus der Perspektive weiblicher Identität. Jeder Versuch, Anne Dudens Prosa aus den Traditionen moderner deutschsprachiger Kurzprosa heraus zu lesen und von hier aus unterschiedliche Genrespielarten vom Prosagedicht über das ‚Denkbild' bis zum Essay zu unterscheiden, bedarf also der Ergänzung des gattungsgeschichtlichen Erkenntnisinteresses durch die Analyse durchgehender ‚Problemkonstanten' (Bachmann) des Werks; erst in der Zusammenschau von Sujets und Schreibweisen erschließt sich die markante Signatur von Anne Dudens Kurzprosa als eigenständige Fortschreibung von Traditionen der Frühromantik und Moderne.

Anmerkungen

[1] Theodor W. Adorno, *Noten zur Literatur*, Suhrkamp: Frankfurt a.M., 1981, S. 21.

[2] Vgl. mit Bezug auf Anne Duden Susanne Baackmann, *Erklär mir Liebe. Weibliche Schreibweisen von Liebe in der deutschsprachigen Gegenwartsliteratur*, Argument: Hamburg, 1995 (Argument-Sonderband, N.F. 237), S. 146 ff.

³ Johann Wolfgang von Goethe, *Werke* (Hamburger Ausgabe in 14 Bdn.), Bd. 12, hrsg. von Erich Trunz und Hans Joachim Schrimpf, dtv: München, 1982, S. 322 f.; vgl. Goethes Brief an Carl Jacob Ludwig Iken vom 27. September 1827 in Johann Wolfgang von Goethe, *Briefe* (Hamburger Ausgabe in 6 Bdn.), Bd. 4, hrsg. von Karl Robert Mandelkow, dtv: München, 1988, S. 250.

⁴ Vgl. zu Anne Dudens musikalischer Poetik in ihren früheren Texten grundlegend Suzanne Greuner, *Schmerzton. Musik in der Schreibweise von Ingeborg Bachmann und Anne Duden*, Argument: Hamburg, 1990 (Argument-Sonderband 179).

⁵ Achim von Arnim, *Werke in 6 Bänden*, Bd. 1, Paul Michael Lützeler, Hg., Deutscher Klassiker Verlag: Frankfurt a.M., 1989, S. 575 (*Gräfin Dolores*).

⁶ Novalis, *Werke*, Gerhard Schulz, Hg., Beck: München, 1981², S. 427, 527; Friedrich Schlegel, *Kritische Schriften*, Wolfdietrich Rasch, Hg., Hanser: München, 1971³, S. 38 f.

⁷ Kvetoslav Chvatík, Mensch und Struktur. Kapitel aus der neostrukturalen Ästhetik und Poetik, Suhrkamp: Frankfurt a.M., 1987, S. 17.

⁸ Siehe Ingeborg Bachmann, *Werke*, Christine Koschel, Inge von Weidenbaum, Clemens Münster, Hgg., Piper: München und Zürich, 1982², Bd. 4, S. 60: ‚Musik und Dichtung haben nämlich eine Gangart des Geistes. Sie haben Rhythmus, in dem ersten, dem gestaltgebenden Sinn.' (*Musik und Dichtung*) Vgl. Greuner, *Schmerzton*, S. 63 f.

⁹ Siehe Franziska Frei Gerlach, Schrift und Geschlecht. Feministische Entwürfe und Lektüren von Marlen Haushofer, Ingeborg Bachmann und Anne Duden, Erich Schmidt: Berlin, 1998, S. 311.

¹⁰ Siehe Ulrich Fülleborn, *Das deutsche Prosagedicht. Zu Theorie und Geschichte einer Gattung*, München 1970; Ulrich Fülleborn, ‚Einleitung', in: U. Fülleborn, Hg., in Zusammenarbeit mit Klaus Peter Dencker: *Deutsche Prosagedichte des 20. Jahrhunderts. Eine Textsammlung*, Fink: München, 1976, 15-43; Dirk Göttsche, ‚Denkbilder der Zeitgenossenschaft. Entwicklungen moderner Kurzprosa bei Marie Luise Kaschnitz', in: Dirk Göttsche, Hg., *„Für eine aufmerksamere und nachdenklichere Welt." Beiträge zu Marie Luise Kaschnitz*, Metzler: Stuttgart, 2001, 79-104; Cornelia Ortlieb, *Poetische Prosa. Beiträge zur modernen Poetik von Charles Baudelaire bis Georg Trakl*, Metzler: Stuttgart, 2001.

¹¹ Marie Luise Kaschnitz im Gespräch mit Ben Witter: ‚Um die Dorfkirche mit Marie Luise Kaschnitz. Spaziergänge XV', in: *Die Zeit*, 3.5.1968, S. 62.

¹² Bachmann, *Werke*, Bd. 4, S. 230.

¹³ Vgl. zum Begriff ‚Denkbild' in diesem Sinne Eberhard Wilhelm Schulz, ‚Zum Wort „Denkbild"', in: *Wort und Zeit. Aufsätze und Vorträge zur Literaturgeschichte*,

Neumünster 1968, 218-252; Heinz Schlaffer, ‚Denkbilder. Eine kleine Prosaform zwischen Dichtung und Gesellschaftstheorie', in: Wolfgang Kuttenkeuler, Hg., *Poesie und Politik. Zur Situation der Literatur in Deutschland*, Stuttgart 1973, 137-154; Burkhard Spinnen, *Schriftbilder. Zu einer Geschichte emblematischer Kurzprosa*, Aschendorff: Münster 1991.

[14] Vgl. exemplarisch Hans-Jürgen Schings, Hg., *Der ganze Mensch. Anthropologie und Literatur im 18. Jahrhundert. DFG-Symposion 1992*, Metzler: Stuttgart, 1994 (Germanistische Symposien, Bd. 15).

[15] Theodor W. Adorno, *Minima Moralia. Reflexionen aus dem beschädigten Leben* (*Gesammelte Schriften*, Bd. 4), Wissenschaftliche Buchgesellschaft: Darmstadt, 1998, S. 43.

[16] Marie Luise Kaschnitz, *Gesammelte Werke*, 7 Bände, Christian Büttrich und Norbert Miller, Hgg., Insel: Frankfurt a.M. 1981-89, Bd. 3.

[17] Vgl. Dirk Göttsche, ‚Denkbild und Kulturkritik. Entwicklungen der Kurzprosa bei Botho Strauß', in: *Text + Kritik*, 81: *Botho Strauß* (Neufassung, 1998^2), 27-40.

[18] Vgl. zur Problematik autobiographischen Schreibens bei Anne Duden Georgina Paul, „‚Life-writing': Reading the Work of Anne Duden Through Virginia Woolf's ‚A Sketch of the Past'," in: Mererid Puw Davies, Beth Linklater, Hgg., *Autobiography by Women in German*, Peter Lang: Oxford, Bern, Berlin, Bruxelles, Frankfurt a.M., New York, Wien, 2000, 291-305.

[19] Max Horkheimer und Theodor W. Adorno, *Dialektik der Aufklärung. Philosophische Fragmente*, Wissenschaftliche Buchgesellschaft: Darmstadt, 1998 (Theodor W. Adorno, *Gesammelte Schriften*, Rolf Tiedemann, Hg., Bd. 3).

[20] Adorno, *Noten zur Literatur*, S. 20, 27, 12 f.

[21] Ebd., S. 25, 27, 10, 28.

[22] Ebd., S. 20 f.

[23] Ebd., S. 24, 28, 30 f.

[24] Ebd., S. 31.

[25] Ebd., S. 26, 21.

[26] Maurice Merleau-Ponty, *Das Auge und der Geist. Philosophische Essays*, hg. und übers. von Hans Werner Arndt, Hamburg 1984, S. 124 (zitiert nach Z 140).

[27] Vgl. hierzu den Beitrag von Teresa Ludden in diesem Band.

[28] Vgl. Frei Gerlach, *Schrift und Geschlecht*, S. 377 ff.

[29] Ebd., S. 393.

Margaret Littler

Trauma and Terrorism:
the problem of violence in the work of Anne Duden

Anne Duden's representation of violence poses problems for the feminist critic analysing the constructions of a female writing subject. On the one hand Duden is explicitly concerned with the trauma of recent German history and of violence against women; on the other hand her poetological works present writing itself as violent, as an act of 'terrorism' which is fundamentally in conflict with life, especially life as a woman. This paper explores the representation of violence and images of abjection in relation to language and subjectivity in 'Übergang'. It relates this discussion to the elaboration of an uncompromising modernist aesthetic in Duden's more recent work, in which the theme of suffering coincides with the 'extremism' of writing in sometimes disturbing ways, as Duden confronts her readers with the violent legacy of German identity.

Anne Duden's prose debut *Übergang* (1982) centres on a founding traumatic event, the effects of which continue to resonate throughout her later work. The title story is the autobiographically-based account of a violent attack in which the female protagonist's mouth and jaw are badly damaged and of the medical reconstruction which seeks to remove all traces of the violence yet which is experienced as equally violent. It is a remarkable account of trauma, both the shock of the event itself and its devastating after-effects. It is the structure of trauma, unintegrated in memory or understanding, yet remaining unbearably present to the traumatised subject, that implicitly links the protagonist's individual experience to her indirect knowledge of the Holocaust. The almost perverse relief associated with the loss of language and temporary liberation from the imperative of female beauty has led feminist critics to interpret the text in Lacanian terms as a critique of the patriarchal symbolic order and a retreat into an intense pre-oedipal, unmediated experience of the body.[1] Violence against women is an ongoing concern in Duden's subsequent work, as is its association with the legacy of National Socialism and with the destructive urge in mankind's relationship to nature.[2] The appeal of this constellation of themes to a feminist readership is understandable, but potentially problematic, as Stephanie Bird has shown: the tendency of women readers to identify with female protagonists can obscure crucial moments of ambivalence, especially in depictions of violence in Duden's work.[3]

This ambivalence comes into sharper focus in Duden's poetological essay 'Zungengewahrsam. Erkundungen einer Schreibexistenz' (1999), in which she reflects on the development of her writing in terms of the relationship between violence and language:

> Die Sprache hat [...] mehr mit Ent- als mit Behauptung zu tun. Mehr mit Zerreißen und Zerrissenwerden als mit Zusammenfügen, Zusammengehören oder -hörigkeit; mehr auch mit Schweigen als mit Ausplaudern. Mehr mit Verlust als Gewinn, mehr mit Gewalt und Krieg als mit Sanftmut und Frieden. (Z 35)

While writing would appear to be the attempt to symbolise and thus remove the psychic blockage of trauma, it is also described here in terms of 'terrorism', 'exterritorial, terroristisch, extremistisch' (Z 12). It is both motivated by compassion for the world and only possible in a radical separation from the world of everyday life. The tension between writing and life is explicit also in her prose of the 1990s (in particular the 1995 volume *Wimpertier*), where images of violence become central to a specifically modernist aesthetic. The development (which Duden herself identifies) from biographically-grounded prose to the almost complete elision of the subject in her more recent poetic texts can be seen in Kristevan terms as a movement towards a 'rhetoric of the pure signifier'.[4] While 'Übergang' may be read as a 'trauma narrative' of sorts, which attempts to accommodate the traumatic event into a life story, in Duden's later work, trauma becomes the basis of an aesthetic existence, a 'Schreibexistenz' founded on poetic language, not as the 'vehicle of understanding', but as 'the locus of what cannot yet be understood.'[5] This progression can be understood in terms of what Shoshana Felman has described as 'the performance of a testimony', first psychoanalytical and then poetic, in which the subject of trauma actively pursues the disintegration of the self, then of language, in the attempt to bear witness to a truth which she does not own.[6] I propose to reconsider the images of violence in 'Übergang' and more recent work in the light of this progression, and to explore Duden's poetological reflections on her status as a female writing subject from the perspective of recent feminist ontology, not strictly compatible with the Kristevan reading indicated above. I shall also be questioning the ethical implications of the aesthetic position elaborated in Duden's more recent work. The relationships between violence, victimhood and femininity which were read as critical of patriarchy in the last decades of the twentieth century may be less palatable to feminist readers at the beginning of the twenty-first.

1. The Subject of Trauma in 'Übergang'

The evidence of traumatic symptoms in the protagonist of 'Übergang' is immediately apparent, in the numbness following the facial injury, in her state of hyperarousal accompanied by the apathy of surrender, and in the dreams which torment her sleep. Firstly one is struck by the absence of pain associated with the injury, attributable to shock, and the inability of the psyche to register what has happened to the body. Then there are the protagonist's persecution anxieties in hospital, where all blacks (whether passers-by or the reassuring anaesthetist) recall the black GIs who attacked her.[7] At the same time she feels impotent to defend herself, as expressed in her last thoughts before succumbing to the anaesthetic before the operation to reconstruct her jaw: 'Ohnmacht, über die die Macht hinweg walzt, Terror, gegen den dein Wille ein Hauch ist' (Ü 72). Finally the traumatic event recurs in horrific dreams, which intrude unannounced into the narrative, such as that in which the protagonist faces a threatening group of neo-Nazis intent on killing her (Ü 84). The recurrence of all-too literal images of the traumatic event are generally attributed to the fact that it has never been integrated into either conscious or unconscious understanding, thus it not recalled as memory but remains unbearably present to the traumatised subject:

> Das frisch Geschehene ließ sich einfach noch nicht handhaben, weder durch Erinnerung noch durch Verdrängung. Entweder es schlief, bewußtlos unruhig und überwältigt vom eigenen Schmerz, oder es war bei vollem Bewußtsein und überwach, wenn der Schmerz keine Ruhe und keinen Schlaf zuließ. (Ü 89)

In addition to these symptoms of trauma in the protagonist, a 'trauma narrative' emerges in the fragmentary life story which appears in the form of italicised flashbacks after the violent attack. These reveal the painful process of female socialisation in immediate post-war Germany, including both the distortions of a female ego-ideal and the repression of the unspoken knowledge of the Holocaust.[8] The aim of this narrative, however, is *not* recovery, whether in the sense of memory or of cure, and this is what accounts in large part for the radical impact of the text and for its immediate appeal to feminist critics who saw in it also a critique of the place accorded to women in the patriarchal symbolic. Indeed, the state of hyperarousal and vulnerability characterising the traumatised subject of 'Übergang' becomes an aesthetic ideal in Duden's more recent poetic work.

The relationship of trauma to the genesis of the subject, particularly as suggested in images of abjection in the text, provides a link to Duden's later work, in particular to her view of writing as 'terrorism'. Julia Kristeva's essay on abjection *Powers of Horror* (1980) draws on the Lacanian account of subject formation. This entails separation from the mother and alienation in language, which then stands in for the real. Kristeva posits an intermediate entity, however, which permanently threatens the attainment of this symbolic position: the abject, which is neither subject nor object, and which must be expelled to create the logical space which the subject will occupy. For her, separation from the mother and the demarcation of body boundaries is achieved through a process of expulsion at the level of the pre-oedipal imaginary. However, it is recalled in the expulsion of all excreta and body fluids, which are the object of such revulsion because they are reminders of our corporeal beginnings and are thus a legacy of the pre-linguistic real.[9] The abject reveals the cost and the fragility of subjective integrity:

> The abject is the violence of mourning for an 'object' that has always already been lost. The abject shatters the wall of repression and its judgements. It takes the ego back to its source on the abominable limits, from which, in order to be, the ego has broken away - it assigns it a source in the non-ego, drive, and death.[10]

Kristeva's essay focuses on the condition of 'borderline subjects', those who have never fully entered the symbolic and fail to differentiate completely between subject and object, inside and outside. They are prone to mystical or aesthetic discourses as ways of keeping the abject under control. Twentieth-century modernist writers such as Georges Bataille or Antonin Artaud are, for Kristeva, subjects who confront abjection and recover from it by means of writing. The association of abjection with the discourse of aesthetic modernism is common to Kristeva and Duden, and I shall return to it in due course.

Abjection is the ultimate figure of transition from inside to out, and thus a central concern of Duden's 'Übergang', which renders so painfully clear the tenuousness of the inside/outside distinction and confronts us with the possibility of the narrative subject's 'sliding back into the corporeal abyss out of which it was formed'.[11] Once the violent attack has dislodged her subjective anchoring in the symbolic, the distinctions between conscious and unconscious, subject and object, even life and death become porous. The corpse is a recurrent figure in 'Übergang', the protagonist occupying a place between the dead and the living as she lies in her hospital bed attached to a drip which is both gallows and umbilical cord: 'Ich war aufgebahrt in der Hölle meiner selbst' (Ü 72). Indeed, Duden states in 'Zungengewahrsam' that the narrative standpoint of the volume *Übergang* was that of 'der tote Leib' (Z 59), indicating an early stage in the process of the elision of the narrative subject in her later work. The dead body is also for Kristeva a figure of abjection, a residue of the unsymbolised real, not signifying anything we can comprehend and thus unbearable to confront: 'refuse and corpses *show me* what I permanently thrust aside in order to live. [...] There, I am at the border of my condition as a living being. My body extricates itself, as being alive, from that border. [...] the corpse, the most sickening of wastes, is a border that has encroached upon everything'.[12] So the image of the corpse in 'Übergang' can be seen as just one instance of the text's circling around the horror of abjection, the uncontrollable seeping of the body suggesting an irreversible dissolution of the subject, succumbing, it would seem at the end of the text, to the stasis of the death drive. From the first realisation of the extent of the protagonist's injuries, we are spared no details of the damage: 'Sie hob eine Hand, um ihre Lippen zu berühren, berührte aber stattdessen aufgerissenes und geplatztes Weiches und lose darin hängende Zähne' (Ü 65). In the violent description of coming round from anaesthetic and being addressed as a subject, the protagonist's vomit (explicitly 'living on' after it leaves her body) demonstrates once more what has to be expelled in order for that subject to reclaim its space:

> Erinnerung - Anstrengung - Identität. Das Geschoß hatte einen inneren, zentral gelegenen Sack durchschlagen, eine bis dahin sicher abgekapselte Blase. Mit unwiderstehlichem Druck drängte ihr Inhalt aufwärts - es war zu spät, es gab kein Aufhalten mehr. Er preßte sich quallig ausdehnend die Kehle hoch - ich möchte tot sein - , riß den bandagierten Höllenrachen, der nichts als geschlossen und bewegungslos sein wollte, mit wüster Kraft und Gewalt auf, so daß ein Stechen, Ziehen, Rucken und Schneiden die hintersten Winkel des Gehirns durchfetzte, und wälzte sich dann als schleimig schwarz-rote Substanz wie Rotwein mit darunter geschlagenem Ei in eine Wanne. In der Nierenschale schwappte er eine Weile hin und her, eine Masse *noch lebenden* Aufruhrs. [...] Ich war angekommen. (Ü 75; emphasis: ML).

The repeated urge to vomit experienced by the protagonist when her mouth is forcibly closed during medical treatment is also associated with being physically and psychologically silenced: 'Eine aufgebrachte, tobende Sprachlosigkeit wollte sich die Seele aus dem Leib schreien und wurde am Ausgang, an der Schwelle zum Ausdruck immer wieder zurückgeschickt' (Ü 92-93). The theme of the repressed scream is ambiguous; both a cry of protest, and a gesture of expulsion, it has a crucial importance for the development toward an ever more eliptical, poetic style which could be seen to locate Duden more firmly in the tradition of twentieth-century modernism.[13] Kristeva sees modernist writing as an assault on the integrity of the subject-object boundary, which she likens to a fragile membrane. This 'thin film constantly threatened with bursting' is preserved by realist narrative, but when the subject's boundaries are threatened, no such narrative is possible any more:

> [T]he unbearable identity of the narrator and of the surroundings that are supposed to sustain him can no longer be *narrated* but *cries out* or is *descried* with maximal stylistic intensity (language of violence, of obscenity, or of a rhetoric that relates the text to poetry). The narrative yields to a *crying-out theme* that, when it tends to coincide with the incandescent states of boundary-subjectivity that I have called abjection, is the crying-out theme of suffering-horror. [...] If one wished to proceed further still along the approaches to abjection, one would find neither narrative nor theme but a recasting of syntax and vocabulary - the violence of poetry, and silence.[14]

What Kristeva calls the 'theme of suffering-horror' persists in Duden's work (particularly in the volume *Wimpertier)*, but it is increasingly accompanied by 'the violence of poetry, and silence', most obviously in the move towards poetry in the volumes *Steinschlag* (1993) and *Hingegend* (1999). In the context of the European avant-garde, Kristeva differentiates between 'the novelist's verisimilitude' and the 'inhumanity of the poet', by which she implies that narrative reinforces subjective stability, but avant-garde texts destabilise and threaten the subject's coherence. They do so, for Kristeva, by affording us access to the *jouissance* of the pre-signifying drives, that is to a condition preceding subject formation but of which traces remain circulating in language.[15] *Jouissance* here connotes both the pleasure of the archaic attachment to the maternal body before the emergence of the subject *and* the pain of separation; accordingly the *jouissance* awakened by images of the abject mingles both the pain of separation and horror at the threat of loss of identity associated with pre-Oedipal pleasure, traces of which remain circulating in language.[16] This may begin to offer an explanation of the apparent tension between suffering as theme and violence as aesthetic project in Duden's work, between horror of, yet secret pleasure in the abject. What remains to be explored further is the question of how the increasing destabilisation of the subject and the tension between traumatic pain as theme yet pleasure in the violence of poetic language relate to her position as a woman writer.

2. 'Zungengewahrsam' and the female writing subject.

The three-part poetological essay 'Zungengewahrsam. Erkundungen einer Schreibexistenz' confronts us immediately with the ambivalence of writing:

> Auch das Schreiben ist ein Gewaltakt. Oft genug zumindest ist es ein gewaltgeladener Auftakt zum Text, den dann, später, auch wenn er es in sich hat, mit all dem nichts mehr verbindet. Der Text ist der Text, das Gewordene, anders Gewordene. Die Verbindung ist gekappt, die Nabelschnur zerschnitten. Der Text atmet allein, von sich aus. Ob er nun gelesen wird oder nicht. (Z 11)

These opening lines combine the notion of writing as giving birth and producing the alterity of the text, with the idea of writing as an inherently violent gesture. The metaphor of birth for artistic creativity is neither new nor necessarily related to a female creative subject, and Duden's use of the birth metaphor is characteristically ambiguous. The text/child is completely cut off once expelled, not an other to be nurtured and protected. Later in the essay the offspring is itself by no means unequivocally sympathetic:

> Keine Erzählung hat begonnen und keine Geschichte, entstanden ist nur ein Sprach-Schrift-Gebilde mit der Veranlagung zur Vielstimmigkeit, ein mehrstimmiger Textkörper, durchaus auch mit Monstrosität begabt: eine unblutige Ausgeburt, während der Verfasserin das Blut ausgeht, die Tränenflüssigkeit, die Knochensubstanz, das Unterhautzellgewebe und so weiter. (Z 45)

While the image of a monstrous and polyphonic text is certainly a challenge to monologic meaning, it also indicates a sacrifice of life to language, the body of the writing subject given up for the 'Mitgift' of the text. The passage continues according to the retrospective logic of signification, the writing subject's entire life being interpreted *ex post facto* as the production of texts, which come to replace that life. The close inter-dependence of text and writing subject implied here is further underlined by references to Levinas, whose ethical notion of the subject as hostage to the other is explicitly invoked (Z 16). The text is the other to whom the writing subject is responsible, indeed, which calls the writing subject into being. But there is another form of 'Geiseldrama' cutting across the relationship with the text, namely that of the female writing subject with other selves:

> Levinas sagt: 'Der Andere geht mich an. [...] Ich bin des Anderen Geisel. [...] Man anerkennt den Anderen, insoweit man sich als Geisel betrachtet. Das Wichtige ist dabei, daß ich die Geisel bin.' Dieser Gedanke ist mir nah und äußerst vertraut, vertraut wie wahrscheinlich unzähligen Frauen, für die er eine lebenslange, und sei's nicht zu Bewußtsein kommende, Praxis ist, derart, daß sie nicht zu Sinn und Verstand kommen. Für mich als Schreibende, immer Zum-Schreiben-kommen-Wollende, ist er eine Unlösbarkeit, eine Aporie. Und genau daraus resultiert dann ein Schreiben als Gewaltakt, zumindest ein Schreiben mit gewalttätigem Auftakt. (Z 16)

The aporia in question is that between the *female* subject as subject-in-relation and that of the *writing* subject, which must be autonomous and free. This resonates with recent feminist interest in the ontological status of the female subject, in particular with the work of philosopher Christine Battersby, who challenges the notion of identity as self-contained and always in opposition to other entities. Instead she envisages 'the persistence of an embodied self through mutation, birth and change' and sees selfhood in ontological terms as attained gradually, and unavoidably, in relations of power, dependence and responsibilty to others. For her, female subjectivity is individual but non-autonomous.[17] But for Duden, all writing must begin with an 'Über*setzungs*akt': 'Es setzt ein mit dem Sich-Abstoßen vom Terrain und Terror des Geiseldramas und setzt, schon schreibend, *über* zum Terrain der Ungebundenheit' (Z 17). Implicit in this, therefore, is the necessity to relinquish a female subject position in order to become a writing subject. The third part of the essay declares provocatively: 'Das Schreiben ist absolut, etwas an sich Totalitäres', which introduces another aporia. Writing does violence to everyday life, but everyday life is itself 'gewalttätig': 'Schreiben wird Enthauptung der gewalttätigen Ordnungen und Hierarchien des Tages, Entfesselung, Lösung der Bindungen' (Z 51).

The texts in question are not reassuring 'narrative' ('Der Paßgang gemächlicher Gattungen', Z 42) which, according to Kristeva, merely reinforces the subject in its oedipal position,[18] but multi-layered, polyphonic texts, in which meaning is never fixed. They bear close relation to music, which often represents a utopian alternative to language in Duden's work. In 'Übergang' music is 'die Nahrung, die ich wirklich brauchte' (Ü 74), as opposed to the ubiquitous violence swallowed by the protagonist's unconscious. It affords the only relief in her traumatised state. The polyphony of late-medieval music represents an ideal also in 'Zungengewahrsam' due to its capacity to express intense pain and joy without inflicting any damage: 'Der Umgang mit Sensibilität,

Empfindlichkeit, Erregbarkeit, mußte nicht tödlich ausgehen' (Z 56). Music allows the subject to be porous, not enforcing the subject/object boundaries with which language works, and it resonates in the body as well as in the mind. Thus where words can be experienced as gunshot, penetrating the subject and requiring of it a position, music's 'arrows' are harmless: 'Sie traf auf und traf einen, mit Pfeilen, die nicht verwunden konnten, weil sie im Auftreffen schon in bloße Wellenschwingung sich verwandelt hatten' (Z 58). Music is also prized for creating space, a theme which recurs frequently in Duden's work.[19] But it is also music's capacity to express the inexpressible, and its proximity to madness, which makes it serve as a model and ideal for Duden's writing:

> Die Musik schien von vornherein, aber besonders vom Anfang des Schreibens her gesehen, ein direktes, selbstverständliches Verhältnis sowohl zur Vernunft als auch zum Wahnsinn zu haben. Sie schien von großer Durchlässigkeit, schien die Dinge nicht auseinanderhalten und vor allem den Wahnsinn, oder was dafür gehalten wurde, und damit eine ganze Gefühls- und Ausdruckswelt, nicht verbergen, übertönen oder gar verleugnen zu müssen (Z 54).

The notion of madness as a relative and potentially creative state is reminiscent of modernism and in particular of the work of Antonin Artaud. Famed for his own mental instability and for his taboo-breaking Theatre of Cruelty, he set out to combat the complacency of early twentieth-century theatre, which he saw as serving only to flatter its bourgeois patrons. He aimed to assault the audience with action on stage which had the immediacy of dream-contents, not displaced and encoded as in Freud's model, but raw and profoundly disturbing. The idea was to confront spectators with ugliness and evil, after which they would feel relieved, 'as if awakening from a nightmare, the evil and terror cleansed away'.[20]

Duden's identification with at least some aspects of Artaud's aesthetic may be concluded from her quotation of his words at the point of 'Zungengewahrsam' where she identifies what she sees as her own literary trajectory, from the point of view of the 'corpse' in *Übergang* to the elision of the subject in the poetry of *Steinschlag*: 'Etwas wie Gesang stand an, ein Wechsel zur größten Eigenwilligkeit von Stoff und Ton. Die Person ist der Schrift nicht mehr im Wege, sie ist von ihr eingeholt und wird von ihr beiseite- und zurückgelassen' (Z 59). The relative absence of the narrative subject in her more poetic texts makes possible the expression of extreme intensities of perception and emotion, which both Duden and Artaud relate to childhood.[21] Writing of this development in her work, Duden quotes Artaud: 'Ich schreie im Traum,/doch ich weiß, daß ich träume,/und auf BEIDEN SEITEN DES TRAUMS/lasse ich meinen Willen herrschen' (Z 60).[22] In a more recent interview, Duden reiterates the last two lines of this quotation in the context of her own writing career, which she sees as a tightrope walk without a safety net, an attempt to exist in a place where it is impossible to be:

> Was die Texte allesamt machen, heute vielleicht noch stärker: eine Art Existenz zu gründen in einem Dasein, das in gewisser Weise nicht vorkommt bzw. unlebbar ist - eine Gratwanderung, bei der man zu beiden Seiten abstürzen kann. Antonin Artaud hat einmal gesagt: 'Auf beiden Seiten des Traums lasse ich meinen Willen herrschen.' Es geht um diese Unlebbarkeit, das Unerträgliche, um ein großes Loch, das die Gegenwart ist. Es gibt darin keine Halterungen.[23]

The images of writing as a 'Gratwanderung' and of a gaping abyss suggest that the impossible state of vulnerability which her texts articulate, can be sustained only as a writing subject. Put differently, poetic language can rescue the 'borderline subject' from the fascinated fixation on the abject, in the absence of redemption via religious experience. This would accord with Kristeva's view,

> that contemporary literature, in its multiple variants, and when it is written as the language, possible at last, of that impossible constituted either by a-subjectivity or by non-objectivity, propounds, as a matter of fact, a sublimation of abjection. Thus it becomes a substitute for the role formerly played by the sacred, at the limits of social and subjective identity.[24]

The question remaining in my mind is whether Kristeva's 'a-subjectivity' can in any way be said to be female. Poetic language is, for Kristeva, a reconciliation with what we separate from in order to become subjects, an attempt 'to tap that pre-verbal "beginning" within a word that is flush with pleasure and pain'.[25] But although Kristeva posits an unsettling of the symbolic by writing which somehow acknowledges a debt to the archaic mother, what she identifies in the writing of the (exclusively male) avant-garde is no more than the symbolic *jouissance* which circulates in language as a result of the subject's renunciation of the maternal bond.[26] The 'feminine' it celebrates has little to do with female subjectivity as construed by Battersby.[27] In terms of Duden's aesthetic, the question is whether the 'terror' of symbolisation is challenged in writing which also celebrates the pleasure in the text, a pleasure in part derived from the sublimation of abjection and horror. The tension between the poetic text as sublimation of abjection, and the abject/horror as 'theme' with a specific

The problem of violence in Anne Duden's work 53

historical referent will be explored in the following discussion of one of Duden's poetic texts.

3. 'Arbeitsplätze'. Impossible places to be.

In many ways the short text 'Arbeitsplätze' from the 1995 volume *Wimpertier* enacts in poetic form the literary development traced in the essay 'Zungengewahrsam'. It is prefaced by a quotation from Artaud's 'Fragments from a Diary in Hell', which points once more to the uncompromising focus on suffering in Duden's work: 'ich habe den Bereich des Schmerzes und des/ Schattens gewählt/ wie andere den des Glanzes und der Anhäufung/ der Materie./ Ich arbeite nicht im Raum irgendeines Bereiches./ Ich arbeite in der einzigen Dauer'. (W 90) Duden's text begins with a humorously literal interpretation of the writer's occupation as a completely irregular and unregulated form of work, one in which there is no designated 'workplace'. Nonetheless, two 'places' *do* occur in the text, Berlin and 'Norddeutschland', constituting sparse but recognisably biographical references to Duden's own development as a writer. The subject who is 'schwarz vor Wissen' (W 94) is reminiscent of that in 'Übergang', and the knowledge itself is associated with images of dismemberment and abjection: 'Jeden Tag stach es [das Wissen ML] mich ab, stückweise/ in Berlin zum Beispiel/ und schärfte dadurch den Blick für die untoten Stellen/ in den Landschaften der Städte/ am Fuß der Betonmauern/ wo sich Sand, Hundekot und Monatsblut mischen' (W 96). Yet this sensitivity to the horrific detail of everyday life is a necessary prerequisite for the development of the writing subject, whose physical being is subsumed by language:

> Sie [die Worte, ML] benötigen das absolute Gehör des Schmerzes
> die Kryptästhesie der Knochen
> und die Alarmbereitschaft der Grubenorgane.
> Sie brauchen auch natürlich mein Blutwasser
> und meine Tränen
> um erweichen zu können.
> Sie brauchen meinen lebenden Körper mit Haut und Haar. (W 102)

In this text, as in 'Zungengewahrsam', language is ambiguous, both violent and compassionate, an alien power yet one to which the subject gladly submits. Language can lay siege to the subject, pouring out of her mouth, 'wie einen Anfall/ - Buchstabenschaum vor dem Mund - versuche ich solches Reden zu handhaben/ etwas, wofür ich nicht kann/ und nicht zur Rechenschaft gezogen werden will/ ein Notfall, den es möglichst ohne viel Aufhebens zügig durchzustehen gilt' (W 92). She is a subject 'spoken by' language, but at the same time impelled to symbolise the as yet unsignified knowledge of suffering, personified as timid creatures cowering in tunnels, in unequivocally abject terms:

> Aufgeriebenes ehemaliges Leben, pulverisiertes Blut
> in ausgetrockneten, rissigen Flußbetten
> molchiges Gewürm und ineinander verschlungen Schleimiges
> in Schwemmländern
> feingemalener Sand und Staub
> an den Küsten der Meere verflüssigten Schmerzes
> die bis auf den Grund geleert werden müssen.
> Weiterpulsierende augenlose Körper, die darauf warten
> endlich ihr Herz abgeben zu können
> und dann aufgelöst und fortgespült zu werden. (W 93)

In the face of these images of dereliction, it is words that come to the rescue ('ich krieche auf ihre Anwesenheit zu' W 103), but it is also the subject which bears responsibility for forming these images and words. Gradually the 'ich' of the text comes to identify with a 'Sprachexistenz', personified as an indeterminate, dreamlike figure, and, like the 'ich' of 'Übergang', a 'survivor':

> Dämmerzustand Zwitterwesen Traumfigur
> die seit eh und je
> in ihrem eignen Narkosezustand nach schwerer Krankheit
> überlebt.
> ....
> Ich muß ein Gehör entwickeln für das was sie hört
> einen Blick für das was sie sieht
> und Buchstaben, Silben, Worte für das
> was sie unhörbar sagt (W 103)

This figure defies all binary oppositions, is ageless, genderless, a 'Pflanze, die im Behältnis eines menschlichen Körpers/ in menschliche Haut gehüllt/ dem Wüstenboden entwächst' (W 105). It achieves a momentary unity of word and gesture, an ideal of reconciliation between language and the unspoken knowledge of the body.

What is less clear is how this utopian figure relates to the notion of a female writing subject, and to the gendering of violence present here, as elsewhere in Duden's work. The notion of the body as a container has important implications for gendered subjectivity for Battersby, as it implies that matter is inert and incapable of radical novelty. She criticises as hylomorphism the belief, underlying much of western metaphysics, that change comes about by active form imposing itself on passive matter.[28]

Yet Duden's writing, which appears constantly to draw attention to the materiality of the body and of language, also represents language as inert matter, only subject to formation by the creative mind: 'Ich würde, glaube ich, nicht schreiben, [...] wenn die Sprache selbst nicht der Gegenstand der Auseinandersetzung für mich geworden wäre. So wie Cézanne seine Bilder gemalt hat, so geht es auch mir primär darum, an einer Materie und mit einer Materie zu arbeiten, die man nur selber so formen kann und formen muß'.[29] In 'Arbeitsplätze', where there are gestures towards female subjectivity, they are in the references to 'weibliche[n] Lebenslinien' (W 95) and to the guilt of two abortions, performed by 'Schlächterärzte'. The female subject position does appear to be primarily that of identification with the passive victim, while men are characterised as the criminal perpetrators of the destruction which transfixes the poetic subject's gaze, and which renders all the more valuable the rare moments of male compassion. The example given for this provides a specific historical referent for the ubiquitous violence in Duden's work. The testimony of Holocaust survivor Filip Müller is invoked as a lasting and unflinching witness to the suffering of the Jews in concentration camps.[30] His text, with its 'tastend gewissenhafte[r] Wiedergabe' (W 99) is credited with symbolising the unspeakable horror and finally laying it to rest:

> das Wissen
> fängt nach innen und außen zugleich zu fließen an
> und überkommt
> überströmt
> die Worte zwischen hier und noch dort
> so daß auch sie schwach werden
> untergehen wollen
> zurückweichen
> sich absinken lassen bis unter die Flut
> sich ins Schweigen zurückbetten
> und dem Unsagbaren endlich den Vortritt lassen
> in einem Schlucke, einem kurzen Anflug von Schluchzen (W 100)

The use of Müller's text as example of 'die männlichen Tränen' (W 98) is both understandable and faintly troubling, given his status as a Jew whose survival was due to his enforced assistance in mass murder.[31] The words from his text quoted in Duden's poem refer to his decision at one point to go into the gas chamber and share the fate of the other Jews, a decision which, as we know from his testimony, he did not act upon.[32] It is perhaps precisely the ambiguity of his stance, coupled with the voyeuristic unease experienced on reading the acounts of camp survivors, which underlies

Duden's choice of his example in this text. It both makes explicit the historical referent of horror and suffering in her work and acknowledges the degree of complicity involved in the use of suffering to construct a writing identity.[33] This is how one might explain the appearance of images from Müller's text in the subject's account of her own literary endeavour, which could otherwise be deemed an unacceptable appropriation:

> Nachts, wenn wahrheitsgemäß nichts anderes geblieben ist
> wird meine Arbeit auch zur Schreckenszelle
> in der das bißchen Bewegungsfreiheit und Sauerstoffvorrat
> für den kleinsten Rest von Leben
> nicht auszureichen scheint.
> Dann glaube ich mir kein Wort mehr
> in der Enge der sechs nackten Wände
> weil wirklich alles verloren und nichts gewonnen ist
> und die Wortfäden
> wie dünnflüssiger Speichel
> aus halbgeöffneten und bewußtlosen Mündern
> sich kraftlos aufs Kopfkissen legen. (W 100-101)

The lines which follow indicate an awakening, as if the appalling images have been the content of nightmares, but the references also to writing recall Artaud's aesthetic of cruelty, in which the spectator emerges 'cleansed' by the experience of unspeakable horrors. On a literal level, Müller's horrific images merely haunt the subject's dreams; but given the figurative level on which this text operates, there is a danger of eliding the reality of the death camps with the *jouissance* of the poetic encounter with the real.

4. Conclusion.

Duden's depictions of trauma are in many ways all the more interesting for the fact that recovery from trauma is not sought. Her work offers insights into the violence on which the symbolic is founded, and into the normalisation of violence in the world of late twentieth-century western culture. In relation to her poetic trajectory I have been concerned to identify ambiguities in the depiction of violence which can be explicated in psychoanalytical and aesthetic terms; the advent of the subject in the symbolic order of language is both a defense against trauma *and* in itself traumatic, involving expulsion from the supposed bliss of the maternal bond. Thus depictions of horror can be interpreted both as mourning for what has been lost, and as a re-finding of *jouissance* circulating in language. I hope to have demonstrated something of the poignant complexity of her writing, which sometimes pushes language to its limits to articulate 'eine unmögliche Daseinsmöglichkeit'.[34] While this can be understood in Kristevan terms as a challenge to symbolic subjective stability, from Battersby's perspective it suggests an extreme metaphysical pessimism. Duden's poetological writings highlight a radical incompatibility between the female self-in-relation and the writing subject. The images of birth and the hostage, for example, are not used to propose the body's capacity for radical change, nor an interdependent individuality based on imbalances of power, but rather to emphasise the agonising sacrifices facing the woman writer. The insistence on the fragility of the subject's position in relation to the object, made most explicit in images of fluidity and the tacky self-other boundary are not used, as by Irigaray, to posit new ways of thinking female identity. Instead, they remain the object of fascinated disgust, sustaining the subject in contemplation of what it abhors. Horror and violence are the source of both the trauma and the terrorism in Duden's uncompromising aesthetic, which forces us to confront sometimes uncomfortable dilemmas, not least how adequately to commemorate the victims of the Holocaust. The extremism of Duden's stance lies in repeatedly confronting her readers with this violent legacy of German identity, while also demonstrating how closely violence, subjectivity and textuality are linked.

Notes

[1] Sigrid Weigel's psychoanalytical reading endorses what she sees as a deconstruction of symbolic constructions of femininity: Sigrid Weigel, *Die Stimme der Medusa. Schreibweisen in der Gegenwartsliteratur von Frauen*, (1987) Rowohlt: Reinbek, 1989, p. 124.

[2] Some feminist critics have criticised Duden for a too-easy identification with the victims in a victim-oppressor dichotomy. See Ricarda Schmidt, 'Arbeit an weiblicher Subjektivität. Erzählende Prosa der siebziger und achtziger Jahre', in: Gisela Brinker-Gabler, ed., *Deutsche Literatur von Frauen, 2, 19. und 20. Jahrhundert*, Beck: Munich, 1988, 459-477; Elsbeth Dangel, 'Übergang und Ankunft. Positionen neuerer Frauenliteratur. Zu Anne Dudens *Übergang* und Verena Stefans *Wortgetreu ich träume*', *Jahrbuch für Internationale Germanistik*, 22.2 (1990), 80-94. As Stephanie Bird's work shows, the victim-oppressor relationship in Duden is more complex than these critics suggest.

³ Stephanie Bird, 'Desire and Complicity in Anne Duden's *Das Judasschaf*', *Modern Language Review*, 93.3 (1998), 741-753.

⁴ Julia Kristeva, *Powers of Horror. An Essay on Abjection*, (1980) translated by Leon S. Roudiez, University of Columbia Press: New York, 1982, p. 23.

⁵ Cathy Caruth, 'Introduction II', in: C. Caruth, ed., *Trauma. Explorations in Memory*, John Hopkins University Press: Baltimore, 1995, 151-157 (here: p. 155).

⁶ Freud famously pointed to the fact that 'the speaking subject constantly bears witness to a truth that nonetheless continues to escape him, a truth that is, essentially, *not available* to its speaker'. (Cited in: Shoshana Felman, 'Education and Crisis, On the Vicissitudes of Teaching', in: Shoshana Felman and Dori Laub, *Testimony. Crises of Witnessing in Literature, Psychoanalysis, and History*, Routledge: New York, London, 1992, 1-56, here: p. 15). Felman draws parallels between Freud's dream work and Mallarmé's contemporaneous account of the poetic revolution in France, seeing both as radical exponents of the liberating force of disintegration.

⁷ Leslie Adelson was the first critic to detect in this an insensitivity to race, in particular in view of the metaphorical appropriation of 'darkness' connoted as feminine later in the text. See Leslie A. Adelson, 'Anne Duden's *Übergang*: Racism and Feminist Aesthetics', in: L. Adelson, *Making Bodies, Making History. Feminism and German Identity*, University of Nebraska Press: Lincoln, London, 1993, 37-55.

⁸ For a detailed Lacanian reading of this aspect of 'Übergang' see the chapter on Duden in: Brigid Haines and Margaret Littler, eds, *Contemporary Women's Writing in German. Feminist Perspectives*, Oxford University Press: Oxford, forthcoming. A distinction should be noted here between the recurrence of *traumatic* knowledge (which has never been integrated into the psyche) and recollection or retrieval of *repressed* memory.

⁹ If Lacan's view of the subject is seen as fundamentally a relationship to the other (as language, as desire, as *jouissance*), then the abject challenges it, allowing of no clear subject/object distinction. But if the abject is seen as the residue of the real in the symbolic, then Kristeva actually shares one of Lacan's most persistent preoccupations with the material effects of language. See Bruce Fink, *The Lacanian Subject. Between Language and Jouissance*, Princeton University Press: Princeton NJ, 1995, p. 28.

¹⁰ Kristeva, *Powers of Horror*, p. 15.

¹¹ Elizabeth Grosz, 'Julia Kristeva', in: Elizabeth Wright, ed., *Feminism and Psychoanalysis. A Critical Dictionary*, Blackwell: Oxford, 1992, 194-200 (here: p. 198).

¹² Kristeva, *Powers of Horror*, p. 3.

[13] Also on this motif see Margaret Littler, 'Diverging trends in feminine aesthetics: Anne Duden and Brigitte Kronauer', in: Arthur Williams, Stuart Parkes and Julian Preece, eds., *Contemporary German Writers, their Aesthetics and their Language*, Peter Lang: Bern, 1996, 161-180. In this reading the scream is the welling-up of unconscious knowledge which fails to find a release.

[14] Kristeva, *Powers of Horror,* pp. 140-141.

[15] Kristeva describes the 'inhumanity' of the avant-garde in thematic as well as stylistic terms: 'In the wake of a black lineage where Lautréamont or Artaud is inscribed, inhumanity discovers its appropriate themes, contrary to all lyrical traditions, in horror, death, madness, orgy, outlaws, war, the feminine threat, the horrendous delights of love, disgust, and fright' (Kristeva, *Powers of Horror*, p. 137).

[16] What Kristeva sees as traces of pre-symbolic maternal drives in avant-garde texts, other Lacanian theorists (such as Bruce Fink, Paul de Man) interpret as an integral feature of language itself, the materiality of linguistic structures in the unconscious, which account for both the pain of traumatic recollection and the pleasure of poetic texts.

[17] Christine Battersby, *The Phenomenal Woman. Feminist Metaphysics and the Patterns of Identity*, Routledge: New York, 1998, pp. 6-7. See also the chapter by Teresa Ludden on this theme.

[18] '[A] narrative is, after all, the most elaborate attempt, next to syntactic competence, to situate a speaking being between his desires and their prohibitions, in short, within the Oedipal triangle' (Kristeva, *Powers of Horror,* p. 140).

[19] See for example Duden's essay on the music of Carlo Gesualdo (1560-1613), 'O dolorosa sorte', in: *Der Wunde Punkt im Alphabet*, Rotbuch: Hamburg, 1995, pp. 7-12. His music delineates whole landscapes and gives expression to intensities of pain and love which are beyond reason and its binary mode of thinking. See also in the same volume: 'Über erdgebundene Engel' and 'Im verlorenen Ton'. It is possible also to see in Duden's depiction of music and visual art the kind of challenge to Kantean subjectivity which underlies Battersby's feminist ontology. This would render a more positive reading, but one which in my view takes too little account of the trauma and suffering in Duden's work.

[20] Colin Russell, 'A New Scène Seen Anew: Representation and Cruelty in Derrida's *Artaud*', http://130.179.92.25/arnason_de/colin.html

[21] Like Duden, Artaud valued the intensity of childlike perception, which was what he sought to recapture in theatre. See Artaud, ' Of Art and Death', in: *Collected Works vol I*, translated by Victor Corti, Calder and Boyars: London, 1968, 87-93 (here: p. 91). See also Duden, 'Nachschrift', *Wimpertier,* 113-115 (here: p. 114).

[22] The quotation is from Artaud's 'Seraphim's Theatre', a text originally intended for inclusion within *The Theatre and its Double* (1938) which famously expounds his notion of Theatre of Cruelty. 'Seraphim's Theatre', Antonin Artaud, *Collected Works vol. IV*, translated by Victor Corti, Calder and Boyars: London, 1974, pp. 113-117.

[23] Interview with Claudia Kramatschek, 'In den Faltungen der Sprache', *neue deutsche literatur*, 48.2 (2000), 32-44, (here: p. 33).

[24] Kristeva, *Powers of Horror*, p. 26.

[25] Kristeva, *Powers of Horror*, p. 61.

[26] Bruce Fink defines symbolic *jouissance* as 'the residue of the drives' which is sacrificed when we become speaking beings. Fink, *The Lacanian Subject*, p. 99.

[27] Battersby is concerned to envisage a model of subjectivity based on interpenetration, interdependence, and radical material change, as distinct from a model of autonomous (masculinised) self predicated on a 'network of exclusions (abjection)' Battersby, *The Phenomenal Woman*, p. 89.

[28] Battersby's critique of Derrida and Lacan is based on their debt to Kantean thought, which can only posit a self *in* its body in relation to an *other* outside it, leaving him unable to think otherness within the self (Battersby, *The Phenomenal Woman*, p. 97).

[29] Interview with Kramatschek, p. 38.

[30] Müller was one of the Holocaust survivors interviewed by Claude Lanzmann for his film 'Shoah'. He was a Czech Jew born in Sered in 1942, and interned as a schoolboy in Birkenau and Auschwitz. In Auschwitz he was recruited to work in the gas chambers and crematoria for three years. His book *Sonderbehandlung. Drei Jahre in den Krematorien und Gaskammern von Auschwitz* (1979) is one of the most detailed sources of information on the camps. (An English translation exists under the title: *Auschwitz Inferno. The Testimony of a Sonderkommando*, translated by Susanna Flatauer, Routledge & Kegan Paul: London, 1979).

[31] Also troubling is the implicit feminisation of Müller in his 'exceptional' status as compassionate man, which could be said to reproduce an anti-Semitic stereotype.

[32] Müller's words, quoted in Duden's text (W 100), are: 'Abstellen. [...] Was sollte man leben, für was? Und da ging ich in die Gaskammer, mit denen, und entschieden zu sterben. Mit ihnen', Claude Lanzmann, *Shoah* (Fr. 1985), Claassen Verlag: Düsseldorf, 1986, pp. 219-220.

[33] In this respect I concur with Stephanie Bird's Lacanian interpretation of *Das Judasschaf*. She argues that 'the genocide of the Jews in particular enables her to adopt and sustain her role as victim, a position that is further justified by her reference to

The problem of violence in Anne Duden's work 61

other instances of destruction and pain. [...] It is in terms of this symbolic identification that her relationship to atrocities can be viewed as one of complicity. Her complicity does not reside in aiding and abetting the oppressors, or feeling sympathy for what they do; it resides in her dependence on the horror that violence provokes and a dependence on others' and her own suffering for structuring her identity' (Bird, 'Desire and complicity', p. 752).

[34] Interview with Kramatschek, p. 33.

Stephanie Bird

Considering Ethics in the Short Prose of Anne Duden

Anne Duden's short stories depict pain and intense suffering, yet most are not explicitly concerned with the historical and social basis through which the suffering of the individual woman might be understood. This paper analyses the 'status' of the suffering; whether it is linked to a particular moral concern, or whether it raises more general questions about how we understand ourselves as ethical subjects. I draw on Emmanuel Levinas's ideas to argue that the stories stage the intolerability of the ethical burden on the individual, but that by their uncompromising depiction of anguish they succeed in putting the reader into question.

Anne Duden's stories are immensely troubling. This is due not only to the extraordinary and shocking descriptions of pain, despair and anguish, the immediacy with which the narrators' suffering becomes all-enveloping. Another troubling aspect of the texts is the 'status' of the suffering they depict. The stories explore physical and mental anguish and the ways in which they can be represented, but do they also express a concern with the cause of suffering, with its social and with it its ethical dimension? Clearly in the story 'Übergang' and in *Das Judasschaf* individual female anguish is placed in the context of the atrocities of the German past and the violence that continues to saturate contemporary society. However in many of the stories in the collections *Übergang* and *Wimpertier*, such a historical and social basis for understanding individual anguish is largely absent while at the same time the narrators in varying degrees seem to link their own suffering to a position of privileged moral insight. Thus, for example, they often claim to have a heightened awareness of repressed knowledge and denied pain, to which others do not have access. This is perhaps most clearly illustrated by the narrator's comment in 'Chemische Reaktion', when she asserts that 'Der Unterschied war einfach und logisch: sie hatten ein Ziel und sahen nichts anderes, ich hatte kein Ziel und sah alles andere.'(Ü 55-6) It is the relationship between suffering and ethical demand that is of particular interest here. I wish briefly to explore whether suffering is linked to a particular moral injunction or purpose, whether it functions in the service of a specific argument or social critique, thereby in some measure manifesting a didactic aim; or whether through the emphatic absence of concern with cause, the text raises (more abstract or more fundamental) questions about how we understand ourselves as ethical subjects.[1]

Terror, threat and despair are often presented as external impositions upon the protagonists from the outside, and are often associated with imminent violence. The whole collection of stories in *Übergang* follows the italicized pronouncement:

> *Ich bin ständig auf der Flucht vor anderen Menschen. Sie haben nur eins im Sinn: mich auszubeuten oder umzubringen. Sie fangen immer mit ein und derselben Sache an. Erst reißen sie mir die Augen aus und befestigen sie an sich selbst.* (Ü 7)

This statement, offered without explanation, focuses only on the narrator's perception and sets the tone of most of the following stories. They too concentrate on the narrators' perceptions, their extremes of emotion, their sense of imminent or actual abuse. The lack of an explanatory framework and the apparent disparity between mundane cause and catastrophic effect, for example in the story 'Tag und Nacht', have the effect of distilling the emotions into the essence of terror or anguish.

Common to most of the stories is the insistence that the narrator's suffering is inflicted from the outside. In 'Tag und Nacht' the threat is posed by an initially nameless horror, 'das Kommende: diese, ihrem Wesen nach gewalttätige, Annäherung'. Here, the 'Ungeheuerlichkeit' (Ü 113) is the new day. The story 'Chemische Reaktion' begins with the narrator firmly situating 'den Wahnsinn' outside herself, embodying the physical threat it poses in the form of 'eine Armee im Anmarsch, nein, nicht auf mich, sondern auf all die Orte, an denen ich mich abends und am nächsten Tag aufhalten oder die ich passieren würde.' (Ü 50) And in 'Der Auftrag die Liebe', the narrator personifies love in order to describe the physical attack it makes upon her. She does not know what love is, but does know the violent effect it has; 'Nur hat sie mich fest im Griff. Sie hält und schlägt mich, sie treibt mich um, sie richtet in ihrer Abwesenheit Angriffe gegen mich [...]. Sie ist in allen Körper- und Nichtkörperteilen zugleich.' (Ü 117) Even in those stories where the intense suffering manifests itself in the physical fabric of the individual female body and in which anguish is described almost exclusively in terms of body tissue and fluids, the emphasis is on the body as the victim of an external force. Something, and this something with the stories, appears in the body, imposes itself, forces, pushes through, bites or ruptures the living fabric. In 'Herz und Mund' this thing is the bitterness which has replaced the narrator's heart, which, when she goes to bed

> drückte irgendwie von unterhalb meines Grundwasserspiegels [...], drückte alles hoch, bis zu den Augen und Schläfen. Zwischen Kehle und Augenhintergrund eingesperrter heißer Schleimbrei. (Ü 44)

In 'Fleischlaß', the narrator's agony is conveyed first in terms of a female wolf, bear or large cat tearing her up: 'Ganze Stücke Fleisch, Muskeln, Eingeweide, Knochen riß sie heraus, würgte sie hinunter, erbrach sie in meine schlingernde Bauchhöhle.' (W 17) Subsequently the narrator describes being taken to hospital, where, instead of blood-letting for her condition, the doctor recommends flesh-letting. He advises her lover; 'Beißen Sie ihr alle zwei Tage ein großes Stück Fleisch aus ihrem Körper. Das wird sie nicht wollen, aber es ist lebensnotwendig und tut ihr gut. [...] Sie wird natürlich davor zu fliehen versuchen.' (W 18) One final example is in 'Fancy Calling It Good Friday'. When the narrator is lying next to her sleeping lover after being reunited with him, Truth makes an appearance:

> Jetzt, wo ich auf dem Rücken lag, kroch die Wahrheit langsam über mich, tastete jeden einzelnen Poreneingang ab, testete die Durchlässigkeit der anderen Öffnungen, [...] richtete die Härchen an der Haut steil auf und jagte Schauer über den ganzen Körper hin. (W 35)

This truth, which remains undefined, is described as an 'enge, mörderische, [...] verlogene Wahrheit' (W 35), and within minutes the narrator feels 'zersetzt und zerfressen' (W 35). Once again, the narrator is having something done to her, the body is having something done to it.

As I mentioned earlier, many of the stories depict the effect of violence and perceived threat on a protagonist who is already in despair or 'unheilbar krank' (J 67) and not on an exploration of cause. The relationship of suffering to its origin is unknown, forgotten or not an issue. Thus the immediate cause of suffering is a violent attack, either figuratively (madness like an army, truth or love) or actual. So in 'On Holiday' the narrator's incurable pain is caused by 'kriegerische[ ] Auseinandersetzungen' (Ü 129), and in 'Wimpertier', the description of violence and a screaming then sobbing tongue culminates in the statement: 'EINE FRAU WIRD BESEITIGT.' (W 28) Similarly, the context of personal anguish within which these attacks occur, and which compounds (and sometimes enables) their devastating effect, remains unexplained. Not that the narrators are attempting to hide the cause of their suffering or make it deliberately obscure. If they reflect upon it, it is usually a mystery to them too. At a point in 'Die Jagd nach schönen Gefühlen' when the narrator is feeling better she comments; 'Oft versteh' ich mich dann nicht mehr. Wieso habe ich so gelitten, warum hat es mich so erwischen können' (W 22). In 'Fassungskraft mit Herzweh' she feels that her life has contracted and that she is being pressed together; 'Ich weiß nicht, wann die Wandlung stattgefunden, über welchen Zeitraum sie sich hingezogen hat.'(W 31)

The intense and exclusive focus on the moment of terror, despair and pain is radical in its effect and, in Erich Fried's view, in itself beneficial: '[Der Leser] braucht etwas, worin er sich wiederfindet, was ihn wenigstens die Berechtigung und Würde seiner Betrübnis versichern kann'.[2] Yet even preceding the positive effects that identification with the narrator's plight may have for the reader, many of the narrators themselves seem to point towards the ethical importance of their suffering by linking it with a position of privileged moral insight and greater awareness than they see in those around them. Thus the narrator of 'Arbeitsgänge' has access to '[d]as Wissen der Untoten, besonders der weiblichen' (W 45), and in 'Das Landhaus' the scientists, who as representatives of academic knowledge set in opposition to 'das Wissen' and the suffering of the body, are viewed with suspicion and disdain. Theirs is a knowledge which can be categorized and put away, so they cannot possibly have lives:

> Das ließ mich vermuten, daß der männliche und der weibliche Wissenschaftler möglicherweise nichtmal miteinander redeten, und daß alle Energie, Freude, Lust und ähnliches, aber auch alle Traurig- und Schwierigkeit in die schon beschriebenen Karteikästen ging. (Ü 16)

In 'Chemische Reaktion' the narrator notices that some of the leaves on the trees have something wrong with them, but no one else notices this, even though they could. This observation leads seamlessly into her defining the difference between her and others:

> Aber niemand nahm es wahr [...]. Ich konnte deutlich erkennen, daß sie alle ein Ziel vor den Augen hatten, damit sie in der Welt nicht irrten [...]. Ich hatte das ja nicht. Der Unterschied war einfach und logisch: sie hatten ein Ziel und sahen nichts anderes, ich hatte kein Ziel und sah alles andere. (Ü 55-6)

Thus in many of the stories a particular constellation of themes is identifiable whereby a profound and violent confrontation with something that radically threatens the protagonist is coupled with a state of suffering. And this suffering is then itself inseparable from what seems to be a heightened ethical awareness to which the encounter gives rise. Fried has pointed to the therapeutic effect of Duden's stories on readers who identify with the narrators' suffering:

> Das Buch kann einen die Angst, die man meist zu vermeiden sucht, so gut kennen lehren, daß man mit seiner Hilfe vielleicht lernen kann, sich wenigstens zuweilen von Angst [...] zu befreien oder doch Abstand zu ihr zu gewinnen.³

It is worth considering, however, whether it is possible to see in the stories an ethical dimension that does not depend upon a relationship of identification between reader and narrator as Fried presupposes. Can the stories be understood as a radical exploration of a lived ethical response to the world, a response which is yet nigh on impossible to sustain in the demand it makes upon the subject? I wish to ask this question in relation to the work of Emmanuel Levinas, to whom Duden refers in 'Zungengewahrsam'. (Z 16) I shall explore whether Duden's stories stage both the fundamental encounter with the undefinable other that makes us ethical subjects, and, in a crucial elaboration of Levinas's thought, the difficulty, if not the intolerability, of that encounter.

Levinas attempts to do what Wittgenstein argued was impossible, namely to use language to articulate an ethics which is totally prior to and different from our understanding of ourselves.⁴ Levinas distinguishes ethics from ontology, arguing that hitherto our understanding of ethics has been subsumed into the language of ontology with its focus on and privileging of the Self. He characterizes western philosophy as the philosophy of the same; its focus is on the ego and the autonomy of the self and in order to preserve this 'marvelous autarchy', the self is involved in the perpetual process of either denying the other or assimilating it, the 'transmutation of the other into the same'.⁵ As a result, ethics has been no more than another systematization of knowledge, typfied perhaps by Kant's Categorical Imperative. In total contrast, Levinas sees ethics as preceding and exceeding knowledge, as unknowable and undefinable, and as that which casts us as ethical subjects before we become knowing subjects. In Levinas's ethics, the other is no longer suppressed or taken over by the same, but remains consistently other. No relation is possible with the other, since the very notion of relation suggests understanding or engagement with, communication which again reduces the other to the economy of the knowable. It is in the face of the other that pure alterity is presented to us, and Levinas insists upon the ethical nature of the self's confrontation with alterity. For in the visitation of the face, which Levinas variously describes as 'stripped of its form', 'naked', 'denuded', 'a distress',⁶ '[c]onsciousness is called into question',⁷ and the 'egoism of the I' is overwhelmed:⁸ 'a face imposes itself upon me without my being able to be deaf to its call or without my being able to stop holding myself responsible for its distress. Consciousness loses its first place.'[9] This moment is constitutive of all subjectivity, for '[t]o be an I means [...] not to be able to escape responsibility [...]. But the responsibility that empties the I of its imperialism and its egoism [...] confirms the uniqueness of the I.'[10] This encounter, the putting into question of the Self, demands an ethical response; 'In the face to face, the Other gives my freedom meaning because I am confronted with real choices between responsibility and obligation towards the Other, or hatred and violent repudiation.'[11]

The ethical obligation is not a matter of choice. The encounter with the other is what constitutes the subject who consequently exists for the other and not for itself. Nor can the obligation be reciprocal since any expectation of reciprocity would presume understanding of the other. Levinas is uncompromising in his conceptualization of the extreme asymmetry of the encounter. The responsibility of the self for the other is absolute, is a 'bond prior to every chosen bond', and as such is 'the state of being a hostage'.[12] The limitlessness of the self's responsibility means that the 'I [...] is [...] what in a permanent sacrifice substitutes itself for others and transcends the world.'[13] Central to Levinas's very definition of man is thus this inescapable fact of self as hostage, through which the uniqueness of the self is also affirmed:

> But this responsibility [...] which the ego cannot escape (I for whom another cannot be substituted) designates the uniqueness of the irreplaceable. [...] But man also has to be conceived on the basis of the responsibility more ancient that the *conatus* of a substance or inward identification, a responsibility which, always summoning from the outside, disturbs just this inwardness. Man has to be conceived on the basis of the self putting itself, despite itself, in place of everyone, substituted for everyone by its very non-interchangeability. He has to be conceived on the basis of the condition or uncondition of being hostage, hostage for all the others who, precisely qua others, do not belong to the same genus as I, since I am responsible even for their responsibility.[14]

When reading Duden's stories in parallel with Levinas's ideas, they often seem like a critical literary exploration of the implications of his thought. Thus the stories stage the encounter between self and unknowable other, an other which throws the self into question. This other remains unknown, does not have a cause and undermines any hope the narrators have of leading a 'normal' existence. The suffering and anguish are profound, but with them come the heightened awareness that is common to so many of the narrators, and in this link we can perhaps see evidence of the notion of responsibility which is so central to Levinas's thought. This responsibility manifests itself in the narrators' heightened awareness and sensitivity towards the horrors that are immanent in everyone's daily existence, even if others choose to remain ignorant of them. The coupling of a radical encounter with an unknown other with this heightened sense of responsibility is clearly seen in 'Chemische Reaktion', in which the narrator, after describing the strange attack of the day before and her accumulating pain, is suddenly appalled to see a dying cat. Whereas some onlookers are standing around, some continue to do their shopping, and even the bus-driver is unsure 'ob auch Sterbende in die Arche gehörten'(Ü 57), the narrator immediately identifies with the dying cat; 'Mein bitteres Unglück streckte sich ihr entgegen, zuckend, schluchzend'(Ü 57). Her pain is overwhelming: 'Da traf mich endlich das ganze Ausmaß der Niederlage'(Ü 57).

Another important dimension of the suffering of the narrators which has resonances with the work of Levinas is the degree of passivity which they show; they are overwhelmed by negative forces and seem unable to resist. In 'Die Jagd nach schönen Gefühlen', for example, the narrator claims that love is the feeling that saves her from drowning, from 'das temporäre Verschwinden meiner Selbst.' (W 21) But she is unable to save herself; 'ich brauche Rettung, ich muß gerettet werden, jedesmal aufs neue. Und die Rettung muß von außen kommen, denn aus mir kommt sie nicht mehr.' (W 21) (This statement finds quite literal representation in 'Das Landhaus', in which the overwhelmed and collapsed protagonist is saved by a man after the failure of her own efforts, presumably the lover who took her there). She claims that 'im Grunde ist mir nicht mehr zu helfen. Die tägliche Summe der Unerträglichkeiten bleibt konstant.' (W 25) In 'Fleischlaß' the narrator appears resigned to her anguish; 'Ja, also hier sitze ich, in der Todesfalle aller Tage, und finde nicht mehr zurück'(W 14), and to return to 'Chemische Reaktion', it is not the narrator who is driven to action through her identification with the cat, but the bus driver who acts by telling a policeman of what has occurred.

Such passivity might be seen as problematic when considering the ethical dimension of Duden's stories, especially as it is combined with the narrators' claims to privileged awareness. So in 'Chemische Reaktion' the narrator is deprecating about the apparent insensitivity of others, yet waits for others to respond while she herself is absorbed by her own pain: 'Da traf mich endlich das ganze Ausmaß der Niederlage, ich brach zusammen und sah mir dabei auch noch zu.' (Ü 57) Such passivity must of course remain problematic if ethics is seen to be related to a course of action. However, if the stories are read with Levinas in mind as staging the encounter with the other, then the theme of passivity fits with Levinas's insistence on this encounter as pacific:

> The face in which - the absolutely other - presents himself does not negate the Same, does not do violence to it as do opinion or authority [...]. This presentation is preeminently nonviolence, for instead of offending my freedom it calls it to responsibility and founds it.[15]

In this way it is possible to understand passivity not as a failure to respond, but as a mode of response which allows for the fundamental perception and awareness of responsibility by the subject to occur.

In fact I think that this is a very idealistic reading, and not one that adequately takes into account another aspect of the text, namely the concurrent and apparently contradictory emphasis on violence and the image of the fight. The fight is as important for understanding the stories as passivity, for it reinforces the involuntary nature of the violent attacks, of the suffering of the protagonists and of the knowledge which they must bear. The fight shows that the narrators are themselves torn between resisting the anguish which is articulated through the body, yet knowing that they cannot comply with the perpetual denial of violence and pain upon which normal existence depends. In 'Chemische Reaktion' the narrator does battle with the 'army' directly: '[ich] mußte also insgeheim zurückschlagen, mich wehren, ausweichen, mich verbergen, ducken'(Ü 50). In 'Fleischlaß' she speaks of the battle as though between two selves: 'Ständig mußte ich Streit schlichten, denn ich vertrug mich nicht. [...] Nur noch sekundenweise hatte ich mich in der Gewalt.' (W 15) In 'Wimpertier' the body has been drained of substance because the narrator needs 'allen Gallert [...] für den einen entscheidenden Kampf' (W 27), and in 'Fancy Calling It Good Friday' the Truth creeping across her body brings with it a danger which she must escape, a confrontation which she calls '[eine] Schlacht' (W 36).

How do we reconcile these two moments in the stories? I would like to suggest that in the seemingly incongruous interaction of passivity with the fight we see the protagonists torn between two possibilities of responding to the demand of the other. If Levinas emphasises the encounter with the other as pacific, Duden refuses any drift towards idealization and exposes the intolerability of the ethical burden for the individual. The moment of 'being put into question' is shown to lead to heightened awareness, but the subject also wishes to resist the insatiable demand for responsibility and the anguish that the encounter with radical alterity produces. As Duden writes in 'Zungengewahrsam', 'Natürlich muß man sich verweigern -

natürlich kann man sich nicht verweigern: "Geisel des Anderen"'. (Z 17) In this first section of 'Zungengewahrsam', Duden describes her familiarity with Levinas's concept of the hostage, but goes on to assert the need to escape from the position of being hostage to the other: 'Entweder man nimmt Urlaub vom Geiselsein oder überläßt es, mehr oder minder schlechten Gewissens, einfach anderen, um zum Schreiben, ja überhaupt zum Denken und Nachdenken kommen zu können.' (Z 16-17) The need to escape from the burden of substitution is thematized in *Das Judasschaf* in the protagonist's ability to 'enter' the paintings, and in *Übergang* in music's ability to offer relief from suffering. Perhaps what makes many of Duden's other stories so shocking is that they do not offer their protagonists this moment of escape, but stage the full agony of concurrently resisting but also carrying the burden of being hostage.

Finally it is worth asking why the other is depicted so shockingly in the stories. The clue to this lies in Fried's emphasis on the effect of the stories on its readers, which was discussed above. For whereas Duden refers to her need to escape from the burden of being hostage in order to write, no such escape is being offered to the reader of these stories. Although as Fried argues, it is possible to identify with the anguish of the narrators, I would suggest that the stories continue to shock and alienate the reader with their depiction of encounters with an ungraspable other and thus in their own way put the reader into question. It is this which makes them ethical stories and not moral tales.

Notes

[1] All references to the text *Übergang* (Rotbuch: Berlin, 1982) will be given in parenthesis as Ü followed by the page number. References to *Wimpertier* (Kiepenheuer & Witsch: Köln, 1995) will be given as W.

[2] Erich Fried, 'Mein Gedächtnis ist mein Körper. Anne Dudens Erzählungen', *Die Zeit*, 13 May 1983, p. 45.

[3] Fried, *Die Zeit*, p. 45.

[4] Ludwig Wittgenstein argued in his *Tractatus Logico-Philosophicus* (1929) that language is correlated with things and that it therefore has a factual limit. 'Wittgenstein believed that ethical, aesthetic and religious discourse lie beyond those limits. [...] [H]e said about the *Tractatus* in a letter to L. Ficker: "The book's point is an ethical

one… My work consists of two parts: the one presented here plus all that I have *not* written. And it is precisely this second part that is the important one. My book draws limits to the sphere of the ethical from the inside, as it were" – that is , from inside factual language.' David Pears, 'Wittgenstein', in: Nicholas Bunnin and E. P. Tsui-James, eds, *The Blackwell Companion to Philosophy*, Blackwell: Oxford, 1996, 685-701 (here: p. 689).

5 Emmanuel Levinas, 'Philosophy and the Idea of Infinity', in: *Collected Philosophical Papers*, transl. by Alphonso Lingis, Duquesne University Press: Pittsburgh, 1987, pp. 49-50. Richard A. Cohen discusses the conventions of translating Levinas's use of *autrui* and *autre* with a capital 'O' and a small 'o' respectively, but in this paper I follow Alphonso Lingis in his consistent use of the lower case.

6 Levinas, 'Meaning and Sense', in: *Collected Philosophical Papers*, p. 96.

7 Ibid., p. 97.

8 Ibid., p. 97.

9 Ibid., pp. 96-97.

10 Ibid., p. 97.

11 Colin Davis, *Levinas. An Introduction*, Cambridge: Polity Press, 1996, p. 49.

12 Levinas, 'Language and Proximity', in: *Collected Philosophical Papers*, p. 123.

13 Ibid., p. 124.

14 Levinas, 'No Identity', in: *Collected Philosophical Papers*, p. 150.

15 Levinas, *Totality and Infinity*, transl. by Alphonso Lingis, Duquesne University Press: Pittsburgh, 1987, p. 222-3.

Teresa Ludden

Material Movements in Texts by Anne Duden

There has been scant attention paid to the philosophical influences on Duden's work which this essay examines through the intersections of Duden's texts with radical philosophy (Adorno, Irigaray and Deleuze). When viewed in a theoretical framework, the striking dissolutions of selves and bodies in Duden's texts may be seen less as an expression of a 'female reality' than as a challenge to the conception of a rational, unified, disembodied self and of the consequent subject-object relations in Western culture. I argue that the texts articulate experiences which re-draw the oppositional model, expressing instead fluid interactions between self and world. However, self and world do not become merged, and I turn to Duden's aesthetics to reflect on the in-between space where dualisms cease to function and re-configurations become possible.[1]

> Aber Material ist stumm. Wo kämen wir hin, wenn wir auch noch aufs Material hören würden.[2]

The above quotation from the text 'Herz und Mund' comes towards the end of a difficult text in which we read of a traumatised narrator and her experiences in hospital while recovering from extensive facial injuries.[3] It expresses the narrator's frustration that she literally cannot speak because the destroyed mouth is now 'eine zugestopfte Fleischteilhöhle mit daruntergemengten brockigen Ersatzteilen' (wires and plastic etc.) and that her subjectivity and the suffering of her body, the 'Rollstuhlklumpen' ($Ü^2$ 45), are not acknowledged or heard by the hospital staff. Her body, which appears to have no means of articulating its pain, is reduced to dead, silent matter.

On another level, however, the quotation reveals Duden's awareness of the silencing of the body in Western culture and the positioning of matter and the body as inert and silent in dominant accounts of formation of selves. In this text and the ones I examine below, there is a questioning of oppositional structures where the active subject is dis-embodied and privileged over passive objects and where movements immanent to matter and the body are not recognised. The way matter and the body are written in Duden's texts suggests that they are not brought under the control of a rational active mind but have an agency of their own. This does not mean that there is a simple reversal of the opposition whereby object/matter becomes active and the subject/mind passive.

Rather the movements of matter entail a shift in perspective where the notion of activity itself is transformed. The critique of oppositions also frequently involves an intense and fluid mode of relating to the environment on the part of the narrator and thus a complicated narratorial stance. For instance in 'Herz und Mund' the structure of an active subject or mind and a subordinate object or passive matter is disturbed. The narrator – who would normally be a subject – is positioned as matter which is, however, far from silent. It is matter which is speaking to itself, feeling and perceiving and it is from this perspective that the text is narrated. The question 'where will we end up if we listen to matter' is therefore mock rhetorical, for we are listening to matter, to the movements of the narrator's body throughout *Übergang*. However, the question is also a challenge to a culture which privileges the qualities of a dis-embodied active mind. Where else might we end up if we listened to the movements of matter?

I shall examine what happens to the subject-object binary in Duden's texts when we are presented with matter that moves and articulates this agency. By tracing this theme through examples taken from *Übergang, Das Judasschaf* and *Zungengewahrsam*, I will argue that the writing frees us from a framework which can only think the subject as active and the object as passive. Indeed, we find many places where dualisms do not function at all, and in order to understand the quality of this writing and the experiences of the narrators we need to replace the concepts of distinct subjects and objects with a more dynamic understanding of *relations* between subject and object, self and other. But firstly, I will briefly summarise the arguments of philosophers who criticise the hierarchical and violent subject-object relations which predominate in and define Western culture.

Horkheimer and Adorno in *Dialektik der Aufklärung* criticise Western Enlightenment culture for privileging active subjects over passive objects and repressing other possible modes of relation between individuals and between humans and nature. They write: 'Die mannigfaltigen Affinitäten zwischen Seiendem werden von der einen Beziehung zwischen sinngebendem Subjekt und sinnlosem Gegenstand [...] verdrängt.'[4] The subject-object binary here appears as an imposition on multifaceted affinities and differences which are repressed. This dualistic oppositional structure describes one model of identity construction in which the active Enlightenment subject is defined in opposition to passive, inert matter. It is this concept of self which the feminist philosopher, Luce Irigaray attacks in her *Speculum of the Other Woman* through her questioning of the transcendental subject. This subject can 'sustain himself only by bouncing off some objectiveness, some objective'.[5] In other words it is only through the relation with opaque matter (which is posited by the meaning-giving subject) that the subject can be made into a single coherent self and the ground for thought and action. The problem with the subject, for Irigaray, is that it is an abstraction which claims to transcend and so denies its connections with the material world:

> Rising to a perspective that would dominate the totality, to the vantage point of the greatest power, he thus cuts himself off from the bedrock, from his empirical relationship with the matrix that he claims to survey.[6]

Irigaray is playing with the multiple meanings of 'matrix', encompassing as it does *mater*, matter, (m)other and earth which she sees as etymologically connected. For her the constitutive split between subject and object is created by the subject's distancing himself from earth/mother/woman/object which he 'masters' and supposes to be inert, flat, static. Irigaray's account of this mode of formation of self also stresses that the subject not only transcends its connections with the material world but needs to posit matter as permanent and changeless in order to create a stable sense of self. Other contemporary feminist philosophers have also questioned the role given to matter, the objective world and nature in the philosophical tradition of the West and the boundaries which are erected in this tradition between inside and outside, self and not-self. As a result, a false image of the body as a stable, seamless whole is also constructed which supports the division between self and other.[7]

Such inside-outside binaries do not function when we come to look at the experiences of the narrator in *Übergang* and *Das Judasschaf*. Nor are we presented with an unchanging 'whole' body. Moments when noises engulf the house or room in which the narrator is located are described as occurrences which break down boundaries between self and the environment. In 'Tag und Nacht', for example, the narrator is awoken early in the morning by the noise of an aeroplane. As the outside noise violently intrudes, the division between inside and outside is exploded because the noise is everywhere ('ein trudelndes Überall', Ü^2 97) and possesses all space. The wave of sound is described as shattering space and as dismantling the boundary between self and other along with the tangible boundaries of the body in images which suggest painful breakdown (the narrator is described as 'enthäutet', Ü² 97). So here the house and the body are no longer stable barriers which protect the self but are radically permeable. Also, a division between an active self which hears and sounds which are heard is undermined as the noise impinges on the narrator's consciousness and she is unable to control it or shut it out. The section of text closes with an image of fluidity between self and environment as the wave of sound 'spült an die Membran, zwängt und drückt sich darein' (Ü² 99). It is as if the body is itself experienced as a membrane or an open pore, a boundary which is constantly moving, washed over by the ebb and flow of the sounds.[8]

Similar aural-chaotic experiences occur in *Das Judasschaf*. For instance in the first chapter the narrator floats in an ambiguous realm on the boundary between sleeping and waking. The narrative conveys the experience of hearing sounds from outside whilst in this state and again boundaries between inside and outside and the boundaries of the body are disturbed:

> [D]ie Person wachte nicht und sie schlief auch nicht [...] Der Kopf war etwas anderes. Ein grosses transparentes und schalldurchläßiges Gefäß [...] Er dehnte sich, immer noch weiter, nach außen und nach innen. Bis er alles berührte und von allem berührt wurde [...] Das Gefäß nahm doch ununterbrochen auf. (J² 17)[9]

The head, described as a transparent container permeable to sounds, appears 'other' and dislocated from the body. Hearing, it seems, involves dispossession and bodily disintegration. The image suggests a vulnerable openness to the environment with the head as a permeable boundary which renders notions of an active subject redundant: controlling or organising the external world are not options and 'listening' to the noise does not entail a conscious choice of a subject who can bestow cohesion or unity upon the world. The de-personalised 'Gefäß' is not in control of the influx of sounds – the head here is not conceived as a point of organisation or as privileged locus of reason. The narrator's relations with the outside world on the border between sleeping and waking do not appear to be accounted for according to the transcendental model where the self is stabilised and constructed as central through the process of separation from the environment. The description of the 'Gefäß' is not redolent of a transcendental subject who projects the world by organising it into categories or a mind which decides on action or imposes meaning. As it soaks up the sounds flooding into the room, the head is itself changing, moving, expanding and being re-drawn by the experience ('er dehnte sich nach außen und nach innen') Hearing thus also involves material changes to the body – its boundaries are not static but moving until 'it touches everything and is touched by everything'. Because it is moving, the narrator's head does not establish a boundary between subject and object. Rather the division breaks down between inside and outside as space becomes dislocated, which also means that there is a dissolution of a separate entity 'head'. But this lack of a *separate* head which may transcend the sounds and organise them does not entail a cessation of a mode of activity – the 'Gefäß' has a kind of reflex energy and continues unceasingly to drink in everything ('es nahm doch ununterbrochen auf'). The verb 'aufnehmen' suggests ingestion of food or fluids and thus that the head is not an abstract entity but part of a body; its energies are bodily. It also suggests that the sounds become part of the body's alimentary system while the body becomes a component of a pulsating flow of sounds from outside:

> [...] in alle Richtungen [lag] sich streckend und dehnend, von Linien überzogen und durchwebt, unterhöhlt und ausgebuchtet, überspannt und uferlos das Geschehende. Schritte, langsame und schnelle über und gegen den Stein, hohe Schwalbenschreie, verschwindend und schon wieder zurückkommend. Stimmen über Stimmen [...] Die der Kinder hell. Sie überschlugen sich, kreischend und schreiend, noch nicht unterschieden in oben und unten. (J^2 18)

As in 'Tag und Nacht', the room does not form a barrier but is criss-crossed by a web of sounds which are not filtered or organised into a hierarchy but overlap each other in a realm of undifferentiation. It is as if the head is crossed by the multiple lines of an assemblage of un-ordered sounds and voices and the expanding head dissolves its separate identity by becoming sound. The external sounds appear as the active elements while the 'Gefäß' acts as a sponge changing with the modulating sounds. However, the sounds are on some level received by the semi-conscious 'Gefäß'/body but without this head-body being able to make sense by imposing order ('noch nicht unterschieden in oben und unten'). The terms involved in the encounter no longer exist as distinct entities. Rather than the presentation of a separate entity 'head' located in a separate entity, 'room', which is cut off from the outside world, the boundaries between all the elements become blurred. Thus we get a multiplicity of *connections* between head, room and the sounds of the city street rather than discrete units, a multi-faceted entity of head-room-sounds.

But perhaps it is because I am using examples of sounds which interrogate the inside-outside dichotomy that the active subject - passive object dualism appears not to function. For sounds are not objects and cannot be said to be 'matter' which may be posited by an active subject. So what if we look at examples where the narrators *see?* What happens when the narrators who are positioned with body/matter – see the objective world which according to Adorno, Horkheimer and Irigaray is *also* positioned as matter/object, 'other' to the self? Will the visual relation to the world give us some kind of anchorage. For according to Christine Battersby in *The Phenomenal Woman* vision and sight are the perceptive norms in Western philosophy. Subjects can control what is seen more effectively than sounds and can manage the influx of visual data by processing it into discrete units:

> [...] the field of vision has a focal point, and edges defined as such in reference to the gaze [...] sight seems teleological: directed by the end and the desires of the 'I'. The fact that we focus our eyes on what is ahead of us [...] means that for the subject trained from childhood to orient himself via sight, the data yielded by vision seem to come in discontinuous and manageable bundles. For the most part we never even notice the crowding in of simultaneous visual data that requires the 'forgetting' of visual irrelevancies [...].[10]

Sight is linked to reason and control over external materiality which can be categorised in a way which confirms the subject's separateness and superiority over that which is seen. For Irigaray, too, the transcendental subject's specular relation to the world is stabilising as it is primarily through visual relationships that the 'I' establishes distance from the world as it is mapped and posited as object. But for Duden's narrators looking involves the body, movement, crossing boundaries, destabilisation and dissolution:

> [D]ie Blicke [taumelten] immer wieder aus mir heraus, versuchten, sich auf Wasserflächen zu legen und an Gesichter zu heften oder wenigstens eine ruhige Horizontlinie entlang zu gleiten. Aber die Helligkeit ließ nichts zu, keinen Ort und keinen Aufenthalt. (J^2 8)

This quotation from the first chapter of *Das Judasschaf* when the narrator arrives in the nameless city (which we retrospectively can figure out to be Venice) is on a concrete level simply a description of being blinded by the sun. However, in the light of our discussion of selves and matter the image suggests that the self's ability to map the landscape is hindered by the intensity of the light which does not allow the gaze to fix itself on objects or spaces. This is not a self who can shore up an identity by fixing or mastering the material world. All possibility of positing a unified point of consciousness melts in the glare of the light and the experience is again described as a destruction of fixed space ('ließ nichts zu, keinen Ort oder Aufenthalt') as there is nowhere – no stable surface – for the narrator to reside. The dynamism of the event of seeing ('die Blicke taumelten aus mir heraus' where the verb suggests erratic uncontrollable movements) conveys a movement of the self outside the boundaries of the body with the body again not functioning as an unchanging container for the ego. The seeing self does not, then, establish distance between self and other but travels towards that which is seen even as these things disintegrate in the brightness. It is a type of seeing which follows the movements immanent to the trees and thus sees 'the crowding in of simultaneous visual data [...] visual irrelevancies' which Battersby says we have been trained to forget:

> Sie starrte auf das gelbliche Grün, den Glanz auf jedem einzelnen Blatt; der Bus riß sie los, weg davon. Sie drehte sich noch um zu den Bäumen [...] Ihre Blicke hakten sich in jedem neuen Grün fest, sie wollten nichts wieder loslassen. Aber der Bus fuhr weiter und ließ immer mehr hinter sich, bis sie nicht mehr auseinanderhalten konnte, ob alles schon vorbei war oder ob sie es immer noch und immer wieder neu sah. (J^2 9)

Here the eyes are a force which competes with the momentum of the bus and they notice the shine on *every* single leaf in *every* new bit of green. It is not that they cannot see but that they see too much – the intense abundance of the natural world. The eyes literally get stuck in the 'external materiality' of the trees and bushes to such an extent that it is as if the bus leaves her behind in the greenery. It is as if the flora of the living of world were a magnet which pulls the eyes towards it. Through the interaction of the forces of glances caught up in the trees and the forward movement of the bus, the body is almost pulled apart. The self seems to exist somewhere between the propelling movement of the bus and backward movement of the glances caught in the trees and is thus not privileged above other movements and forces of the landscape. The narrator in this image appears as a force acted upon by the movement of the bus and by the tree's leaves, which results in a disintegration of a stable, whole body or self. Here there is not just spatial but temporal dislocation as well – she cannot tell 'ob alles schon vorbei war oder ob sie es immer noch und immer wieder neu sah' as the boundaries between past, present and future moments break down because they all occur at once.

It is light in motion which unsettles the self-other dualism in another image in which the narrator looks at trees in the second chapter of

Material Movements in Texts by Anne Duden

Das Judasschaf, 'Panorama Berlin'. Here the infinite movements of the leaves effects a radical movement of the self:

> Die ununterbrochene Bewegung der Blätter [...] - teilte sich meinen Augen schnell mit. Bald flirrte das Laub über meine Pupillen, schwärzlich schon, weil es ja Abend war und das zurückgebliebene rosafarbene Sonnenlicht alle Luft dahinter ausfüllte und durchsichtig tönte. Bis ein kleiner Wimpernschlag mich und die Umgebung austauschte. Die Sonne ging jetzt sofort hinter meinen Augen unter, und im selben Moment hatte ich die Baumkronen unter mir und einen atemverschlagenden Weitblick über die kaltrosa sich hinstreckende schwarz erstarrte Stadt. (J^2 42)

Again the narrator is far from being a stationary reference point who manages the movements of the leaves into ordered units. Indeed the fluctuating movements of the leaves and light actually render organisation impossible and the eyes get so close to the movements that in this astounding image she merges with the environment ('mich und die Umgebung austauschte'). The landscape enters the body as the sun goes down behind her eyes. In an image of interchange the narrator's eyeball and the cosmos exchange places rather than existing as static separate poles in an oppositional structure. The eyes become part of the leaves' movements rather than viewing them from outside until it is as if she becomes tree or can see from the perspective of the tree. At the same time, however, the natural world is not reduced to the movements of the 'I' or vice versa. There is still an entity that sees and articulates the slippery exchanges.

> Wiederholt verloren sie [die Augen] sich im Laubwerk, [...] und kehrten nur widerstrebend und in immer längeren Abständen zu ihr zurück, als wäre da, zwischen Blatt und dem Rest, die Luft nicht auch nur Durchgangslager oder sang- und klanglose Fallgrube. Sie durchliefen die steigenden und sich senkenden und auch den Horizont noch übertretenden Unendlichkeiten der Grüntöne, Schimmer, Stufen und Schatten, auf und ab und seitwärts, von anderen Farbstreuungen und -ansammlungen unterbrochen, aber nie festgehalten. (J^2 127)

For Duden's narrators, then, looking involves leaving the body and not being returned in the same state – here the eyes again get lost in the dynamic system of the 'Laubwerk' and return via various detours in the air. Looking entails multiple journeys through the air which (in this example) is alive with possibilities, not a neutral or transparent medium in which objects may be clearly posited. These journeys are not defined by fixed point 'self' (subject) and fixed point 'other' (tree) – it is not a movement from fixed point a to fixed point b because both are moving and the boundaries between them fluid. Rather the wanderings have a force of their own, open to interruptions and novel intersections of colours and song. The air, too, is replete with movements of sounds, colours, patterns and rhythms, suggesting that the travels of the 'I'/eye do not occur in a vacuum or an empty homogenous space but that this space is itself an active element that is full of sounds, colours etc. in constant flux. The eyes run away and follow the infinite possibilities of nuances, shades, spectrums of colours, levels, shadows, the dispersal and coming together of colours. The narrator, whose eyes follow the fathomless movements of nature and soaring modulations of sounds, appears herself to be an open system alive to the boundless combinations of movements which take her beyond the horizon. What we do not have in any of these images is the distance of perspective or rationality but a 'close-up' of an un-mappable world.

It is not the case that we are presented with a narrator who is simply overwhelmed by a malignant materiality that threatens to consume all sense of self . This formulation would not be accurate as first, there is not a clear sense of self to de-stabilise but a self that is formed and re-formed through the relations with the environment. Second, the landscape's dis-organisation is not simply menacing. The perceiving narrator is not pitted against nature as 'other' but appears to share fluid boundaries with the material world. What these quotations show is that the narrator's relations to the external materiality of the world clearly cannot be understood through the active subject-passive object binary. The images do not suggest that there is a whole body/self who sees, rationalises, acts – it becomes difficult to speak of a distinct entity subject/seer and distinct entity object/seen. The self appears only to be there in the relations *between* the two – i.e. the self is not separate from the trees that she sees but there is still someone who sees. The event of seeing is not directed by a fixed subject towards a fixed object, and the seer's body and self are changed by the relations and movements she is part of. These dynamic relations point to a self that is not just modified by the relations with her environment. Rather, the self *is* a modification, a continuous modification which emerges through processes of *interactions* and *relations* between self and other. Therefore we need a different model which expresses the dynamism of the processes of seeing, the processes of becoming self such as one provided by the French philosopher, Gilles Deleuze. For Deleuze, it is precisely the dynamism of the kinds of interactions we have seen in Duden's texts that undercuts notions of a 'well-constituted subject endowed with independence and activity' in favour of what he calls 'the system of a dissolved self'.[11] This 'system of a dissolved self' would be a good description for the narrators we have seen in the quotations above. Deleuze rejects a 'transcendent application of the syntheses of the imagination' claiming instead that:

> there's nothing transcendent, no Unity, subject (or object), Reason; there are only processes, sometimes unifying, subjectifying, rationalising, but just processes all the same. These processes are at work in concrete 'multiplicities', multiplicity is the real element in which things happen... when you invoke something transcendent you arrest movement.[12]

The short text 'On Holiday' from *Übergang* rejects transcendence in a similar way to Deleuze's theory. There is a lack of 'I' (as the ground of narration) which transcends the landscape as the pronoun does not appear until the last paragraph (and the moment the 'I' appears in the text is also the moment of its breakdown into a wave). Instead, the humans are described as 'Die Insassen' ('männliche' and 'weibliche') of a car so it is their *relation* to the car which is stressed, and in its turn, the car's relation to the rapidly disappearing ground in images which suggest movements between different elements in a system beyond the control of the human 'actors'.

> Für das Auto war es am mühsamsten. [...] Und nie wurde ganz klar, ob es sich noch auf festem Untergrund befand oder bereits unmerklich zu versinken begann in der anthrazitglänzenden, heimlich getriebenen und quellenden Flut. (Ü² 118)

We are presented with a sensation of groundlessness in that the beginning of the text conveys the experience of driving on a mixture of ice and water on land which is in the process of being reclaimed by the sea. Through the unceasing movements of images of nature, the text conveys the sense of a lack of human or privileged ground from which a fixed viewpoint might be established. The subject-object binary breaks down as there appears to be an absence of a subject of narration. There is not a narrator (in the Classic Realist sense) but a *voice* which is dislocated from an origin in a clearly identifiable speaker. Uwe Schweikert is right to state that 'die Texte gleichen unablässig redenden Mündern, unablässig geworfenen Blicken'.[13] However, the voice *is* related to the female occupant of the car for she seems to be a perceiving presence and we also briefly read of the flow of her memories and thoughts. But although we are aware that there is a person in a car looking at the landscape, the *way* the movements of this landscape are expressed means that the images of nature have an agency of their own, un-anchored from an interpretative eye/'I' as unified point of consciousness. The images take over from the thoughts of the narrator, from dialogue, analysis or plot. We are left with the paradox of not having a subject of narration – just narration – the movement of the images, sounds and colours.

> Ein nicht endendes Band von Schleierwolken wehte durch die Ruine und über sie hinweg, verfing sich zwischen den Pfeilern und schlingerte in den Rundbögen, gefolgt von schwerer Dunkelheit, die sich flockig auf die Fundamente setzte und an einigen Stellen bereits das Meer aufgesogen hatte. (Ü² 119)

As in the text 'Das Landhaus', the narrative conveys the experience of the limitless sounds, sights and colours of the drama of nature.[14] Movement flows out of movement without there being a human source for that movement. The 'system of a dissolved self' appears here to include multiple interactions with the movements of the water, the clouds, light, colours, sounds and textures so that, as in the following image, the 'I' resembles an absent presence in the event of snow falling on the sea as darkness falls – there is only receptivity for the sounds of the sea itself and movements and rhythms immanent to the waves:

> [Das Wasser] [...] gab einen gleichmäßigen, federleicht wäßrigen Ton von sich, als gingen viele Tausendfüssler auf ihm und über es hinweg. Berührten jeweils nur flüchtig die tausend Wasserpunkte mit ihren wieviel tausend Zehenspitzen und träten weiter und weiter und nirgends hin. (Ü² 119-120)

Nature appears as a system open to continuous modulation and variation in which

> sich zugleich alles austauschte, veränderte, zusammenwuchs; selbst Burg und Fels verloren jetzt ihre eigenen Konturen, bildeten nur noch ein riesiges verschwimmendes Zentrum im noch riesigeren Sogwirbel. Sie [die Insassen: TL] konnten nicht mehr, sie brauchten nicht mehr zu können, denn sie waren schon wie alles andere. (Ü² 119)

It is no longer a question of the human participants' actions in response to environment or a story which can be told. Instead there is a purely optical and aural situation in which movements immanent to the landscape are intuited. It is as if the impossible imperceptible movements of the mountain are sensed and the earth turning is felt and heard. In a disorientating disappearance of fixed points as darkness falls, the occupants of the car 'become like everything else', part of the swirling mass of movements. This prefigures the end of the text where, in a dream-like passage, water encroaches on and consumes the 'I'. Or rather the 'I' enters into the wave as she literally *turns into* the wave with her body.[15] The image speaks both of the *jouissance* of fluidity and the trauma of unboundedness. It is also an affirmation as it is the moment in the text that the pronoun 'I' appears only to disappear. It is therefore the affirmation of an 'I' that is a not-I, that is only there in the movements.

The individual's relation to nature and the landscape in this text is very different to the Enlightenment Subject's alienated, exploitative and distanced relation to the material world. However, there is not a simple *merging* with nature either, self and world do not become one – nature retains its own movements and otherness. Indeed, the landscape is described so obliquely at times that what is seen appears to elude the grasp of a rational mind.[16] But although nature is beyond the control of the narrator, it is not simply threatening either; even though the people lose their contours and the 'I' becomes a wave, there is not a *destruction* of self through an annihilating encounter as the narrative voice continues. So if there is neither a *destruction* of self nor a *merging* we are left with something in between – with an 'I' which is not-I, with a non-unified self which is, however, liveable – just. And it is this paradox that *Übergang* is about. As Duden herself has said in a recent interview:

> *Übergang* ist somit mein Versuch gewesen - und ich glaube, ich arbeite weiter daran -, eine eigentlich unmögliche Daseinsmöglichkeit auszudrücken, und das geht für mich nur durch und in Sprache, über Schrift.[17]

It is to the 'nicht-denkendes Denken' (Schweikert) or rather the 'nicht-sprechendes Sprechen' of visual art that Duden turns to reflect on some of these aporias. I will now conclude by examining Duden's essay on Clea Wallis' paintings in *Zungengewahrsam*, 'Vergittert im Gefilde oder Contenance angloise', in order to highlight Duden's own thinking on the breakdown of the oppositional structures which are so striking in her fictional work.[18]

By engaging with this art, Duden shows that we are almost obliged to think the groundlessness of a matter which moves and the collapse of the polarities of binary oppositions. For with Clea Wallis' paintings, we have to see and think the movement of the lines which win out over fixed space. Space is *only* made up of movements as the frame-less canvas is covered with floating lines. There is a lack of a stable place for the eye to rest because of the multiplicity of travelling lines:

> Unerträglich, zumal für den, der standhaft zu sein gelernt hat und beharrlich das *Ganze* durchschauen zu müssen meint, das Fluchtverhalten der Blicke; denn die Blicke *in* Clea Wallis' Bilder - und es lässt sich einfach nicht mehr

> sagen: *auf* diese Bilder werden immer wieder zum Flüchten, zu Ausflüchten angehalten und gezwungen. Gewohnte Blickabfolgen lassen sich nicht aufrechterhalten, sie werden abgelenkt, unter- oder sogar abgebrochen. Der Raum ist zu tief, hoch und weit zugleich; die Farben scheinen Licht zu werfen und erhellen doch nur sich selbst. (Z 120)

What is unbearable about it is that we cannot stand still – the paintings undermine a stable viewpoint outside the painting. We cannot see it as a 'whole' or see through it to some accessible meaning. The viewer's eyes are forced instead to follow the lines through their multiple variations, directions and dimensions – moving *into* the three-dimensional painting rather than remaining on the surface. The viewer cannot 'know' from a standpoint outside – an ordered series of gazes which might establish stable subjecthood through distance from the seen object are deflected or jammed or broken. The angles cannot be exploited as focal points because they have no ground, they are themselves moving parts of lines. In order to see the work we must enter it and follow the rhythms and patterns in the canvas – like the narrator whose eyes get caught up in the leaves following the movements immanent to the trees. We have to think through the 'Fluchtverhalten der Blicke' (Z 120), *through* the movements of the eye and body rather than from a perspective that is 'standhaft'. The light (like the light in Venice) blocks the penetration of clear reason/mind and illuminates only the brushstrokes and colours themselves, making the eyes follow the material movements of the paint (the colours). In Duden's formulations, the viewer cannot impose meaning but is pulled into the 'Präsenz der Farben' into a space which, in Duden's words, dances and vibrates with the full presence of all the senses, creating a fantastic 'suspended' dimension.

Duden uses an analogy with music to express the sort of space these paintings create by linking the colours to notes:

> Noten oder Farben, die gleichsam keinen Anfang und kein Ende mehr haben, die mitten im Raum auftauchen und die im Rahmen einer oft sehr ausdauernden Arbeit, eines Werks zwar begonnen, das heißt angestimmt, aufgelegt und -getragen werden, die aber nicht aufhören, nicht schließen, weil sie sich Schicht um Schicht, Zeile um Zeile dann immer schon aufgemacht haben und nicht mehr landen werden. (Z 124)

It is as if she sees the paintings as images of a counterpoint of different voices, as spaces without a centre or hierarchy which allow a simultaneity and polyphony of voices or points of view which are not organised into above and below or drowned out by a dominant voice. So unlike the aeroplane image in 'Tag und Nacht', there is not one overpowering noise which eradicates other voices and movements and which *destroys* space. Instead, they – like music – are 'spaces' without co-ordinates, unstable spaces that are defined completely through the movements of sounds but that do not break down into nothingness. The musical canvases, full of rhythms and movements also refuse fixed oppositions. Duden writes that the paintings are unfathomable for the eye because they bring together opposites, the lines are both transparent and opaque, far and near, present and absent, light and dark. Looking at the painting we can see what she means: the way the lines are painted on top of one another means that we cannot distinguish between opposites. The layering techniques where blocks of coloured lines are painted on top of one another, where light lines cross dark lines, colour is painted on colour, result in uncertainty. It is unclear what the lines are doing, whether they are moving under or over or between. Thus the background-foreground distinction disappears disturbing fixed space and polarities and taking the ground away. For Duden, the pictures collapse polarities and open up a third realm. They

> erinnern an die Rückseiten von Stickereien oder lassen an die Vorderseite eines immer fadenscheiniger gewordenen Stoffes denken, der nun somit Vorder- und Rückseite zugleich zu zeigen beginnt und damit schon ein Drittes. (Z 117)

The paintings appear as neither fore- nor background; they reveal a third thing which does not operate with oppositional structures, a 'Zwischenraum' in between polarities just as the narrators are neither self nor other but a relation between the two. The paintings are thus most material examples of a matter which is moving but not heard and of non-functioning dualisms. They open up an Utopian realm of difference, openness and freedom for Duden. Yet these canvases, as Duden's essay stresses, are also material and concrete presences. ('Möglichkeit [...] dessen Wirklichkeit nicht mehr nur in den Sternen steht', Z 124) Her thoughts reveal that they may be regarded as fantastic possible-impossible realms where usual oppositions are suspended. But rather than collapsing in the face of the removal of oppositions, the polyphonic spaces are upheld through the art and the writing. They thus become spaces not just of the de-stabilisation and collapse of the self but also of possible re-configurations beyond the static subject-object structure.

Notes

[1] I am deeply grateful to Anne Duden for allowing me to interview her at length and for her generous and inspirational responses to my comments and questions. I would also like to thank Ewan Porter for his helpful comments on early drafts of this article, and Judy Purdom for answering my many questions about the philosophy of Gilles Deleuze.

[2] Anne Duden, 'Herz und Mund' in *Übergang,* Rotbuch Verlag: Hamburg, 1982, p.45. Page references in brackets refer to the second edition of this text (1996) = $Ü^2$.

[3] 'Herz und Mund' makes more sense when read as a fragment of 'Übergang' which comes later in the collection and where the narrator's experience of facial injury are similar. In 'Übergang', however, we are provided with more orientation and know that the narrator's face has been injured and partially destroyed in an unprovoked attack in a Berlin nightclub.

[4] Max Horkheimer and Theodor W. Adorno, *Dialektik der Aufklärung,* S. Fischer Verlag: Frankfurt a.M., 1969, p.17.

[5] See especially the section entitled 'Any Theory of the "Subject" Has Always Been Appropriated by the Masculine' in Luce Irigaray, *Speculum of the Other Woman,* trans. Gillian C. Gill, Cornell University Press: Ithaca, 1985, 133-146 (here: p. 133).

[6] Ibid., p. 134.

[7] For more information about this area of Feminist Philosophy see Christine Battersby, *The Phenomenal Woman. Feminist Metaphysics and the Patterns of Identity,* Polity Press: Oxford, 1998, especially Chapters 3 and 4 where Battersby argues that Kantian philosophy produces a model of self, the transcendental self, where everything 'outer' is in space and other to the self. This means that inner bodily space falls outside Kant's framework for spatiality and temporality.

[8] For a different reading, see Joanna Bossinade, 'Original Differentiation. The Poetics of Anne Duden' in: Chris Weedon, ed., *Post-war Women's Writing in German: Feminist Critical Approaches*, Berghahn: Providence, R.I. and Oxford, 1997, 131-155. Through the prism of Freud and Derrida, Bossinade reads the aeroplane's penetrating noise as the phallus and as entry into the Symbolic; the shocking event levels out meaning and takes away the narrator's power of speech. She does not focus on the paradox of the narratorial voice coming from the 'spinning space' of shattered meanings and hence does not see creation as well as destruction.

[9] Anne Duden, *Das Judasschaf,* Rotbuch Verlag: Hamburg, 1985, second edition, 1997, p.17. Page references in brackets refer to the second edition of this text (1997) = J^2.

[10] Battersby, *The Phenomenal Woman*, p. 177.

[11] Gilles Deleuze, *Difference and Repetition,* trans. Paul Patton, Columbia University Press: New York, 1994, p.118 and p.78.

[12] Gilles Deleuze, *Negotiations*, trans. Martin Joughin, Columbia University Press: New York, 1995, pp.145-146. The introduction of Deleuzian thought need not be seen as a rejection of the feminist criticism of, for instance, Luce Irigaray. Instead the two bodies of thought can be conceived as complementing each other in the project of re-thinking models of selfhood which do not depend on the oppositional structures mind/body, self/other, subject/object. See Ian Buchanan and Claire Colebrook, eds., *Deleuze and Feminist Theory*, Edinburgh University Press: Edinburgh, 2000.

[13] Schweikert writes this in his excellent 'Nachwort' to the second edition of *Übergang,* 132-138 (here: $Ü^2$ 137). He also discerns a type of 'nicht denkendes Denken' at work in Duden's writing where a bodily memory enables 'alle Begrifflichkeit in Bildlichkeit zurückzuverwandeln'($Ü^2$ 134).

[14] See *Übergang,* ($Ü^2$ 11- 46).

[15] There is a movement towards 'Ich' and identity as the text gradually incorporates more definition of 'der weibliche Insasse' becoming 'die Frau' and 'sie'. 'Sie' emerges from the car (and as a grammatical pronoun) at the moment when the island is submerged and fluidity wins out over form: 'sie [hatte] ein deutliches Rückwärtsgefühl [...]. Sie drehte sich um und sah das uneingezäunte und ununterbrochene Meer [...] Die Insel war natürlich nicht mehr da, und es gab keinen Horizont.' ($Ü^2$121) 'Sie' then flows into 'ich' in a dream-like passage in which the water partially encroaches and then completely covers her body: '[D]ie zweite Woge [...] so hoch ich sehen konnte [...] Durch die Drehung meines Oberkörpers stieß sie leicht an das linke Schulterblatt. Ich blieb stehen, sie berührte mich nun überall auf einmal und brach über mir und mit mir zusammen.' ($Ü^2$ 122).

[16] For instance, the writing does not immediately convey to the reader what is being seen: 'Die Insassen gingen auf etwas Grosses zu, das ihnen keine andere Möglichkeit liess. Wie ein riesiger Schiffsbug, der sich allmählich an Land gehoben und geschoben hat [...] lag es da, einen ort- und zeitlose Endlichkeit.' ($Ü^2$ 118)

[17] Anne Duden, Claudia Kramatschek, 'In den Faltungen der Sprache', *Neue deutsche Literatur 48* (2/2000), 32-44, (here: p. 33).

[18] In *Zungengewahrsam*, Kiepenheuer und Witsch: Cologne, 1999, 114-124. Page references in brackets refer to this text = Z.

Juliet Wigmore

Visions of Nature in Texts by Anne Duden
Metaphor, Metonym, Morphology

This article discusses the portrayal of nature in three texts by Anne Duden and contends that it plays a significant role in her work. In 'Ein Landhaus', a fictional text, nature metaphorically reflects psychological processes in the protagonist. In the essay 'Unter einem Dach' natural elements depicted in an architectural phenomenon stand metonymically for the role of a suppressed and transcended culture. In the third text, a painting depicts natural growth in relation to the development of a written ethical culture, which appears to emerge morphologically, as natural growth out of the earlier culture.

Nature and natural growth feature strongly in many texts by Anne Duden, including both her works of fiction and her essays on topics concerned with art. This article will examine the role played by nature in her work, first in relation to her early fictional text 'Ein Landhaus', from the collection *Übergang* (1982). Thereafter the discussion treats the author's representation of nature in commentaries on art subjects from the 1990s, taken from the collection *Zungengewahrsam* (1999). The texts to be considered are therefore of two quite different types: in the first, a work of fiction, it is the narrator's perspective on nature which is foregrounded and becomes an important means of raising ethical issues. In this text, as will be shown, nature also plays a major role in the structure and progression of the narrative. The later texts, by contrast, take the form of discursive essays and focus explicitly on cultural and ethical aspects implied by the depiction of nature in various works of art. I intend to show that the two different approaches to nature in Anne Duden's writing are linked by similar underlying concerns, and that the early text anticipates some aspects of the later ones. Common to all the texts to be considered is the fact that they implicitly treat nature in terms of the long established dichotomy between nature and culture, a basic tension which allows for different types of interplay in the various texts.

'Ein Landhaus'
In 'Ein Landhaus' (Ü 9-43) the development of events and the experiences of the female protagonist are extensively dependent on her perception of the natural surroundings in which she finds herself. Nature is represented as a material reality, and it plays a role as a stimulus to the changes taking

place in the protagonist. At the same time, the perceptions and representation of nature act as a metaphorical sign to the reader. Within the narrative, these changes are also measured in part by the contrast between the protagonist's perceptions and behaviour on the one hand, and those of outsiders on the other, and the contrast between these two perspectives presents further, more general implications about society.

The representation of nature in the story occurs primarily through the perception of the first-person narrator, an unnamed young woman who has arrived from a nearby town to look after the house during the owners' absence. Her initial impression of the 'Landhaus', so overgrown that it is difficult to detect it amid the surrounding garden, suggests that nature, far from being something 'natural' and inherently familiar, is actually something totally unfamiliar to the protagonist. In this sense it represents a metaphor for a new departure in her thinking. Like the forest in a *Märchen*, this location represents the unknown, a place in which the human subjects get lost until rescued by adulthood, or by a fairytale prince. Even the title 'Landhaus', is ambivalent: besides its usual connotations of 'Haus auf dem Land', there are suggestions that, similar to the 'Brothäuslein' in *Hänsel und Gretel*, it is a 'Haus *aus* Land', so overgrown is it by the vegetation around it that it seems to be actually part of the nature that surrounds it. The oxymoron suggested by the title 'Land-Haus' also evokes an underlying tension between nature and civilisation, a 'Schwellenort zwischen Natur und Kultur'.[1]

An important pointer for interpreting the role of nature in this story is given with the protagonist's initial encounter with the couple who normally occupy the house. They are described as 'Wissenschaftler' and, like the protagonist herself, they remain nameless, suggesting that their professional classification is more important than their individuality. The woman of the couple is, indeed, referred to throughout as 'der weibliche Wissenschaftler', never as 'die Frau', for instance, with the implication that she fits a category as much as the research materials that she and her husband assiduously classify. Although gender issues remain implicit rather than explicit, there is one notable difference between the male and female patterns of behaviour: when the protagonist arrives at the house, the 'männliche Wissenschaftler' has already departed to start work speedily on his research, whereas the 'weibliche Wisenschaftler' is the one who remains behind to greet the new arrival, suggesting that she is more concerned about house and home, and so too with the forces of nature that surround it. With respect to gender, there is also a structural parallel between the separate departures of the two 'Wissenschafler' on the one hand and the protagonist and her lover on the other. They arrive together at the Landhaus, but the man then departs next day, leaving the woman behind to deal with events provoked by the house. This arrangement implies that the female figures are more concerned by the issues raised by the house and its problematic situation between the wildness of nature and control through 'Wissenschaft', as well as the further-reaching unconscious fears of the protagonist to which these polar opposites correspond. However, it is equally clear that Duden does not merely echo the traditional and often simplistic or misogynist equation of nature/ female versus civilisation/ male, a scheme which has usually been used as part of a framework in which women were controlled by men:

> From ancient to modern times, nature - the object of scientific study - has been conceived as unquestionably female. At the same time it is abundantly clear that practioners of science - scientists themselves - have been overwhelmingly men.[2]

Feminist analyses generally adopt one of two perspectives on these polarities: on the one hand, the (usually essentialist) approach has tended to identify women with nature but to re-evaluate the connection, making it a source of women's power or separateness from the patriarchal scheme; on the other, feminist thinkers have attacked patriarchal perspectives which use the equation of women with nature to exclude them from activities based on reason, and thus also from power. Anne Duden, however, avoids both stereotyped approaches.

The conflicting tendencies of nature and wildness as opposed to science and control become evident to the protagonist, and through her, to the reader, after the departure of the 'Wissenschaftler'. With their 'Karteikasten' representing an ordered and classified existence, as well as regular working practice, the couple live inside the house and have erected defences against the overgrowth of nature outside. Indeed, they appear to be oblivious to the threat that the protagonist perceives in this wilderness. Such is their confidence that they are normally unconcerned about leaving the house bathed in light, uncurtained, and thus in full view at night, whereas the protagonist's response is to set up makeshift curtains. The reader may therefore wonder why they have engaged a housesitter , unless they too unconsciously sense a danger. A clue to the essence of the threat is provided by the insistence of the 'weibliche Wissenschaftler' on the importance of looking after the deep-freeze, in case it should malfunction and start to thaw. They, the academic couple, are dependent upon it and its cooked, deep-frozen contents to sustain them while working. The effect of the image is initially banal and ironic; yet its cultural implications are interpreted, unconsciously at least, by the protagonist who describes it as a 'Massengrab' (Ü 13), an image which suggests both repressed memories of the specific German 'Vergangenheit' and also that eternal vigilance is required to preserve it and keep it out of currency. With regard to the dichotomy between nature and civilisation, the food metaphor evokes the anthropologists' classification in terms of the raw and the cooked.[3] In the 'Landhaus' the cooked and frozen contents threaten to thaw and become subject to the processes of decay and thus to the laws of nature, an image suggesting the precariousness of their preserved state and their susceptibility to transition. The frozen 'knowledge' which sustains the couple implies criticism of a lifestyle which is unnatural, depends upon suppressing nature and can be seen as a metaphor for repression. The protagonist is only permitted access to the surface level of the deep-freeze: she is invited to consume food packed in the top layer only, but she must not deprive the academic couple of the deeper levels of their frozen sustenance. By contrast, she is exposed to the 'raw', unfrozen, aspects of nature outdoors, which allow her deeper fears to surface.

The idea of the freezer as a metaphor for repressed knowledge, with difficult or forbidden access, again evoking prohibitions imposed in *Märchen*, has a parallel in the well-ordered and comprehensive music collection, in which many recordings are still factory-sealed. To the protagonist's surprise, the collection lacks the one recording for which she searches and which she hopes will raise her spirits. The absent piece suggests that the range of music is limited and that it too lacks life. Thus even the more artistic side of the academics' life is subject to stringent control, reinforcing the idea that the well-ordered environment is actually stultifying and life-denying.

The conflict between nature and technology, symbolised by the deep-freeze, is represented, equally ambivalently, when the narrator attempts to practise self-hypnosis, as a means of escaping the fears aroused by over-exposure to 'nature'. On this occasion, the means of linking and contrasting the two conflicting elements is acoustic. The narrator imagines she hears the machines of industrial production, which drown out the intrusive sounds of nature, yet seem no less destructive and fearsome to her. Reminiscent of a scene from Fritz Lang's film *Metropolis*, she perceives herself to be controlled by the machines and forced to comply with the demands of over-production of goods which are devoid of meaning: 'Das Produzierte war monströs, weil es sich zu nichts in Beziehung setzen ließ' (Ü 38). It is, in other words, in every sense unnatural. This episode, which can be interpreted as a negative metaphor for modern society and civilisation, allows her to experience a sense of relief when the vision disappears and she once again perceives the sounds of nature. It is this contrast which reconciles her to nature and allows her to accept her exposure to it. The first sound she now hears is the piercing tone of the finch, a leitmotiv in the story, which breaks into the noise of machinery which had previously drowned out the natural sounds. The finch is one of two birds that are mentioned repeatedly: its counterpart is the cuckoo, suggesting a nagging, repetitive call, and together they underpin the idea that the narrator's deep-seated fears can no longer be repressed. Natural sounds, it appears, are less fearsome than the repression of them.

Similar ambivalence about nature can be detected in the protagonist's perception of the massive tree growth, which on the one hand threatens to engulf her. Yet the trees to which she refers explicitly are the 'Lebensbäume', *thuja articulata*, a species of cypress conventionally planted in cemeteries. Besides their linguistic connotations of 'life', these evergreen trees suggest a triumph over natural decay and the permanent presence of the free-growing nature that they represent in the garden of the 'Landhaus'. As such, they contrast with the deep-freeze, containing sustenance with limited shelf-life.

Nature also elucidates the wider context of the narrator's experiences, through the disparity which emerges between her perceptions and those of the local community. From her description of the location of the house, for instance, the village baker does not recognise the place, but it is unclear whether this is because the house is actually so overgrown as to be unseen or because her description is inappropriate. The latter interpretation is subsequently supported by her encounters with the post office: although the staff also do not recognise the house from her description, next day she receives a postal delivery in the normal way, suggesting that it is purely her perception of the house that is abnormal and psychotic. The fact that she experiences nature and the house differently from the local people suggests that wider elements of society are oblivious to the sense of threat perceived by the protagonist. The isolation that she experiences in the house is thus not only the trigger for her fears to surface but also indicates that her experience is 'different' from that of society at large; it suggests a generalised critique of culture and cultural memories.

In keeping with the overtones of the *Märchen* tradition mentioned earlier, in the last paragraph of the story, a man arrives and appears to awake the narrator from her bad dream. This 'rescue' from the nightmare recalls the tale of the Sleeping Beauty, in which the woman sleeps until she is mature, or ready to be awakened. However, rather than acting as a sexual metaphor, as this traditional story is often interpreted, the situation in 'Ein Landhaus' appears to reflect the protagonist's experience in relation to nature. The new arrival, whose identity is not made explicit, appears to be the man she describes as her lover at the beginning, now transformed into the generalised 'ein Mann' who addresses her in the 'du' form. The final outcome is ambivalent and indicates that the protagonist is no mere sleeping beauty, to be redeemed by a fairytale prince. Instead, when the man urges her to leave with him, she questions his demand: her words 'Wohin denn? suggests that she is ready to move on, not merely back to her starting point. At the same time, her question may imply that she sees no necessity or purpose in leaving, perhaps because she is now able to accept the experiences she has undergone in the 'Landhaus'. The consequences of her encounter with nature and its accompanying terrors appear to be largely positive, and nature, which gives rise to personal and cultural fears, is also the source of potential regeneration.

Ambiguities in the relationship between nature and culture, as well as points of contact and conflict between them are also a salient feature of texts about art from Anne Duden's more recent collection, *Zungengewahrsam* (1999). Unlike the situation in the fictional text, where the protagonist's experiences are the creation of the author, in the texts about art objects created by other artists, the significance is indicated by the author's selection of both the particular work of art and the focal points for interpreting it. It is reminiscent of Claire Baldwin's comment in an article on the role of art in Duden's novel *Das Judasschaf*: 'Ekphrasis, as a representation of a representation, is essentially a self-reflective mode'.[4] That is, the art object represented reflects the author's own concerns and perspectives; this applies also to Anne Duden's treatment of nature in her essays on art themes. Although the essays of *Zungengewahrsam* were first published individually, several texts are linked thematically by the fact that the author focuses on the role played by nature in the works discussed and on their wider cultural implications.

'Unter einem Dach'

The text 'Unter einem Dach' (Z 75-90) explicitly addresses aspects of the relationship between nature and culture, which the author sees manifested in English cathedral architecture. The text centres on the decorated bosses, high up at the top of the vaults of Norwich cathedral, now predominantly Gothic in style, but whose origins go back to 1086.[5] The author describes the decoration of the bosses and the apparent conflict of loyalties between the Christian cultural context in which they were executed, and which represents modern civilisation, and an earlier, pagan culture, which was more explicitly nature-based and which was suppressed by the new world order. Duden focuses on the fact that, amidst the Christian symbols, there are also bosses which depict wild things, such as dragons and especially the head of the Green Man, a figure found in most cathedrals. The author highlights the mysterious aspect of the Green Man, whose role may have been as a fertility symbol or as a revival of earlier tree worship (Z 87). This figure often seems to be sprouting vegetation, but even the face of Christ sometimes appears to have pagan overtones and to resemble 'ein männliches Medusenhaupt' (Z 86). Examples of two bosses are reproduced in the text. These and other apparently pre-Christian elements are curious in view of the fact that they were executed between the thirteenth and the fifteenth century. Anne Duden interprets the bosses as implying that awareness of an earlier culture may have lingered covertly. The masons who carved them, probably in situ, would not have expected them to be seen by people standing below. Duden suggests that the carvings may have been prompted because the masons felt the need to pacify nature, which they saw being exploited for the building of the cathedral, by quarrying and cutting down trees, for instance. This vision of gothic architecture as being intimately related to natural growth reflects a perspective on this style seen since the eighteenth century; in German it notably evokes Goethe's view of Strasbourg Minster, when, in 1773, addressing the architect Erwin von Steinbach, he wrote:

> die ungeheure Mauer, die du gen Himmel führen sollst, dass sie aufsteige gleich einem hocherhabnen, weit verbreiteten Baume Gottes, der mit tausend Ästen, Millionen Zweigen, und Blättern wie der Sand am Meer, rings um der Gegend verkündet die Herrlichkeit des Herrn, seines Meisters.[6]

Both the *Sturm-und-Drang* and Romantic perspectives on Gothic architecture present it less as a civilising force overcoming nature than as a form of natural growth, as is also seen in the ruins depicted in Romantic landscapes, for instance, which more evidently reflect upon the human condition.

In Duden's text, the bosses express a tension between overt symbols of Christianity, the modern hegemonic culture, and pagan elements which live on as a sub-culture within it. The fact that some of the bosses depict foliate heads - whether of Christ or of the Green Man - in forms which hark back to an animistic tradition, suggests that they are objects of cultural transition, a meeting point between two traditions, as well as the more literal architectural meeting point between the ribs of the vaults. They reflect Duden's abiding fascination with moments of transition, with 'Schwellenorte', and the concealed, repressed and transitional figures are thus reminiscent of the explicitly entitled *Übergang*. The bosses in 'Unter einem Dach' can be seen as a parallel to the struggle worked out in the individual protagonist in 'Ein Landhaus', for whom too the tension between nature and civilisation is evocative of cultural memories, although there they have more specific historical reverberations in addition to the personal, psychological threat that they represent for the protagonist.

A further aspect highlighted in Duden's description of the bosses is the fact that when the cathedral was built - and until the introduction of artificial lighting - the bosses were not accessible to the naked eye of people standing below, both because they were too high up and because it was too dark to see them. Even now, Duden comments, they are not easy to observe, despite the introduction of mirrors and lighting. The reference to the light effects echoes the role of light and dark in 'Ein Landhaus', where the lighting provides pointers to the relationship between internal and external factors in the house and the protagonist. There, for instance, the academic couple, who allow total clarity by lighting their house when it is dark outside, are in fact less enlightened than at first appears, since they represent control and suppression of the darker forces to which the narrator exposes herself. In Leslie Adelson's analysis, the use of darkness in 'Das Landhaus' stands for the repression of women's hidden experience and subjectivity.[7] It is similarly appropriate as a metaphor for the hidden cultural factors revealed in 'Unter einem Dach'.

The focus on the bosses as a small detail of cathedral architecture allows the author to represent symbolically an aspect of the relationship between nature and culture, past and present. The bosses act as a metonym for the cathedral as a whole, its cultural location and the ethical tradition it represents.

'Wildwuchs'

A second text from *Zungengewahrsam*, 'Wildwuchs' (Z 109-112), treats certain comparable ideas to those expressed in 'Unter einem Dach', but it concerns a different art form. The title 'Wildwuchs' immediately evokes natural growth and suggests a similar kind of untamed environment to that represented in 'Ein Landhaus'. The essay concerns a very intricate painting by Albrecht Altdorfer, called *Die beiden Johannes*, which is reproduced in black and white in *Zungengewahrsam*. The title given to the picture, probably painted in 1511, alludes to the fact that it depicts St John the Evangelist and St John the Baptist, together with other features of Christian iconography. The saints are juxtaposed anachronistically within an all-pervasive natural landscape, and it is this which is the focus of the author's attention in the essay, as it has also been for other art critics who have written about the painting. Indeed, one art historian comments that this tradition follows Raselius, who described the picture in 1598, when he responded to the 'landscape, abundant with lush vegetation, rather than to the portrayal of the saints, who are painted as if they were of the same matter as the moss, the flowers, the trees, and animated by the same lifegiving force'.[8]

Anne Duden highlights the fact that the wild landscape, with its forests and choppy sea, is clearly Germanic, and, as she says, the figures of the two saints appear to be growing out of the landscape itself. Duden describes the two men depicted as 'wilde Männer' who are 'gut aufgehoben' in this wild landscape. The emphasis placed on their wildness evokes John the Baptist's self-designation, as recorded by the other St John, as 'a voice crying in the wilderness' ('eine Stimme eines Rufers in der Wüste').[9] However, the allusion relates not merely to the biblical framework. Altdorfer painted this picture at a time when interest in the Germanic wilderness had been aroused by the rediscovery of Tacitus' *Germania*, published in Nürnberg in 1496, a work which contributed to the humanist revival at that period. Following Tacitus, we may also see the landscape as 'non-Italy and non-Rome':

> [Tacitus'] picture of the topography, manners and religious rituals of the barbarian tribes is, in all essential respects, that of a not-Rome [...] Nowhere is this more evident than in his description of the German habitat.[10]

This perspective highlights the historical and geographical cultural transplantation or grafting that has taken place here. It is thus reminiscent, through a different medium, of the depiction in 'Unter einem Dach' of

Christian images which have been grafted on to wilder, pagan ones, and thus the continued existence of the latter.

The artist Albrecht Altdorfer is credited with having produced the first 'independent' landscapes in European painting, with reference to a few surviving paintings and drawings that are virtually empty landscapes, 'the settings for missing stories'.[11] The painting of the two St Johns, though not a landscape in the specialised sense, is usually discussed in the same context as Altdorfer's true landscapes, because it too makes use of landscape style as something more than a mere backdrop to the Christian symbols in the foreground and higher planes. Indeed, Altdorfer has been interpreted as a 'transitional' figure:

> For a number of modern art historians, who came to see the Renaissance as a kind of prefiguration of the Romantic crisis, Altdorfer straddled a threshold of intellectual history.[12]

While art critics, including Christopher Wood, cited above, urge caution in approaching Altdorfer from a post-Romantic perspective, the symbolic, cultural importance of the landscape in this painting is evident.

Anne Duden's interest in the landscape and detailed depiction of the plant-life in particular in this painting emphasises the close, indeed morphological, connection of the two saints with nature. She suggests that a 'reading' of the painting is possible, in the way one might read a text: 'Die Lektüre ist folgsam und treibhaft zugleich und läßt sich treiben überdies. Sie folgt den eingeschlagenen Blickrichtungen; sie geht von links nach rechts und oben nach unten [...]' (Z 110). Yet, this reading ends in the overpowering landscape. The nature of the connection between the natural setting and the human figures in the picture is summarised in the last sentence of the essay in which the author refers to the saints as follows: 'Die Nachbarn, oder vielmehr die Benachbarten, deren Namen sich decken, einander - und diese Welt und deren Ende - im Wort aufheben' (Z 112). The phrase 'im Wort aufheben' echoes the first sentence of this text: 'sie scheinen gut aufgehoben in ihrer - etwas ungewöhnlichen Nachbarschaft' (Z 109). The linguistic ambiguity of the word 'aufgehoben' is invoked, too, in the sense that the wildness of nature is on the one hand overcome by the Christian era, but at the same time it is 'preserved' by reminders of it in the prophet, the evangelist and their intimate connection with nature, reminiscent of the situation in 'Unter einem Dach'. The phrase from the final sentence 'etwas ungewöhnlichen Nachbarschaft' alludes to the somewhat incongruous juxtaposition of the two foregrounded figures, 'die Benachbarten'. The crucial element of the final phrase is 'im Wort', which evokes St John's gospel, which gave priority to the 'Word': 'Im Anfang war das Wort',[13] where the word is synonymous with the divine creator. The putative relationship between the two St Johns is suggested at the beginning of Duden's essay as that of a shared knowledge, symbolised in the picture by the Christian symbolic figures on the upper plane, knowledge which the author depicts as a 'Wirkungsbereich aus Neben- Mit- und Nacheinander'. The picture shows, in her words, the 'Wildwechsel alten, neuen und sich just bildenden und herausstellenden Wissens' (Z 109). In this scheme, the old knowledge is represented by the natural phenomena; the new knowledge is that depicted by the figures of Madonna and Child; the knowledge in the process of formation is shown by the process of writing the gospel, of actually creating new knowledge in relation to old knowledge. In this respect, the author's perspective also suggests a general implication about the nature of writing and the role of the writer.

In this constellation, St John the Baptist remains an ambivalent figure. On the one hand, he is the first human subject of St John's gospel, and thus the evangelist is curiously juxtaposed, confronted with the object of his narrative. By the time the account was set down, John the Baptist was long dead, and his beheading was the subject of a picture by Altdorfer, painted in 1512, a year after the probable date of the *Two St Johns*. The sense of timelessness evoked by the incongruous juxtaposition of the two figures reflects the timeless validity of the subject matter. From a traditional point of view, this would include the Christian doctrine of eternal life, which it reflects and which conflicts with the laws of nature, represented in the picture by the plants, which, following the natural lifecycle, grow and die. Although the evangelist is known as the writer who prioritised the Word, so too John the Baptist, the voice crying in the wilderness and the last of the prophets in the Old Testament tradition, can be regarded as representative of the *spoken* word. He is a precursor of the written word, subordinated to the enduring form of the written word, of *logos* and modern thought. This knowledge, including scientific knowledge and reasoning, treats nature as the object of study and control.

The text focuses on the very detailed depiction of the natural landscape, particularly highlighting individual, identifiable plants. The author emphasises the strength of the natural growth in relation to the iconic male figures who represent the Word, but who at the same time are visibly emerging from and are still intimately attached to the old knowledge and nature. Duden describes the plants, whose properties for healing and destruction had been analysed earlier by Albertus Magnus (1200-80) and in Altdorfer's own time by his younger contemporary Paracelsus. It has been suggested that Altdorfer was familiar with these ideas, which were current in his own time. Yet, they also evoke a more ancient form of knowledge, more intimately based in nature than the scientific remedies of modern time. Reinhild Janzen singles out three herbal plants for discussion, relating to specific areas of the painting.[14] The plant that grows beside the evangelist is sage (German 'Salbei'). Traditionally the plant had anti-illusionary properties and so it is an appropriate invocation or symbol of the writer seeking knowledge and truth. On the opposite side, next to John the Baptist, is a plant closely associated with him, mullein, known as King's Candle, ('Königskerze', 'Wollkraut') which in Austria is burnt on St John the Baptist's feast day to protect animals, an allusion reflected here perhaps in his protective role towards the symbolic lamb. Most problematic and ambiguous is the plant that occupies the central foreground, henbane, German 'Bilsenkraut', and as Duden calls it 'Schlaf-[...] Dullkraut' (Z 109). In Albertus Magnus' system, this plant was a toxin and induced sleep. Its negative properties seem to conflict with those of the lamb, and perhaps acts as a warning. The painting thus symbolically shows up the organic connectedness between nature and the dominant ethical culture which replaced traditional thinking, but which is still accessible.

These symbols suggest the equivocal relationship between ancient beliefs and the modern culture which replaced them, similar to the situation portrayed in 'Unter einem Dach', yet more ambivalent because of the juxtaposition and simultaneity depicted in the two-dimensional frame. Even the relationship between the conventional and static figures on the upper plane and those below is subject to multiple interpretation. The symbolic Madonna and Child is the lynch-pin that holds the other figures together and provides the spiritual link between the two saints. The figure of the sheep, or symbolic sacrificial lamb, represents sacrifice and death, hence, perhaps, the warning herb that stands in front of it. This is, on the one hand, in the evangelist's terms, the Word made flesh, and the line of light between the Madonna and child and the sheep below suggests the bond between body and matter on the one hand and intellect or spirit on the other. Yet the other line, crowned by a victory flag, indicates the opposite, the triumph over death.

The emergence of the new ethical knowledge depicted here is reflected in the second of Anne Duden's poetics lectures published in

Zungengewahrsam, where she states, 'Das Fleisch wird Wort' (Z 39), to express the process of writing as a form of maturity. As a reversal of the evangelist's ordering of this phrase, the reciprocal relationship between flesh and word, between nature and ethical culure is invoked, with the implication that writing transcends nature, similar to the situation depicted in *Die beiden Johannes*. In the same context, Anne Duden uses the image of the female monster, the Medusa, who like John the Baptist, was silenced by being beheaded and Duden comments that writing is more concerned with 'Ent- als Behauptung' (Z 34). That is to say, what is silenced is as important as what is said. In the context of the natural phenomena depicted in these texts, suppressed cultural knowledge, or the closed book, as in the picture, still exerts power and remains eloquent.

Notes

[1] Anne-Kathrin Reulecke, 'Anne Duden', in: *KLG*, Text und Kritik: Berlin, 1995, p.4.

[2] Lorna Schiebinger, quoted in: *Women. A Cultural Review*, 1:1 (1990), p. 101.

[3] Claude Levi Strauss, *The Raw and The Cooked*, Pimlico: London, 1969 (orig. 1964). Discussed in relation to gender studies in Carol P.MacCormack, 'Nature, culture and gender: a critique', in: Carol P. MacCormack and Marilyn Strathern, eds, *Nature, Culture and Gender*, CUP: Cambridge, 1980, 1-24.

[4] Claire Baldwin, 'Speaking of Art. Ekphrastic Reflections in Postwar German Literature', in: Robert Weninger and Brigitte Rossbacher, eds, *Wendezeiten. Zeitenwenden. Positionsbestimmungen zur deutschsprachigen Literatur 1945-1995*, Stauffenberg: Tübingen, 1997, 131-149 (here: p.133).

[5] Eric Fernie, *An Architectural History of Norwich Cathedral*, Clarendon: Oxford, 1993.

[6] J.W.Goethe, 'Von deutscher Baukunst', in: Edna Purdie, ed., *Von deutscher Art und Kunst*, Clarendon: Oxford, 1964, p.125.

[7] Leslie Adelson, 'Anne Duden's *Übergang*. Racism and Feminist Aesthetics. A Provocation', in: *Making Bodies, Making History*, University of Nebraska Press: Lincoln and London, 1993, p.45.

[8] Reinhild Janzen, *Albrecht Altdorfer. Four Centuries of Criticism*, UMI Research Press: Ann Arbor, 1979, p.24.

9 John/ Johannes, I, 23.

10 Simon Schama, *Landscape and Memory*, HarperCollins: London, 1995, p.81. See also p.93.

11 Christopher S. Wood, *Albrecht Altdorfer and the Origins of Landscape*, Reaktion Books: London, 1993, p.13.

12 Wood, *Albrecht Altdorfer and the Origins of Landscape*, p.26.

13 Johannes, I, 1.

14 Janzen, *Albrecht Altdorfer. Four Centuries of Criticism*, pp.81-82.

Wiebke Sievers

Grenzen der Übersetzung
Anne Dudens *Übergang* in englischer und französischer Sprache

This article will show that Anne Duden's literary project to express an ‚impossible possibility of being' clashes with contemporary translation practice. In the light of these clashes I attempt to reread Anne Duden's *Übergang*. Starting with an introductory exploration of these premises this article will turn to a critical discussion of the different marketing strategies used for the English and the French publication. Finally I compare and contrast the two translations of the text 'Herz und Mund' concluding that Anne Duden's writing of otherness calls for a new understanding of translation.

> Das erste Kapitel des Schreibens beginnt [...] zwischen grellstem Licht und tiefster Dunkelheit. Die Geschichte der Worte setzt ein in der Verlorenheit, sie setzt auf das Verlorene. Auf das Wissen, daß nichts mehr zu gewinnen ist, aber alles dableibt, versteckt in Worten, in Bildern, die vor allem die einstigen Gefühle, die Empfindungen, die Blicke, die Potenzen der Welt aufbewahren bis zum Tag ihrer *Übersetzung, Übersetzung* in die Auferstehung, in den Text, aber auch die Bitternis, die Empörung, die Trauer und Wut. Das erste Kapitel des Schreibens beginnt am und beim Übergang. (Z 32, Hervorhebung: WS)

In diesen Worten fasst Anne Duden in ihrem Prosaband *Zungengewahrsam* den einsetzenden Schreibprozess. Schon das Schreiben selbst beinhaltet also für sie eine Übersetzung im Sinne einer Befreiung der in Wörtern und Bildern gefangenen Daseinsmöglichkeiten, die in der ‚ununterbrochenen Versklavung durch Werktätigkeit, auch Arbeit genannt oder Geldverdienenmüssen' unterdrückt werden (Z 32). Dementsprechend versucht Duden in ihren Texten die Grenzen dieses Alltäglichen zu durchbrechen, um damit in die Grenzbereiche unserer Wahrnehmung vorzudringen und ‚die Möglichkeiten unseres Ausdrucks bis ins Unmögliche hinein – oder vielmehr zurück – zu erweitern.'[1] Dieses fortlaufende Projekt, ‚eine eigentlich unmögliche Daseinsmöglichkeit auszudrücken'[2] erfordert, um im Bild der Übersetzung zu bleiben, ‚ein Überschreiten und Verwandeln der Grenzen der übersetzenden Sprache', wie Jacques Derrida dies in seinen Ausführungen zu Walter Benjamins ‚Die Aufgabe des Übersetzers' beschreibt.[3] Genau damit sind jedoch die Probleme für die Übersetzung von Dudens Texten in andere Sprachen schon vorprogrammiert, denn die gängige Übersetzungspraxis dient aufgrund ihrer Orientierung an den Normen und Konventionen der Zielsprache weniger der innersprachlichen Grenzverschiebung als der sprachlichen Konservierung. Die jeweiligen Ausgangstexte werden in das Korsett der übersetzenden Sprache gezwängt und damit dem Zielpublikum der Übersetzung ein transparenter Blick auf den Ausgangstext vorgegaukelt. Unterstützt wird diese Praxis von einer Literaturkritik, die zum einen nur selten auf die Übersetzung eines Textes eingeht und diese zum anderen nur dann lobt, wenn sie den Normen der Zielsprache gerecht wird.[4] Dass diese Übersetzungspraxis - wie übrigens auch die Literaturwissenschaft[5] - in der Auseinandersetzung mit Dudens Texten an ihre Grenzen stößt, äußert sich in erster Linie darin, dass bisher als eigenständige Veröffentlichung Dudens sowohl im Englischen als auch im Französischen nur der Prosaband *Übergang* erschienen ist. Zudem wird die Analyse der beiden Übersetzungen zeigen, dass aus dieser Praxis Grenzziehungen gegenüber dem Fremden in Dudens Texten resultieren. Das Fremde, das sich in diesen als Außer-Ordentliches, wie Bernhard Waldenfels es nennt, den bestehenden sprachlichen und konzeptuellen Ordnungen entzieht und diese damit gleichzeitig in Frage stellt, wird in den Übersetzungen in diese Kategorisierungen zurückgeführt und auf diese Weise ein- und ausgegrenzt.[6] Dieser Versuch der Rückführung in bestehende Systeme zeigt sich bei der französischen Publikation schon in den Veröffentlichungsstrategien, die in Form der Klappentexte und Illustrationen im ersten Teil dieses Aufsatzes im Vordergrund stehen sollen. Anschließend folgt eine Detailanalyse der Übersetzungen von ,Herz und Mund', in dem die alltägliche Gewalt gegenüber dem auch sprachlich aus der bestehenden Ordnung ausgeschlossenem Anderen aus der Position dieses Anderen vor Augen geführt wird. Dabei versucht Duden die binäre Opposition zwischen Ich und Anderem in der Sprache aufzulösen und damit zu zeigen, dass jedes Ich ein Anderes impliziert und umgekehrt: Nach Maurice Merleau-Ponty ist dies ein ‚Grundlegender Polymorphismus, der bewirkt, daß ich den Anderen nicht *vor* den Augen des Ego konstituieren muß; er ist schon da, und das Ego ist ihm abgerungen.'[7] Auch diese Auseinandersetzung mit der in der Sprache angelegten Gewalt geht in der gängigen Übersetzungspraxis verloren. Gleichzeitig beleuchten jedoch die Unterschiede zwischen der englischen und der französischen Version von Dudens *Übergang* die im Ausgangstext angelegte Differenz und bilden damit die Grundlage für eine Neuinterpretation. Den Abschluss des Aufsatzes bilden einige Überlegungen zu alternativen Übersetzunskonzepten, mit denen der

Ausgrenzung des Fremden in der Übersetzung von Dudens Texten begegnet werden kann.

Übergang im Licht seiner unterschiedlichen Veröffentlichungen

Anne Dudens *Übergang* wurde zunächst 1985 in englischer Sprache unter dem Titel *Opening of the Mouth* in der Übersetzung von Della Couling bei Pluto Press in Großbritannien und Australien veröffentlicht. 1987 erschien dann bei Alinéa in Aix-en-Provence unter dem Titel *Traversée* der französische Text Pierre Furlans und Dominique Jallamions. Schon diese Reihenfolge ist eher ungewöhnlich, denn im englischsprachigen Raum lassen sich deutsche Texte normalerweise ungleich schwerer an den Verlag bringen als in Frankreich.[8] In diesem Fall lässt sich jedoch die englische Erstveröffentlichung sicherlich unter anderem darauf zurückführen, dass Anne Duden selbst in Großbritannien lebt. Zudem unterhält sie aufgrund ihrer früheren Tätigkeit bei Rotbuch Kontakte zu englischen Verlagen mit ähnlichen Schwerpunkten und Zielvorstellungen, zu denen eben auch Pluto Press gehört.[9] Allerdings konnten auch diese Voraussetzungen nicht verhindern, dass ihre zweite deutsche Veröffentlichung, *Das Judasschaf,* deren Übersetzung in *Opening of the Mouth* von Pluto Press noch angekündigt wurde, dann nie in englischer Sprache erschien - wahrscheinlich aufgrund ökonomischer Probleme und einer daraus resultierenden Nischenbildung von Pluto Press im Sachbuchbereich. Auch von Dudens französischem Verlag Alinéa sind keine weiteren Veröffentlichungen ihrer Texte zu erwarten: dieser musste 1993 Konkurs anmelden und wurde daraufhin aufgelöst.[10]

Schon die Strategien, die von den beiden Verlagen bei der Veröffentlichung ihrer Übersetzungen verfolgt wurden, verraten eine sehr unterschiedliche Positionierung von *Übergang* in der jeweiligen Zielkultur. Die französische Ausgabe stellt den Text in den Rahmen einer autobiographischen feministischen Literatur, die in Frankreich genau wie in Deutschland mit der Frauenbewegung in den siebziger und achtziger Jahren des letzten Jahrhunderts an Bedeutung gewann.[11] So zeigt die Illustration das Gesicht einer Frau und der Klappentext lässt verlauten:

> Entre les paroles du début et celles du fin, Anne Duden retrace ce qui arrive à une femme et ce qui se passe en elle. Pour une grande part, ces choses appartiennent aussi à l'Allemagne, et ne peuvent en être dissociées. Mais, curieusement, elles correspondent aussi aux pensées, aux attentes et aux sentiments les plus profonds et les plus essentiels des lecteurs non allemands.[12]

An diesem Text lässt sich einerseits eine gewisse Unsicherheit in der Beschreibung von *Übergang* ablesen. So werden die Erfahrungen und Gefühle der Frau, die Anne Duden gemäß der Interpretation dieses Klappentextes in einer lebhaften Erzählung dem Vergessen entreißt,[13] in ihrer Wiederaufnahme im folgenden Satz mit der allumfassenden Wendung ‚ces choses' als nur schwer fassbar kategorisiert. In ähnlicher Weise stuft das Adverb ‚curieusement' die den französischen LeserInnen in Aussicht gestellten Identifikationsmöglichkeiten mit diesem fest in Deutschland verankerten Text als unerklärlich ein. Dieser augenscheinlichen Unsicherheit bei der Beschreibung des Inhalts und der Wirkung von *Übergang* wird jedoch andererseits mit einer stark fixierenden Interpretation des Prosabandes begegnet. Ganz selbstverständlich vereint der Klappentext die Ichs in diesem Band in einer einzigen Frau, auch wenn in den acht verschiedenen Texten nie konkret auf ihre Identität verwiesen wird. Teilweise, so in ‚Herz und Mund', wird das Ich nicht einmal eindeutig als weiblich kategorisiert. Der französische Klappentext basiert also auf einem Subjektbegriff, der zum Ausschluss des Anderen, in Form des Weiblichen oder auch Irrationalen, beigetragen hat und dem aus genau diesem Grunde in *Übergang* eine Alternative entgegengestellt wird. Konkret besteht diese, wie die Analyse des Textes ‚Herz und Mund' zeigen wird, im Oszillieren zwischen Subjekt- und Objektposition. Dem männlichen Subjekt wird in diesem Text also nicht mit einem weiblichen begegnet, sondern mit einer Schreibweise, die den Gegensatz zwischen Subjekt und Objekt aufzulösen und damit dem erneuten Ausschluss eines Anderen durch ein abgerungenes Ich, diesmal unter umgekehrten Vorzeichen, vorzubeugen versucht.

Das soll nicht heißen, dass sich *Übergang* nicht als autobiographische Literatur lesen ließe. Ganz im Gegenteil, wie Georgina Paul gezeigt hat, können Anne Dudens Texte sehr wohl im autobiographischen Genre verankert werden, allerdings nur, wenn dieses Genre nicht in seinen herkömmlichen Grenzen als Bildungsroman eines fixen Ich verstanden wird.[14] Genau diese althergebrachte Vorstellung von autobiographischer Literatur scheint sich jedoch nicht nur in der Illustration und im Klappentext, sondern auch in der Titelwahl der französischen Veröffentlichung zu spiegeln. Das Wort *traversée* beschreibt konkret eine Überfahrt, also das Übersetzen an ein anderes Ufer, oder auch das Überqueren eines Gebirges bzw. das Durchqueren eines Landes. Der Begriff beinhaltet also im übertragenden Sinne das Durchlaufen verschiedener Erfahrungen und Stationen mit einem bestimmten Ziel und impliziert damit eine Art von

Identitätssuche, der eine fixe Vorstellung von Identität zugrunde liegt. Der deutsche Titel *Übergang* dagegen betont das Element der Grenzüberschreitung in einem solchen Prozess und umfasst dementsprechend die Phase des Wechsels zu etwas Anderem, Neuem oder auch in ein anderes Stadium, so zum Beispiel den Übergang vom Wachen zum Schlafen.[15] Genau diese Zwischenzustände, wie Duden sie in *Zungengewahrsam* nennt (Z 49), spielen in den Texten des Bandes *Übergang* nicht nur in Bezug auf die Begriffe Subjekt und Objekt eine bedeutende Rolle. Sie bewirken auch die Verschiebung der Grenzen zwischen Drinnen und Draußen in ‚Das Landhaus' (Ü 14, 17), zwischen Traum und Wirklichkeit in ‚Herz und Mund' (Ü 44-45) und letztendlich zwischen Leben und Tod in ‚Die Kunst zu ertrinken': ‚Nach allem blieb ihr nur noch eines: weder unterzugehen noch aufzutauchen. Weder zu schlafen noch zu wachen, weder zu leben noch zu sterben.' (Ü 138) Diese Bedeutung des Wortes Übergang, die in *traversée* nicht enthalten ist, umfasst im Französischen der Begriff *passage*, der ansonsten synonym zu *traversée* verwendet werden kann. Mit *passage* nun wurde in der französischen Übersetzung des Bandes die deutsche Titelerzählung benannt. Damit wird diese im Französischen zum Wendepunkt in den Erfahrungen der Frau erhoben und die Strukturierung des gesamten Bandes nach dem Muster herkömmlicher autobiographischer Literatur mit einem Ausgangs-, Wende- und Zielpunkt vervollständigt. Sicherlich kommt ‚Übergang' die herausragende Bedeutung als Wendepunkt in diesem Band auch zu, denn das jeweilige Ich wird nicht mehr, wie noch in den vorausgehenden Texten, ungewollt und überraschend von diesen Zwischenzuständen überfallen, sondern setzt sich diesen bewusst aus.[16] Trotzdem durchbricht Duden in *Übergang* das Konzept einer zielorientierten Identitätssuche von Anfang an, denn schon die ersten drei Texte, so auch ‚Herz und Mund', bringen die im Titel des Bandes enthaltenen Übergänge zur Sprache. Auch sie beinhalten also ein Öffnen des Mundes für ‚eine unmögliche Daseinsmöglichkeit.'

Damit ist eine der möglichen Bedeutungen des englischen Titels von *Übergang, Opening of the Mouth,* aufgezeigt. Dieser stellt die Suche nach einer neuen Sprache in den Vordergrund. Dabei wird mit der Partizipialform der Prozesscharakter dieses Öffnens und damit der Akt des Schreibens selbst und nicht dessen Produkt betont. In genau dieser Hinsicht weicht nach Meinung Georgina Pauls Anne Dudens autobiographisches Projekt von herkömmlichen Texten dieses Genres ab:

> [...] it is in writing – in the act of writing, not in the text which is merely the relic of this act, in *Schreiben*, then, rather than in *Schrift* – that the self is able

to constitute itself as the sum of its 'moments of being' and in the intensity of the 'moment of being' that is the moment of writing [...].[17]

Die englische Veröffentlichung lässt also schon in ihrem Titel die Vorstellung von einer fixierten Identität, wie sie der französischen Ausgabe von *Übergang* zugrunde liegt, hinter sich. Gleichzeitig wird mit *Opening of the Mouth* ein entscheidendes Element der Titelerzählung aufgegriffen und dieser damit eine besondere Bedeutung im Prozess des Schreibens zugewiesen. In ‚Übergang' zertrümmert eine Gruppe von schwarzen GIs dem Sie/Ich bei einem Überfall den Mund. Gerade dieses gewaltsame Öffnen des Mundes lässt das Ich jedoch zu einer eigenen Sprache finden. Entscheidend ist dafür der Perspektivenwechsel vom Sie zum Ich, der bezeichnenderweise nicht, wie sowohl Sigrid Weigel als auch Leslie Adelson behaupten, mit dem Moment der konkreten Operation und der Rekonstruktion des Mundes eintritt[18] - auch wenn die Wortwahl das zunächst anzudeuten scheint -, sondern mit der ärztlichen Kategorisierung der vorher minutiös beschriebenen Ereignisse als Überfall:

> Mit einem unblutigen, präzisen Schnitt trennte der Arzt mich ab von dem, was war. Ein Überfall also. Hinter dem zentralen Wort sackte alles weg. Es setzte sich augenblicklich an die Stelle dieses Gemisches aus Sequenzen, Wirbeln und Stillständen, aus hohler Dunkelheit und diffuser Beleuchtung, angespannt ruhig verharrenden und abrupt agierenden Körperteilen, Gesichtsarealen und Mauerkanten, aus diesiger Feuchtigkeit und glänzendem Asphalt. [...] Ich konnte nichts damit anfangen. Überfall. Das Loch, das Maul sollte mir gestopft werden, kaum, daß es aufgerissen worden war. (Ü 67)

In dem ärztlichen Ausspruch ‚Ein Überfall also' offenbart sich ein Moment des sprachlichen Verbergens und damit des Verlustes all der vorausgegangenen Vorgänge und Erfahrungen. Mit dem Wort ‚Überfall' wird dem Ich eine klare Bedeutung dieser Ereignisse vorgeschrieben, die jedoch sein eigenes Erleben dieser Momente nicht fassen kann. Genau diese Kluft bewegt das Ich zur Öffnung des Mundes, zur eigenen Versprachlichung seiner Erlebnisse, die das Verborgene ans Licht bringen soll, ohne wiederum zu verbergen. Im englischen Buchtitel wird diesem speziellen Übergangsmoment damit eine besondere Bedeutung zugeschrieben. Der Übergang als Zwischenzustand wird anders als im Deutschen auf ein bestimmtes, den anderen Übergängen zugrunde liegendes Bild spezifiziert. Aber auch im Deutschen wird auf die Titelerzählung durch die Übereinstimmung von Buch- und Erzählungstitel ein Schwerpunkt gelegt und diese damit in ihrer besonderen Bedeutung, die oben schon beschrieben wurde, hervorgehoben. Die Funktion von ‚Übergang' als Wendepunkt wird im Englischen mit dem Titel ‚Transition' betont, der den im Begriff Übergang enthaltenen Zwischenzustand beschreibt.

Die Offenheit in der Deutung von *Übergang*, die sich schon im englischen Titel ausdrückt, spiegelt sich auch im Klappentext und der Illustration dieser Veröffentlichung. So beginnt der Klappentext mit den Worten ‚eight stories', um dann im letzten Absatz die Möglichkeit aufzuwerfen, dass es sich bei diesen ‚Erzählungen' vielleicht doch nur um eine einzige handeln könnte.[19] Damit sieht er also von einer vorgefertigten Interpretation des Textes ab. Und auch die Illustration, ein Ausschnitt aus ‚Christus als Schmerzensmann',[20] der von Anne Duden selbst ausgewählt wurde und sich auch auf ihrer späteren Veröffentlichung *Steinschlag* wiederfindet, lässt sich in vielfacher Weise auf den Text beziehen.[21] Zum einen hat die heftig blutende Wunde im Leib Christi die Form eines Mundes und unterstreicht damit die Titelmetapher. Doch nicht nur der Mund trägt in diesem Text Wunden davon, der ganze Körper ist in seiner Funktion als Gedächtnis eine einzige Wunde, wie dies im Epilog beschrieben wird: ‚Mein Gedächtnis ist mein Körper. Mein Körper ist löchrig.'(Ü 141) Wie in der Analyse von ‚Herz und Mund' deutlich wird, sind diese Wunden auch Folge der sprachlichen Gewalt, die dem Körper als Objekt der Sprache zugefügt werden. In einem weiteren Sinne verweist die gewählte Illustration mit der Passionsgeschichte schließlich auf einen der vielen Intertexte von *Übergang*, die Bibel, die in ihrer Funktion als Speicher einer Vielfalt von verborgenen Bedeutungen innerhalb des westeuropäischen kulturellen Gedächtnisses in Dudens Texten eine besondere Rolle spielt.[22] Auf diesen Intertext wird auch mit der Illustration der deutschen Erstausgabe von *Übergang*, Vincent van Goghs Rohrfederzeichnung ‚Aronstab', angespielt. Bei Aronstab handelt es sich um eine Pflanze, deren Name auf dem lateinischen ‚aron' basiert, das dann volksethymologisch an den Hohen Priester Aron im Alten Testament angelehnt wurde. Dieser stand Moses bei der Befreiung des Volkes Israel aus Ägypten zur Seite und führte, um den Pharao davon zu überzeugen, dass die beiden wirklich im Auftrag Gottes handelten, einen Stab bei sich, der sich vor den Augen des Pharaos in eine Schlange verwandelte.[23] Der Titel dieser Zeichnung beinhaltet damit schon Anne Dudens Projekt, den Wurzeln der Sprache auf den Grund zu gehen. Zudem bildet die deutsche Illustration eine ähnliche Einheit mit dem deutschen Titel wie die englische mit dem englischen, denn in van Goghs Zeichnung verschwimmen die Übergänge zwischen den Pflanzen und ihrem Hintergrund.[24] Der englische Titel dieser Zeichnung, ‚Study of Arums',[25] beinhaltet jedoch weder die Anspielung auf die Bibel noch die in der Sprache verborgen liegenden Bedeutungen. Mit der Wahl eines neuen Titels und einer neuen Illustration wurde also versucht, die Vieldeutigkeit der deutschen Ausgabe in der Einheit von Titel und Bild nachzuahmen. Diese Art des kreativen Umgangs mit dem Ausgangstext ist jedoch, wie die folgende Analyse zeigen wird, in den Übersetzungen eher selten der Fall.

‚Herz und Mund' im Licht seiner unterschiedlichen Übersetzungen
In ‚Herz und Mund' wird der sich stets wiederholende, in der Sprache verankerte gewalttätige Ausschluss des Anderen aus der Position dieses Anderen heraus, also einer eigentlich ‚unmöglichen Daseinsmöglichkeit' thematisiert. Diese Aporie zeigt sich schon in den ersten beiden Sätzen, die in der französischen Übersetzung mit der Einfügung eines Prädikats in die elliptische Konstruktion im zweiten Satz gleichzeitig eine erste Anpassung an sprachliche Normen offenbaren:

> In Schöneberg und Tiergarten liege ich begraben. Mein Herz im zweiten Hinterhof, gebrochen und von meinen eigenen Augen an der Birke und der Platane aufgeknüpft und gehängt. (Ü 44)

> Mon cœur *est resté* brisé dans la deuxième cour, […][26]

Das schon tote Subjekt leistet also Beihilfe zum Mord seiner selbst im alltäglichen Dasein. Mit dem Herz tötet es jegliches Anliegen und damit auch jegliches Zieldenken in sich ab. Zudem unterstützt es den Prozess seiner Objektwerdung jedoch auch darin, dass es sich gegen die Versprachlichung seiner Bitternis, die ihm trotz des verlorenen Herzens erhalten geblieben ist, aus Furcht vor einem erneuten Ausschluss eines Anderen mit allen Mitteln zur Wehr setzt. Trotzdem, und genau darin besteht das oben erwähnte Oszillieren zwischen Subjekt- und Objektposition, lesen wir über dieses Objekt, das im alltäglichen Leben verdrängt wird, einen aus der Ich-Position erzählten Text. Dieser beinhaltet also sowohl die Furcht vor dem freien Sprechen als auch deren Überwindung in dieser spezifischen Art des Schreibens.[27] Der im doppelten Sinne ‚entmündigte' und an den Rollstuhl gefesselte ‚Klumpen', den das Ich in dieser herrschenden Sprache darstellt (Ü 47-48), ohne Herz und mit einem zertrümmerten, bandagierten und deswegen fest verschlossenen Mund erhält im geschriebenen Text sowohl Herz als auch Mund, das heißt eine eigene Stimme, die wiederum paradoxerweise seine Angst vor den Folgen eines befreiten Sprechens zum Ausdruck bringt. So läuft dem Ich die vom fehlenden Herzen zurückgebliebene Bitternis im wahrsten Sinne des Wortes fast über, der eingesperrte heiße Schleimbrei schiebt sich zwischen Kehle und Augenhintergrund, und doch öffnet sich ihm, anders als in Jesus' Ausspruch in der Übersetzung Martin Luthers, nicht der Mund (Ü 44).[28] Von Taten oder Leben, wie sie in der Bach-Kantate ‚Herz und Mund und Tat und Leben' anklingen, ist deswegen im Titel dieses Textes schon gar nicht mehr die Rede.[29] Das Ich ist seinen Anderen auf Gedeih und Verderb ausgeliefert, es ist als Objekt gefangen in einer Sprache, in der sein Zwischenzustand weder beschrieben noch wahrgenommen werden kann. Der Text ‚Herz und Mund' selbst jedoch kann als Beispiel einer neuen Sprache gelten, in der diese Beschreibung und Wahrnehmung möglich wird. Erst eine solche Sprache also kann Herz, Mund und Augen öffnen, wie Duden dies in ‚Vom Versprechen des Schreibens und vom Schreiben des Versprechens' fasst:

> Dabei könnte einem das Herz aufgehen, könnten einem die Augen übergehen und würde der Mund vielleicht überfließen wollen – von gefundener wie sich einfindender, überraschend erscheinender und doch genau sich bildender und immer weiter möglich werdender Sprache. Und man könnte auch einmal aufhören, mitten im poetischen Satz gar, sich vorm Schreiben, als zu großer Aufgabe zum Beispiel, zu fürchten. (V 43)

In ‚Herz und Mund' dagegen bleibt das Ich aufgrund der mangelnden Ausdrucksmöglichkeiten seiner selbst in der herrschenden Sprache, in der das Ich als Objekt gefangen ist, sowie aufgrund der Furcht vor den möglichen Folgen eines befreiten Sprechens sprachlos: ‚Mein *Friedhof* des Herzens ist eine *geschlossene Institution*. Die Schläge und alle anderen Regungen und Bewegungen bleiben *eingekerkert*.' (Ü 45) In diesem Bild graben sich die möglichen Folgen eines solchen befreiten Sprechens in konkreten gesellschaftlichen Repressionen gegen dieses Andere, die sich eben auch in der Sprache niederschlagen, in den Körper des Ich ein. Neben Tod und Gefängnis drohen diesem im Falle der Äußerung seiner andersartigen Gedanken die geschlossene Anstalt für den aus der gemeinschaftlichen Ordnung ausgeschlossenen Wahnsinn.[30] Diese möglichen Strafen, die Andersdenkenden ‚blühen', werden im Text auch an Beispielen festgemacht:

> Blick auf die sich vom Gesicht wegbewegende Hand, die nicht über weichfeste Formen und Flächen hinweggeglitten ist, sondern in etwas nur noch weich Matschiges gegriffen hat. Warm Schleimiges und Glitschiges, auch Mengen

von Speichel, der irgendwo dickflüssig herauskam. Und in ein Kreuz- und Quergerage innerhalb dieser Masse aus Vergänglichem und Kadaver: Zähne, Knochen, Splitter. *Pfahl/ Pfählchen im Fleisch.* Abbildung der Wasserleiche Rosa Luxemburgs. Ein kleiner verrotteter Zahnstumpf-Zaun, Tor zum verwilderten Kadavergarten. Der Schädel eine einzige wulstige Weichteilmasse. (Ü 45-46, Hervorhebung: WS)

In diesen Assoziationen zum eigenen von einem Überfall völlig zerstörten Mund klingt Rosa Luxemburgs Ausspruch ‚Freiheit ist immer auch die Freiheit der Andersdenkenden' bezeichnenderweise im Bild ihrer Wasserleiche an. Der ‚Pfahl im Fleisch' dagegen verweist auf Martin Luthers Übersetzung von Paulus' zweitem Brief an die Korinther und damit auf die Leiden der Apostel vor der Institutionalisierung der christlichen Kirche: ‚Und auf daß ich mich nicht der hohen Offenbarungen überhebe, ist mir gegeben ein *Pfahl ins Fleisch*, nämlich des Satans Engel, der mich mit Fäusten schlage, auf daß ich mich nicht überhebe.'[31] Diese biblische Anspielung offenbart sich jedoch weder im englischen ‚Stakes/sticks in my flesh' noch im französischen ‚Bâton/bâtonnet dans ma chair.'[32] Im Französischen ist die Übersetzung dieser Anspielung schon von daher problematischer, als dass, anders als im Englischen und im Deutschen, keine kanonische Bibelversion vorliegt, in deren Worten die Bibelerzählungen in der jeweiligen Kultur gespeichert, ritualisiert und in jedem Kontext automatisch abrufbar sind.[33] Doch auch im Englischen konzentriert sich die Übersetzerin hauptsächlich auf das Wortspiel, das mit der Übersetzung ‚thorn in the flesh', wie diese Stelle in der King James Bible lautet, wahrscheinlich nicht so elegant hätte gelöst werden können. Damit verlieren die beiden Übersetzungen von ‚Herz und Mund' die vielschichtigen Bezüge des ‚Pfahls im Fleisch' zu seinem biblischen Kontext, die im Folgenden kurz erläutert werden sollen.

In seinem zweiten Brief an die Korinther versucht Paulus die von anderen Predigern beeinflusste Gemeinde Korinth wieder auf seinen Pfad zu bringen. Anscheinend wurde ihm unter anderem vorgeworfen, er sei, da er nicht zu Lebzeiten Jesu berufen wurde, kein wahrer Apostel.[34] Diesen Vorwurf versucht er in diesem Brief zu widerlegen, indem er sich der Repressionen, so zum Beispiel der Geißelhiebe, Auspeitschungen und Steinigungen, rühmt, denen er aufgrund seiner Verkündigung der christlichen Lehren ausgesetzt ist.[35] Allerdings ist ihm dabei durchaus bewusst, dass diese Art der Überhebung den göttlichen Geboten widerspricht und Strafen nach sich ziehen kann. Diese sieht Paulus im ‚Pfahl im Fleisch', der in der Forschung im allgemeinen als eine Krankheit gedeutet wird, antizipiert.[36] Hinter dieser Krankheit verbirgt sich in seinem Weltbild nämlich der ‚Engel Satans', der Paulus in weiser Voraussicht schon einmal ‚mit Fäusten' schlägt, damit er nicht mit den Offenbarungen, die ihm zuteil geworden sind, prahlt. Paulus' Interpretation des Pfahls im Fleisch deckt also die der christlichen Ordnung inhärenten Strafen auf und kündigt damit die bevorstehenden Repressionen gegenüber Andersdenkenden durch die Kirche an, auch wenn deren Anhänger noch selbst als Andersdenkende verfolgt werden. Bezeichnenderweise entzieht Paulus selbst sich dieser Ordnung, indem er sich in diesem auch als Narrenrede bezeichneten Abschnitt seines Briefes der Narrenfreiheit bedient: ‚Was ich jetzt rede, das rede ich nicht als im Herren, sondern als in der Torheit, [...]'.[37] Dieses rhetorische Mittel kann jedoch nur funktionieren, wenn der Narr aus der kirchlichen Ordnung ausgenommen ist. Paulus' Brief ist also fest in jenem logozentrischen Denken verankert, dem der Text ‚Herz und Mund' sich widersetzt.

In seinem Kontext in ‚Herz und Mund' ist der ‚Pfahl im Fleisch' wie das Bild der Wasserleiche Rosa Luxemburgs eine Spur des ewigen Kampfes zwischen der dominanten Ordnung und des aus dieser Ordnung ausgeschlossenen Anderen. Assoziativ schließt er sich im obigen Zitat an die Zähne und Knochenüberreste im Mund an. Hinter den Zähnen, die das nicht in die Ordnung zu integrierende Verborgene und damit Tote wie eine Art Zaun ein- und ausgrenzen, liegt normalerweise die Bitternis des Ich, die Wut über seinen Ausschluss, wohl verschlossen. In ihrem Zustand in diesem Zitat als ‚Zahnstumpf-Zaun' eröffnen sie jedoch einen ersten Blick auf den ‚verwilderten Kadavergarten' und damit auf das ausgeschlossene Andere. Dieser ‚Kadavergarten' erinnert an die Ansammlung von Schädeln und abgetrennten Armen und Beinen auf Vittore Carpaccios Bild ‚Der Heilige Georg im Kampf mit dem Drachen' und damit - in den Worten von Anne Dudens Beschreibung dieses Bildes in ‚Gegenstrebige Fügung' in *Der wunde Punkt im Alphabet* - an die ‚blut- und knochengesättigte Gegend, in der das liquidierte Wissen massenhaft selbstlos wird, eine unerhörte Stimme erhält und als unsagbare Stimme aufgehoben bleibt in geschlechtslosen, untergehenden Mündern.' (A 120) Der Mund des geschlechtslosen Ich in ‚Herz und Mund' ist mit seiner unerhörten und doch verschriftlichen Stimme eins der Opfer des ewigen Kampfes zwischen dem Heiligen Georg und dem Drachen, einem Paradigma des sich ewig wiederholenden Ausschlusses des Anderen.[38] Der Drachentöter hat in ihm seine Spuren hinterlassen, ‚[...] ihm seinen *Pfahl ins Fleisch* stoßend, Fleisch des ungezähmten und ungezäumten Mundes, Maules; das Ungeheuer aufspießend, mundtot pfählend, [..].' (A 121

Hervorhebung: WS) Im und am Mund des Ich als Symbol für die Sprache wird also dieser Kampf zwischen Georg und dem Drachen, zwischen der Ordnung und deren Ausschluss des Anderen ausgeführt. Denn dieser Kampf hat sich auch in die Sprache eingeschrieben, wiederholt sich tagtäglich in ihrem selbstverständlichen Gebrauch und rechtfertigt damit auch die obigen Repressionen:

> [Es geht] nicht gewaltfrei zu in der Sprache, und jedenfalls scheint unserem üblichen Satzbau, unserem gemeinen Satz, ein Engelsturz vorausgegangen zu sein und eine Paradiesaustreibung dazu. Es ist ein Urteil ergangen. Und der gemeine Satz betont das oft genug, um sich zu behaupten. Ihm sitzt der Schreck noch in den Gliedern, die Angst davor für vogelfrei erklärt zu werden. Und die Ahnung, das heimlich gewordene Wissen, daß jeder *Be-* eine *Ent*hauptung folgen kann oder bereits vorausgegangen ist, bleibt ihm als Nachgeburt verschwistert, behält er als Schatten neben, vor, hinter sich. (V 41, Hervorhebung im Original)

Nur im Kampf mit der alltäglichen Sprache kann diese verborgene Seite im poetischen Satz ans Licht gezerrt werden. In ‚Herz und Mund' schreiben sich dieser Kampf mit den in der Gewalt verankerten, vergessenen Wurzeln der Sprache bis zur Grenze des Unerträglichen konkret in den Körper des Objekts dieser Sprache ein. Am einprägsamsten geschieht dies, dem Thema des Textes ensprechend, am Bild der Entmündigung:

> Ich konnte nicht sagen, wie ich litt. *Man hatte mich – ich war entmündigt.* Ich litt also nicht. (Ü 47)

> I couldn't say how I was suffering. *I was without my right of say – it had been taken away.* So I did not suffer then.

> J'étais incapable de dire de quelle manière je souffrais. *On m'avait – j'étais privée du droit de parole.* Je ne souffrais donc pas. [39]

Das Ich ist also ‚entmündigt', das heißt, im allgemein gebräuchlichen Sinne, bestimmter Rechte, so des Rechts auf freie Rede, beraubt, denn es ist von der herrschenden Sprache ausgeschlossen. Doch diese Entmündigung schreibt sich in diesem Text eben auch ganz konkret in den Körper des Ichs ein. Diesem wurde mit einer Eisenstange der Mund zertrümmert - eine Tat, deren Beschreibung in Phrasen wie ‚Vergewaltigung des Kopfes' und ‚Eindringen und gewalttätige Ejakulation' den Objektstatus des Ich in den Rahmen des Geschlechterkampfes stellt (Ü 46). Dieses Aufspüren der gewalttätigen Wurzel des Wortes ‚entmündigt' und seine im Text veranschaulichte Rückführung auf seine konkrete Bedeutung, wird weder im Englischen noch im Französischen nachvollzogen. Beide Übersetzungen entscheiden sich für die allgemein bekannte figurative Bedeutung dieses Wortes und spezifizieren diese auf das Recht auf freie Rede, das dann zumindest im übertragenden Sinne wieder mit dem zertrümmerten Mund in Zusammenhang gebracht werden kann.[40]

Der Entmündigung des (grammatikalischen) Subjekts, also des 'ich', im zweiten Teil des Satzes 'Man hatte mich – ich war entmündigt' entspricht jedoch zusätzlich im ersten das Festsetzen des (grammatikalischen) Objekts, des 'mich'. Das Ich kann sich in der alltäglichen Sprache nicht ausdrücken, ist vielmehr als Objekt von dieser ausgeschlossen und gleichzeitig in ihr gefangen. Die sprachliche Gewalt gegenüber dem Objekt äußert sich also in diesem Satz nicht nur im Vokabular, also im Bild der Entmündigung, sondern auch in der Grammatik. Im Englischen werden diese beiden Sätze, die sich nur sehr schwer in konventionelles Englisch übertragen lassen, gemäß der oben beschriebenen, den sprachlichen Normen verpflichteten Übersetzungspraxis in einen anderen Bezug zueinander gesetzt. Ihre Reihenfolge wird umgekehrt und der zweite mit dem ‚it' nicht auf die Person als Objekt, sondern auf das Recht auf freie Rede bezogen. Damit erhält der Satz zwar zielsprachliche Transparenz, verliert jedoch all jene Deutungsmöglichkeiten, die in der Ausgangssprache verankert sind. In der französischen Übersetzung dagegen bleiben diese nicht nur möglich, sie beinhalten sogar spezifische Elemente der Gewalt in dieser Zielsprache. So kommt das Französische für das Objekt mit dem ‚m' in ‚m'avait' mit nur einem Buchstaben aus, lässt dieses also in diesem ersten Satz fast unsichtbar werden. Zudem wird das Subjekt im zweiten Satz im doppelten ‚e' von ‚privée' aus grammatikalischen Gründen als weiblich kategorisiert, während das Objekt im ersten Satz geschlechtslos bleibt.[41] In diesen beiden Sätzen stellt das Französische dem weiblichen, sichtbaren Subjekt also ein geschlechtsloses, fast unsichtbares Objekt gegenüber. Allerdings scheinen die ÜbersetzerInnen, wie das folgende Beispiel zeigt, mit dieser Gegenüberstellung im Französischen keine durchgängige Strategie zu verfolgen:

> Der Pfleger *schob mich* in den Fahrstuhl, ich konnte nicht sprechen und nichts *erfahren*,… (Ü 46)
>
> The male nurse *wheeled me* into the lift, I couldn't speak, or *ascertain* anything,…

L'infirmier *m'a poussée* dans l'ascenseur. Je ne pouvais ni parler, ni m'informer, ... [42]

Im ersten Satz dieses Zitats ist das Ich genau wie im vorherigen Beispiel sowohl konkret als auch grammatikalisch Objekt der Ereignisse, wird jedoch trotzdem im Französischen als weiblich markiert. Mit einer gänzlich anderen Konstruktion hätte diese in diesem Fall grammatikalisch notwendige Markierung sicherlich vermieden werden können, wenn die Gegenüberstellung von weiblichem Subjekt und geschlechtslosem Objekt von den ÜbersetzerInnen als Merkmal der sprachlichen Gewalt in der französischen Sprache dann strategisch beabsichtigt gewesen wäre. Im anschließenden Satz, in dem das Ich wiederum Subjekt ist, wird noch einmal auf dessen Beschränkung durch die sprachlichen, bildlich konkretisierten äußeren Umstände verwiesen. Dabei umfasst das Wort ‚erfahren' nicht nur das Sammeln oder auch Absichern von Informationen im Gespräch mit dem Pfleger, wie im Französischen bzw. Englischen umgesetzt, sondern auch konkret das Er-Fahren der Welt, also das Steuern des Rollstuhls, den das Ich nicht selbst bewegen kann. Auch in diesem Bild bedingen sich sprachlicher Ausschluss und konkrete Umsetzung gegenseitig, denn das Ich wird als Anderes von einem Pfleger, der es völlig ignoriert, auf ein bestimmtes Ziel, das ihm selbst in seiner Ziellosigkeit unbekannt ist, zugeschoben, ist diesem also völlig ausgeliefert. Daraus resultiert auch die Angst des Ich vor der völligen Auslöschung durch all die Subjekte, von denen es umgeben zu sein scheint:

> Wenn zwei oder drei von ihnen kommen – einer reicht ja schon für einen Klumpen -, um mich endgültig zu beseitigen. Es kommen und gehen so viele Leute. Killer betreten Krankenhäuser doch nicht nur in Krimis. Nicht, bitte. Für den, der ein Anliegen hat, wird alles so einfach. Er erfährt und erreicht genau das, was er will. Mich. (Ü 49)

> It's not just in thrillers that killers get into hospitals. No, please. For anyone so inclined it's all so easy. He finds out and gets to exactly what he wants. Me.

> Ce n'est pas seulement dans les romans policiers que des tueurs pénètrent dans les hôpitaux. Non, s'il vous plaît. Pour celui qui en exprime le souhait, tout devient extrêmement simple. Il découvre et atteint exactement ce qu'il veut. Moi.[43]

Die Angst vor der endgültigen Auslöschung wird in diesem den Text ‚Herz und Mund' abschließenden Absatz mit dem Stabreim bis ins Absurde geführt. Die englische Übersetzerin versucht, diesen Effekt mit dem Reim der Worte *thriller* und *killer* nachzuahmen. Im Französischen dagegen wird die ironische Brechung der Ängste durch dieses rhetorische Mittel unbeachtet gelassen. Doch dieses Tragikomische in ihren Texten wird, wie Anne Duden in einem Interview anmerkt, häufig ignoriert, ‚gerade weil Witz und Aberwitz ineinander übergehen'.[44] Dies ist auch in ‚Herz und Mund' der Fall. So steht das Ich im obigen Zitat Todesängste vor den Anderen aus, eben weil diese als Subjekte anders als das Ich ein Anliegen haben. Ihnen liegt also etwas am Herzen, das dem Ich ja fehlt. Damit wird für sie das alltägliche Leben einfacher, wie die Vorausdeutung des englischen ‚so inclined' und des französischen ‚celui qui en exprime le souhait', auf das sich anschließende ‚it's all so easy' bzw. ‚tout devient extrêmement simple' anzudeuten scheint. Das Anliegen macht diese Menschen nämlich zu zielstrebigen Subjekten, die sich im alltäglichen Dasein der gemeinen Sprache zu Hause fühlen, da diese ihren Erfahrungen entspricht und diese damit auch beschreiben kann. In dieser Sprache erfahren sie das Ich als Objekt, aber machen es damit auch zu diesem ‚mich', gehen also als Sieger und Mörder aus dem sprachlichen Kampf hervor. Diese Interpretation ist im Englischen in der Möglichkeit des Rückbezugs des ‚so inclined' auf die ‚killer' angelegt. Trotzdem wird auch in der Ambiguität der englischen Übersetzung das Anliegen nicht so offen gelassen wie im Deutschen. In beiden Fällen wird dieses Wort auf ein anderes Satzteil bezogen und damit in eine logische Struktur eingebunden. Gerade dies wird jedoch im Deutschen vermieden. Das Anliegen selbst erhält keine genauere Definition, es beinhaltet jegliches Ziel, das einem am Herzen liegt und damit einen Denkweg, eine logische Struktur vorgibt. Im Text ‚Herz und Mund' wird solch einer Struktur jedoch schon am Anfang die Basis entzogen, denn das Ich knüpft sein Herz an einem Baum auf und tötet damit jegliches Anliegen, das eine Struktur vorgeben könnte, in sich ab. Neben der herkömmlichen Vorstellung von Identität wird in ‚Herz und Mund' also auch dem Logozentrismus der Sprache begegnet, der sich in der englischen und der französischen Übersetzung jedoch am Endes dieses Textes wieder einschleicht.

Grenzen der Übersetzung?

Anne Dudens Aufspüren der sprachlichen Gewalt am Körper des Objekts, des Anderen dieser herrschenden Sprache in der Konkretisierung sprachlicher Metaphern wie Entmündigung und der Offenlegung der Subjekt-Objekt-Spaltung in den grammatikalischen Strukturen des Deutschen findet in keiner der beiden Übersetzungen wirklich eine Entsprechung. Ganz im Gegenteil, diese bleiben weitestgehend genau jenen Grenzen der

Sprache verhaftet, die Duden in ihren Texten zu überschreiten versucht. Im Französischen werden *Übergang* schon über die Illustration sowie über den Klappentext und die Titelgebung herkömmliche Elemente autobiographischer Literatur eingeschrieben, denen sich der Text widersetzt. Die seltenen Fälle in denen sich ein innovativer Umgang mit den Möglichkeiten der französischen Sprache anzudeuten scheint, so mit der Markierung des weiblichen Geschlechts, können weniger als Strategie denn als Zufall betrachtet werden. Im Englischen dagegen deuten zwar die Veröffentlichungsstrategien einen innovativeren Umgang mit der Übersetzung von *Übergang* an, doch das Fremde in ‚Herz und Mund' bleibt auch in dieser Übersetzung aufgrund der Orientierung an den zielsprachlichen Normen verborgen. Das heißt jedoch nicht, dass Dudens Texte aufgrund ihrer starken Verankerung im Deutschen unübersetzbar sind. Vielmehr zeigen sie die Grenzen der gängigen, an den zielsprachlichen Normen orientierten Übersetzungspraxis auf, denn sie erfordern, wie schon in der Einleitung erläutert, ‚ein Überschreiten und Verwandeln der Grenzen der übersetzenden Sprache',[45] und damit eine Spaltung der Zielsprache in sich selbst:

> Diese Grenze der Übersetzung verläuft nicht zwischen den Sprachen; sie teilt die Übersetzung und die Übersetzbarkeit an sich selbst, im Innern ein und derselben Sprache. (…) Die Babelisierung wartet also nicht auf die Vielheit der Sprachen. Die Identität der Sprache kann sich nur als Identität bejahen, indem sie sich der Gastfreundschaft einer Differenz sich selbst gegenüber oder einer Differenz des Mit-sich-seins öffnet.[46]

Auch die Vorstellung von einer Identität der Sprache muss also von einem fixen Identitätskonzept, auf der die gängige Übersetzungspraxis beruht, gelöst werden und mit dem Prozesscharakter der Identität, der Differenz in sich selbst angereichert werden, um Anne Dudens aufnehmen zu können. Statt einer Bestätigung und Konservierung eines bestimmten Sprachstandes, bedürfen diese Texte also dessen Differenzierung. Doch damit nicht genug, auch die zeitlich und kulturell determinierte Vorstellung von Treue in der Übersetzung, die sich in der Übersetzungspraxis zwischen den extrem limitierenden Polen der wörtlichen versus der sinngemäßen Übersetzung bewegt,[47] bedarf für die Übersetzung von Dudens Texten einer neuen Auslegung. Da die von ihr ans Licht gezerrten Schattenseiten der Sprache, so das Bild der Entmündigung, nicht universell sind, müssen diese in jeder Einzelsprache neu aufgespürt und anschließend auf den Körper des von dieser Sprache ausgeschlossenen Objekts übertragen werden. Die Texte müssen also die gewalttätigen Wurzeln der Zielsprache aufdecken, was im gängigen Verständnis einer Neuschreibung gleichkommt, andererseits jedoch die einzige Art der Übersetzung ist, die solchen Texten gerecht werden kann.

Anmerkungen

Ich möchte mich bei Anne Duden für ihre ausführlichen Informationen zur Entstehung der beiden Übersetzungen bedanken. Georgina Paul und Ulrike Pütter bin ich für ihre kritischen Anmerkungen zu einer früheren Version dieses Artikels zu Dank verpflichtet.

[1] Suzanne Greuner, *Schmerzton. Musik in der Schreibweise von Ingeborg Bachmann und Anne Duden*, Argument Verlag: Hamburg, Berlin, 1990, S. 5.

[2] Anne Duden, Claudia Kramatschek, ‚In den Faltungen der Sprache', *Neue deutsche Literatur* 48 (2/2000), 32-44 (hier: S. 33).

[3] Jacques Derrida, ‚Babylonische Türme: Wege, Umwege, Abwege', übersetzt von Alexander García Düttmann, in: Alfred Hirsch, Hg., *Übersetzung und Dekonstruktion*, Suhrkamp: Frankfurt a.M., 1997, 119-165 (hier: S. 145).

[4] Eine ausführliche Auseinandersetzung mit den Wurzeln der gängigen Übersetzungspraxis im anglo-amerikanischen Sprachraum findet sich in Lawrence Venuti, *The Translator's Invisibility. A History of Translation*, Routledge: London, New York, 1995. Zur Übersetzungspraxis in Frankreich vgl. u.a. Antoine Berman, *L'épreuve de l'étranger. Culture et traduction dans l'Allemagne romantique*, Gallimard: Paris, 1984, S. 11-17 und die Aussagen des Lektors und Übersetzers Bernard Lortholary im Gespräch mit Marion Graf, Gilbert Musy und Peter Utz, ‚Editer la littérature allemande en France', in: Marion Graf, Hg., *L'écrivain et son traducteur en Suisse et en Europe*, Éditions Zoé: Genf, 1998, 204-209 (hier: S. 209).

[5] Zu den Problemen der Literaturwissenschaft mit Anne Dudens Texten vgl. Franziska Frei Gerlach, *Schrift und Geschlecht. Feministische Entwürfe und Lektüren von Marlen Haushofer, Ingeborg Bachmann und Anne Duden*, Erich Schmidt: Berlin, 1998, S. 17 und 314 (Geschlechterdifferenz & Literatur, Bd. 8). Als problematisch erweisen sich zum Beispiel schon literaturwissenschaftliche Begrifflichkeiten wie ‚Erzählung' oder auch ‚Protagonistin', denn Dudens Texte haben weder im herkömmlichen Sinne eine Handlungsstruktur noch eine agierende Heldin. Deswegen wird ‚Erzählung' in diesem Text ausschließlich für die Titelgeschichte verwendet, der dieser Begriff noch am ehesten gerecht wird, und ‚Protagonistin' ganz vermieden.

[6] Vgl. zum Begriff der Fremdheit, der dieser Auseinandersetzung zu Grunde liegt: Bernhard Waldenfels, *Topographie des Fremden: Studien zur Phänomenologie des*

Fremden I, Suhrkamp: Frankfurt a.M., 1999. In den vier Bänden seiner Studien zur Phänomenologie des Fremden liest Waldenfels Edmund Husserl im Licht seiner französischen Interpreten wie Jacques Derrida, Michel Foucault, Maurice Merleau-Ponty und Emmanuel Levinas.

[7] Maurice Merleau-Ponty, *Keime der Vernunft*, übersetzt von A. Kapust, Fink: München, 1994, S. 281.

[8] Vgl. meinen Artikel zu den unterschiedlichen Voraussetzungen der Veröffentlichung von Übersetzungen in Großbritannien und Frankreich in den achtziger und neunziger Jahren des vorigen Jahrhunderts: ‚German Identities in Transition? The Translation of Contemporary German Fiction in Britain and France', in: Arthur Williams, Stuart Parkes, Julian Preece, Hgg., *German-Language Literature Today: International and Popular?* Peter Lang: Oxford, Bern, Berlin, Bruxelles, Frankfurt a.M., New York, Wien, 2000, 31-48 (hier: S. 31).

[9] Vgl. Barry Turner, Hg., *The Writer's Handbook 1999*, Macmillan: London, 1998, S. 71 und http://www.plutobooks.com/.

[10] Vgl. Pascal Fouché, Hg., *L'édition française depuis 1945*. Electre, Éditions du Cercle de la Librairie: Paris, 1998, S. 845.

[11] Vgl. Elizabeth Fallaize, ‚Introduction: women's writing and the French cultural context in the 1970s and 1980s', in: *French Women's Writing. Recent Fiction*, Macmillan Press: Houndmills, London, 1993, 1-29 (hier: S. 23).

[12] Anne Duden, *Traversée*, übers. von Pierre Furlan und Dominique Jallamion, Alinéa: Aix-en-Provence, 1987.

[13] Das lebhafte Erzählen ist mit der Wiederbelebung des Vergessenen im Wort ‚retracer' vereint. Diese Definition stammt wie auch alle folgenden zu französischen Begriffen aus: *Le Petit Robert*. Le Robert: Paris, 1989.

[14] Georgina Paul, „‚Life-writing": Reading the Work of Anne Duden Through Virginia Woolf's „A Sketch of the Past"', in: Mererith Puw Davies, Beth Linklater, Hgg., *Autobiography by Women in German*, Peter Lang: Oxford, Bern, Berlin, Bruxelles, Frankfurt a.M., New York, Wien, 2000, 291-305.

[15] Die Definitionen deutscher Wörter entstammen dem *Duden. Deutsches Universalwörterbuch,* Dudenverlag: Mannheim, Wien, Zürich, 1996. Zum Begriff ‚Übergang' vgl. außerdem: Elsbeth Dangel, ‚Übergang und Ankunft. Positionen neuerer Frauenliteratur', *Jahrbuch für internationale Germanistik*, 22,2 (1990) 80-94 (hier: S. 81-82).

[16] Besonders deutlich wird die Freude über die Rückkehr aus dem Zwischenzustand in das alltägliche Leben, das in der stereotypen Beschreibung zudem karikiert wird, am

Ende von ‚Chemische Reaktion': ‚Ich begann mich auf einen Nachmittagskaffee zu freuen. Kuchen würde ich mir besorgen, und für den Abend hatte ich eine Verabredung mit einer Kinokarte' (Ü 58).

[17] Paul, „‚Life-writing'", S. 301-2.

[18] Sigrid Weigel, *Die Stimme der Medusa. Schreibweisen in der Gegenwartsliteratur von Frauen*, tende: Dülmen-Hiddingsel, 1987, S. 125 und Leslie Adelson, ‚Anne Duden's *Übergang*. Racism and Feminist Aesthetics. A Provocation', in: *Making Bodies, Making History. Feminism and German Identity*, University of Nebraska Press: Lincoln, London, 1993, 37-55 (hier: S. 46).

[19] Anne Duden, *Opening of the Mouth,* übers. von Della Couling, Pluto Press: London, Leichhardt, 1985.

[20] Das Bild ‚Christus als Schmerzensmann' wird dem unbekannten Meister des Bartholomäus-Altares zugeschrieben. Eine vollständige Abbildung nebst Erläuterungen findet sich in: Rainer Budde, Roland Krischel, Hgg., *Genie ohne Namen*, Dumont: Köln, 2001, S. 382-3.

[21] Vgl. Anne Duden, *Steinschlag*, Kiepenheuer & Witsch: Köln, 1993.

[22] Vgl. dazu den voraussichtlich im Jahr 2002 erscheinenden Aufsatz von Andrea Geier, 'Unterminierte Apokalypse. *Michel, sag ich* von Ulla Berkéwicz und *Übergang* von Anne Duden', in: Verena Lobsien, Maria Moog-Grünewald, *Apokalypse. Der Anfang im Ende,* Heidelberg.

[23] Vgl. Exodus 7. Das Buch Exodus wird mit dem Zitat ‚Zahn um Zahn' auch in ‚Herz und Mund' aufgerufen.

[24] Vgl. Matthias Arnold, *Vincent van Gogh. Werk und Wirkung*, Kindler: München, 1995, S. 299.

[25] Vgl. Johannes van der Volk, Ronald Pickvance, E.B.F. Pey, Hgg., *Vincent van Gogh's Drawings*, Rijksmuseum Kröller-Müller: Otterlo, Arnoldo Mandodori Arte: Milan, De Luna Edizioni D'Arte: Rome, 1990, S. 289.

[26] Duden, *Traversée*, S. 49.

[27] Vgl. dazu auch Hubert Winkels' Interpretationsansatz mit Bezug auf Derridas *Grammatologie*: ‚[Die] Funktion der Stimme, des gesprochenen Wortes, „ein Trugbild [zu liefern], das uns tiefer berührt als die Wahrheit" ist es, der sich die Frau verschließen will, deretwegen der Mund zerstört, geschient, vernäht werden muß. Die Erzählung ‚Herz und Mund' führt vor, wie das Selbstverständnis und mit ihm die subjektkonstituierende sinnvolle Rede erlischt. An ihre Stelle tritt so etwas wie die

Schrift des Körpers, eine Grammatik der Symptome'. H. Winkel, *Einschnitte. Zur Literatur der 80er Jahre,* Kiepenheuer & Witsch: Köln, 1988, S. 46.

[28] Der biblische Intertext zum Titel von ‚Herz und Mund' findet sich in Matthäus 12, 34. In der Übersetzung Luthers lautet diese Stelle: ‚Wes das Herz voll ist, des geht der Mund über'.

[29] Auf diesen Intertext verweist Uwe Schweikert im ‚Nachwort' zu *Übergang* (Ü 132-138, hier: Ü 133).

[30] Spuren dieses Ausschlusses von Andersdenkenden finden sich auch in *Zungengewahrsam*: ‚Die so schreibt – dieses Ich – wäre im Mittelalter noch... man kennt den Spruch, [...]' (Z 13); ‚*Highly disturbed* würde man eine solche *lady in waiting* in England nennen, wo eine Statistik gerade ergeben hat, daß 87% aller Dichter zumindest einmal in ihrem Leben irgendeine Art von Geisteskrankheit gehabt haben, verglichen mit nur 35% aller Politiker' (S. 15, Kursivierung im Original). Die Beschreibung als *lady in waiting* bezieht sich sowohl auf das gespannte Erwarten der Übergänge als auch auf die Tatsache, dass sich das Ich diesen gnadenlos unterwirft.

[31] 2. Korinther 12, 7.

[32] Duden, *Opening*, S. 41, *Traversée*, S. 51.

[33] Vgl. Henri Meschonnic, *Poétique du traduire*, Verdier: Lagrasse, 1999, S. 33-34.

[34] Vgl. Karl Hermann Schelkle, *Der zweite Brief an die Korinther*, Patmos-Verlag: Düsseldorf, 1964, S. 13.

[35] Vgl. 2. Korinther 11, 24-25.

[36] Vgl. Schelkle, *Der zweite Brief an die Korinther*, S. 206.

[37] 2. Korinther 12, 17.

[38] Vgl. Frei Gerlach, *Schrift und Geschlecht*, S. 316-344.

[39] Duden, *Opening*, S. 43, *Traversée*, S. 53. Die Kursivierungen in diesem sowie in den weiteren Übersetzungsvergleichen wurden von mir zur Hervorhebung der im folgenden besprochenen Probleme vorgenommen.

[40] Auf die mangelnde Polysemie in der englischen Übersetzung des Begriffes Entmündigung weist schon Leslie Adelson hin: 'Anne Duden's Übergang', S. 143.

[41] Genau diese Geschlechtslosigkeit bzw. die Unmöglichkeit der geschlechtlichen Kategorisierung ist, wie schon angedeutet, in verschiedenen Texten Dudens Merkmal des ausgeschlossenen Anderen. Vgl. Duden, ‚Gegenstrebige Fügung' (A 77-84, hier: A 80).

[42] Duden, *Opening*, S. 42, *Traversée*, S. 52.

[43] Duden, *Opening*, S. 45, *Traversée*, S. 55.

[44] Duden, Kramatschek, ‚In den Faltungen der Sprache,' S. 33.

[45] Siehe Anmerkung 5.

[46] Jacques Derrida, *Aporien: Sterben – Auf die 'Grenzen der Wahrheit' gefaßt sein*, übers. von Michael Wetzel, Wilhelm Fink: München, 1998, S. 26. In diesem Text dekonstruiert Derrida Heideggers Aussage ‚Der Tod ist die Möglichkeit der schlechthinnigen Daseinsunmöglichkeit' (*Sein und Zeit*, § 50), zu der sich Dudens Projekt der Darstellung ‚einer unmöglichen Daseinsmöglichkeit' sicherlich in Beziehung setzen ließe.

[47] Vgl. Douglas Robinson, *Translation and Empire. Postcolonial Translation Theories Explained*, St. Jerome: Manchester, 1997, S. 50.

Georgina Paul

An Easter of words
Steps towards a reading of Anne Duden's *Steinschlag*

Published in 1993 to reviews that almost unanimously hailed it as a great work, Anne Duden's poem-cycle *Steinschlag* has subsequently never been the subject of a systematic scholarly reading. This essay seeks to end the critical silence by providing an approach to Duden's poem that can open up a path for later readings. It is conceived as a sequence of steps, starting with the 'obscurity' of the poem's meanings and moving on through aspects such as musical composition and the poem's construction of space to the final proposition of the poem's relation to its cultural context.

> STEINSCHLAG hinter den Käfern.
> Da sah ich einen, der log nicht,
> heimstehn in seine Verzweiflung.
>
> Wie deinem Einsamkeitssturm
> glückt ihm die weit
> ausschreitende Stille.[1]

1. Critical silence

To write about Anne Duden's *Steinschlag* is not easy. This is already signalled by the paucity of critical commentary to have appeared in the nine years since its publication on what is undoubtedly a major and significant poem by an author whose work is held in high esteem by the most serious of scholars of contemporary German literature.[2] The reviewers who first responded in 1993 to the cycle's publication were almost unanimous in hailing it as great art.[3] With such a basis, one might have expected a fuller, more reflective response to follow, but since then no systematic readings of the poem have been attempted until the three essays in this volume. There is, it seems, something about *Steinschlag* that evades the critic or that defends itself against critical approach.

It would be simple – too simple – to identify the problem as lying in the poem's 'difficulty', the obscurity of its meanings.[4] Admittedly, the poem has no truck with the accustomed day-to-day order of things, nor its language with the quotidian 'gemeiner Satz' (V 41): to enter this text is to step across a threshold into another room, an other room. 'Schreiben wird Enthauptung der gewalttätigen Ordnungen und Hierarchien des Tages, Entfesselung, Lösung der Bindungen', as Duden writes in the third of her poetics lectures entitled 'Zungengewahrsam', which provide the most extensive, if oblique, commentary to date on the poem and its genesis. (Z 51)[5] In this sense, *Steinschlag* may be understood, in Celan's phrase, as a 'Gegenwort'.[6] But as the mention of Celan already reminds us, Duden's late-twentieth-century poem has at its back – or rather, to the extent that it, like Benjamin's *Engel*, is turned towards the ruinous past, it reflects in its face – a well-established tradition of poetry that is not simple, not transparent in its meanings, that requires, demands even, extreme attentiveness on the part of the reader (that 'Aufmerksamkeit', perhaps, that is the natural prayer of the soul).[7] Not Celan only, but the French symbolists and surrealists on whom he drew when finding his way with words,[8] Rilke also, and Hölderlin, and, on the English side (for Duden is a writer who moves between cultures), T. S. Eliot:[9] the language of all of these poets has seemed 'difficult' in the way that it is intent on a sphere *apart* from the quotidian. But all have found critics and readers prepared to enter into the encounter that the poem requires if the stone is to blossom.

'Difficulty' alone, then, cannot explain the neglect. Sex, I suspect, plays its role, sex and politics. It is notable that Duden's work has hitherto attracted the attention above all of feminist scholars in contexts that lay stress on the sex of the author. *Steinschlag*, as a breakthrough text that takes leave of the narrative personae of Duden's earlier prose work in order to move into the Orphic realm of the singing voice, takes leave also of the female body that is the privileged site of feminist politics.[10] To follow the writer into the Orphic realm means, among other things, to follow her into the male poetic tradition from which the poem gathers resonances, a path which feminist critics are oddly unwilling to take: Franziska Frei Gerlach's fine work on Duden, for example, pursues the links with Bachmann and Haushofer, but blocks out male influences, since her feminist argument requires the woman writer to be in reaction against, rather than honouring, the male tradition.[11] The critical silence around *Steinschlag* is in part a witness to the limitations of feminist criticism in this respect, and the poem itself a reminder of the degree to which all of Duden's work has been in excess of the feminist project within which it has generally been located hitherto.

As Duden indicates in the 'Zungengewahrsam' lectures, *Steinschlag* is the product of a long and agonising struggle towards a new form, a struggle which left a gap of eight years between publications (*Das Judasschaf* appeared in 1985, *Steinschlag* in 1993), and perhaps the most compelling reason for the lack of commentary on the poem to date is that *time* is similarly needed for the silent gestation of an adequate critical response which a work of this complexity asks for.[12] My purpose with this essay is to make a start, to begin to open up a space for a reading of Duden's poem. The essay is conceived as a sequence of steps into the poem's 'otherness', beginning with what first meets the reader as s/he steps across its threshold.

2. Obscurity

> Der Tonfall ein Dauerregen
> gleichmäßig geschnürt Litaneien des Verhangenen
> in denen die Bilder ertrinken
> aus einem Deutschland
> das nie existiert hat.
> Unter vorgezogenem Dach und niedriger Decke
> Antizyklone
> lichtscheu und kalkig bestäubt
> auf engstem Raum beieinander
> während wenige Meter weiter
> grellweiß vor geschuppten Stämmen
> eine steilaufgerichtete Helle steht
> in der nur die hohen und beweglichen Töne
> angeschlagen werden.
> Witterungsunabhängig. (S 7)

It is instructive to find almost all critics of, say, the work of Paul Celan or of T. S. Eliot beginning their elaborations with the aspect of the poems' 'obscurity' or 'Dunkelheit'. The greater the critic, the more he or she is likely to dismiss the difficulty of understanding in order to move the focus onto some other aspect. 'Mit den ersten Worten des Gedichts [...] beginnt die Schwierigkeit des Verständnisses, zugleich aber auch die Möglichkeit, zu erkennen, daß die traditionellen Mittel der Lektüre versagen': this perception of the *opportunity* for the transformation of established reading habits is Peter Szondi's spontaneous response to the challenge of Celan's 'Engführung'.[13] Helen Gardner, meanwhile, lecturing on Eliot's *Four Quartets* in Oxford in 1948, six years after the completion of 'Little Gidding' and thus of the cycle, reminds us of the extent to which Eliot's contemporary readers were also baffled, sometimes irritated by his 'obscurity'.[14] Gardner, that poet's reader, teaches an attitude of contemplation that is not troubled by not at first grasping meaning:

> It is better in reading poetry of this kind to trouble too little about the 'meaning' than to trouble too much. If there are passages whose meaning

seems elusive, where we feel we are 'missing the point', we should read on, preferably aloud; for the music and the meaning arise at a 'point of intersection', in the changes and movement of the whole. [...] Reading in this way we may miss detailed significances, but the whole rhythm of the poems will not be lost, and gradually the parts will become easier for us to understand.[15]

Gardner (reading Eliot) redirects us (reading Duden) from a concern with meaning to a concern with music and with composition. The rigid fixation on semantics, that is the fixation of reason, is dismissed; the space in which significances are at first dark can be experienced rather as a musical space, a shaped, contained atmosphere moved by rhythms, intonations, sound patterns. Indeed, the immediate derailment of grasping reason upon entry into the text signals that this has been a crossing-over into a realm entirely other. '"Reason's click-clack" was replaced by the pure joy of "accurate song",' as the contemporary American poet Kathleen Fraser (quoting Wallace Stevens) writes, recollecting her formative encounter as a child with the language of verse.[16]

3. Movement / musicality

Der Tonfall ein Dauerregen
gleichmäßig geschnürt Litaneien des Verhangenen [...] (S 7)

The first image of the opening poem of the *Steinschlag* cycle draws attention to cadence (*Tonfall*), and what is promised appears to be monotony, regularity, the repetitive structure of the litany. The rhythm has no regular metrical stress-pattern, however; rather, the modulations of speech are reproduced, although prominent alliteration and a perceptible rhythmic beat remove this speaking from the sphere of everyday language, imbuing the whole with an air of solemnity. Scanning the free verse reveals a degree of symmetry in the structuring of the syllables:

```
v   -  v v    - v - v
Der Tonfall ein Dauerregen
   -    v v v   -   v v - v v v   - v v
gleichmäßig geschnürt Litaneien des Verhangenen
v -  v v  - v v  -  v
in denen die Bilder ertrinken
v   v v    -      v
aus einem Deutschland
v  -  v v -   v
das nie existiert hat.
v v  - v - v v   -    v  - v v - v
Unter vorgezogenem Dach und niedriger Decke
```

Steps towards a reading of Steinschlag

```
 - v v - v
Antizyklone
 -    v  v - v v  -
lichtscheu und kalkig bestäubt
 v  - v  -    v v - v
auf engstem Raum beieinander
 v  v  - v v - v  - v
während wenige Meter weiter
 -  -  v  v  - v   - v
grellweiß vor geschuppten Stämmen
v v  -  v  v - v v  - v  -
eine steilaufgerichtete Helle steht
v v  -  v - v  v v - v  v - v
in der nur die hohen und beweglichen Töne
 - v  - v  - v
angeschlagen werden.
 - v v - v - v
Witterungsunabhängig.


v – v v – v – v
– v v v – v v – v v v – v v
v – v v – v v – v
v v v – v
v – v v – v
v v – v – v v – v – v v – v
– v v – v
– v v – v v –
v – v – v v – v
v v – v v – v – v
– – v v – v – v
v v – v v – v v – v –
v v – v – v v v – v v – v
– v – v – v
– v v – v – v
```

Predominant in this opening block of 15 lines is the use of the 3- or 4-stressed line (with the shorter ll.4 and 5 splitting the 3-stressed rhythm across two lines). Only l.6 runs to 5 stresses, lending emphasis to the short (and contrastive) single-word line 'Antizyklone' that follows. In the second block of 20 lines (beginning 'Kein Weg geht am Arbeitslager vorbei'), the lines lengthen initially (in those lines concerned with the 'Arbeitslager') before returning to the established rhythm of 3- and 4-stressed lines. These lines are after all, then, in principle 'gleichmäßig geschnürt', with the occasional long line slowing the rhythm, drawing it out (oppressively), and the shorter lines contrastive, emphatic, other.

The composition is held together most obviously by a network of alliterations: prominent in the opening is the 'g' of 'gleichmäßig geschnürt' which passes on to 'grellweiß vor geschuppten' and to 'gewaltsam geweckt' in the second block of lines. The 'w' in 'grellweiß' and 'gewaltsam geweckt' picks up another prominent alliteration in the opening block: 'während wenige Meter weiter', 'Witterungsunabhängig', passing on to 'Weg' and 'Worte' in the second block. The 'geschuppten' shifts meanwhile into a sequence of 'st' sounds: 'Stämmen', 'steilaufgerichtete', 'steht', linking to 'steinernen' in the second block (as well as the title 'Steinschlag'), also 'Strumpfhosenproduktion', 'stecken [...] in den Verstorbenen', 'Einzelstücken'. Striking in amongst the multiple occurrences of the dominant 'ei' diphthong – 'gleichmäßig', 'Litaneien', 'beieinander', 'weiter', 'grellweiß', 'steilaufgerichtete' – and the long 'e' – 'denen', 'wenige Meter', 'steht', 'beweglich', and, in the second block, 'Weg', 'Karree' – is the aspirated short 'e' of 'Helle', which, though echoing the 'grell-' of 'grellweiß' which describes it, is a suddenly different word amongst the 'Litaneien des Verhangenen' of the opening. The aspiration becomes prominent in the third block of lines with its distinctively different music: 'Haarrisse', 'höchstens', and from 'hellhöriges' and 'heimlich' it starts to associate particularly with 'l':

> [...] hellhöriges aber heimlich bleibendes
> Aufschluchzen
> einiger Kilometer Landschaft
> entlang der Autobahn
> der Autobahn selbst
> wo die Landschaft flimmernd vor Hitze
> sich bis auf sie gelegt hat. (S 8)

(Note also the chiasmus 'Landschaft ... Autobahn ... Autobahn ... Landschaft'.) The 'l' initiates the emphatic rhythm of the line 'Licht Luft Farbe und Form' before the alliterative 'h' returns to close the block: 'herausgehalten haben'. The short 'e', meanwhile, takes on prominence in the fourth block of lines in the key word 'Ekstase', returning in 'Das Ekstatische ein Extrakt' (S 9).

I have begun to take note of blocks of lines (I hesitate to call them stanzas), and further note the differential spacings between these blocks. Thus the first two blocks are separated from each other by a single *Leerzeile*, but the second from the third by three *Leerzeilen*. That the first two blocks belong together is suggested already by the observations of a similar musicality, while the second two blocks are marked by a different set of sounds, as it were a different instrumentation. Within the larger structure of the poem, then, there are phases like thematic blocks in a *musical* composition. If we take the musical analogy further, we might suppose that the lines unpunctuated except by stops are, like Peter Weiss's in his 'Oratorium' *Die Ermittlung*, a form of *Partitur*, or musical score, for speech.[17] The line breaks are breaks in rhythm, and differing measures of distance between blocks of lines indicate lesser or greater pauses between blocks. And if we look for a moment over the whole composition of 'Steinschlag I', the following pattern emerges (the numbers indicate the number of lines in each block; the two vertical bars the breaks created by the triple *Leerzeile*):

15 20 || 18 23 || 16 15 || 22 9 || 18 14 7 || 18 || 12 14

'Steinschlag II' is much shorter, and its pattern looks like this:

17 8 14

The recurrent pattern of 18-line blocks suggests a further compositional principle which will need attention later, as does the fact that both I and II finish with a 14-line block. But in this general structural overview, the entire poem emerges as a pattern of successive spaces. And given our observations vis-à-vis the opening sequence on the passing of sound from one block to the next on the one hand, and a significant alteration of sound from one block to the next on the other, the expectation is raised that the poem will prove to be a sequence of *Klangräume*, with motifs shifting and changing as they pass through the whole structure.

4. Topographies

The musical construction of space, and music as inspiration for a similar form of construction of poetic space, are themes considered in the second and third of the 'Zungengewahrsam' lectures. In this context, Duden inserts a passage from 'Das Landhaus' in *Übergang* where the narrator describes the effect of listening to '[die] vierzigstimmige[..] Motette eines Komponisten aus dem 16. Jahrhundert' (identified in the lectures as Thomas Tallis's 'Spem in alium') in the following way:

> Erst öffnete sie einem eine Kammer, dann einen Raum, der zu einem weiteren größeren Raum führte, und so immer weiter, bis man halb träumend, halb wach wahrnahm, daß man mittlerweile durch alle Räume und Mauern und Dächer hindurchgeschleust war und fortgetragen von einer einzigen großen

> einsammelnden und aufhebenden Bewegung, einer Luftwoge, die einen schließlich mitnahm ins Offene und einen dort ruhig und gleichmäßig beatmete.(Z 52 and Ü 23)

This description of the musical composition and its effect corresponds to the compositional structure of the opening poem in the *Steinschlag* cycle as already identified: the poem as a pattern of successive spaces. The blocks of lines, as the component parts of the sequence, are not, however, sound chambers alone. Returning to the semantic level, we may find that our eyes are in the meantime beginning to adjust to the obscurity, and we can see that the poem is also constructing a sequence of topographical figures, is perceptually defining its spaces. In the first five lines of the poem, this is not prominent: here, only the word 'Deutschland' summons up a national, politico-historical, and – since the language of the poem is German – linguistic space. That it is a 'Deutschland, das nie existiert hat' (S 7) could be read as an acknowledgement that this Germany is a construction of the mind; and since (to look forward for a moment) the figure of Hölderlin will appear late in this opening poem of the cycle, the reading is possible that what is being summoned up is Hölderlin's longed-for Germany as a land of the gods, and that it is the images of this that have drowned in the 'Litaneien des Verhangenen'. The significance of the poem's construction of *poetic* space will be considered later.

The remainder of the first block of lines, however, posits an enclosed, constrained interior room – 'Unter vorgezogenem Dach und niedriger Decke [...] auf engstem Raum beieinander' – which, 'lichtscheu', is juxtaposed with an apparently exterior space (exterior because of its 'geschuppten Stämmen') characterised by a dramatically vertical light: 'während wenige Meter weiter / grellweiß vor geschuppten Stämmen / eine steilaufgerichtete Helle steht'. This latter is also a space marked by a particular sound: 'in der nur die hohen und beweglichen Töne / angeschlagen werden'. If these first fifteen lines are understood as the proposal of a theme, as in the opening bars of a musical composition, then it is not only cadence and tone that are given importance, but also the construction of contrasting topographies.

Over the fourteen compositional blocks that make up 'Steinschlag I', there emerge a series of juxtaposed scenes perceivable (at least in part) in *social* terms, inhabited as they are by different kinds of characters: the workers, the 'leisure class', the dead, the poet/Ich. In block 2 (S 7f.), the 'Arbeitslager', spatially defined by the 'steinernen Karree mit den schweren Eisentoren', is peopled by a workforce of those 'zusammen in die Auferstehung getrieben' who reappear in block 4 as the 'Lebenslänglichen' (S 9), i.e. are likened to prisoners. The poem's first reviewers recognised in the 'Arbeitslager' a reference to the camps of the Holocaust, but this immediate association accrues further layers through the reference to 'Strumphosenproduktion' and the 'braunkohlenfarbene[r] Engel', summoning memories of the (women's) prisons of the German Democratic Republic as much as of the Nazi period.[18] Or, since the landscape of the poem, as this gradually unfolds, is decisively contemporary, all the figures in this topography of the 'Arbeitslager' may be seen as tropes within the scenery of late industrial society, with its underclass of alienated shiftworkers. In this sense the compacting of associations – Holocaust, GDR, contemporary industrial society – serves to emphasise a relentless historical continuity.

Contrasted with the workers of block 2 are the 'Leichtfüßigen' or 'Vertreter der leisure class' introduced in absentia in block 5 ('Weit und breit kein Leichtfüßiger in Sicht / kein Vertreter der leisure class', S 9), becoming dominant, however, in blocks 7 and 8 (S 10-11). This class ('Schicht'[19]), satirised as 'hingegeben ahnungslos' ('sie [...] kriegen bloß ganz leichte Schläge ab / nur die die das Schicksal ohnehin austeilt / und ohne deren Zugabe der Lauf der Welt eintönig würde', S 11), is recognisable as a comfortably-off middle-class, essentially unacquainted with grief, a 'chattering class', whose 'sprudelnde[r] Wortschatz' is 'den Heimwiederaufbereitungsanlagen entnommen' (S 10-11). But the 'Leichtfüßigen', as dictators of cultural production, also have a more sinister role, namely the policing of (poetic) language and its associated profounder emotions: 'Laut Gesetz muß jede verbliebene Anschaulichkeit / abgegraben und ihnen ausgehändigt werden / zwecks Ausdünnung bis Beseitigung der Metaphern /daraufhin sich einfindender Leidenschaft / und unumwundener Befriedigung' (S 11). The laconic 'Ein Vollzugsprivileg' that comments upon this 'duty' links the 'Leichtfüßigen' to figures later in the cycle: notably to the 'streng verkniffenen Recken' (S 39) of the third poem, 'Nacht neben Nacht über Tag', St. George-style characters whose object of attack is the offensively multiplicit, thus dragon-like, and feminised poem (or poet).

In between the concerns of the 'Leichtfüßigen' in blocks 5, 7 and 8 is inserted, in block 6, a graveyard scene that sets a memorial to the dead: 'Seit zwei Jahren tote Cathy / dreiundzwanzigjährig' (S 10). '[V]om Vater in die Erde gejagt gesteckt festgetreten', the dead and violated Cathy initiates a theme that recurs later in the cycle of the 'feminine' (to be understood in its broadest cultural sense) as victim of an aggressive (male-connoted) power, here buried in a site inserted between the world of the 'Arbeitslager' and that of the 'Leichtfüßigen'.

In block 3, meanwhile, the first of the three 18-line blocks in this part of the poem, there is an initial significant interruption of the emerging pattern of contrasting social groups and topographies: '[e]ingezwängt in schmalste Zeitritzen' (S 8) is the sudden 'größte Weite', the 'Aufmerken', 'Aufschluchzen', '[e]igentlich nichts weiter als die Regung / ganz alltäglicher Mischungsverhältnisse / Licht Luft Farbe und Form' (S 8). This perceptual possibility, alliteratively connected, as I suggested earlier, to the 'steilaufgerichtete Helle' of block 1, is associated with landscape as opposed to cityscape: here a landscape seen from the motorway (recall the chiasmus: 'Landschaft ... Autobahn ... Autobahn ... Landschaft', S 8). This space of the other to both the 'Lebenslänglichen' and the 'Leichtfüßigen' is the space of the ecstatic, the necessarily brief space in which, for a flash, we are beside ourselves: 'Das Ekstatische ein Extrakt / eingeklemmt / erkaltet verhärtend in Spalten / Abgründen der Zeit' (S 9).

If the 'Leichtfüßigen' are (as already indicated) the policers of poetic language, the poetic 'Ich' who enters the poem at block 9, the second of the 18-line blocks, with the line 'Unterdessen atme ich Steine' is naturally cast in opposition to them. Gradually the poem removes her from the city sphere of the 'Leichtfüßigen' into a landscape marked by repeated thematic variations on the words of the poem's title 'Stein' and 'Schlag'. The names Durance and Aix (blocks 12 and 13, S 13-14) fix this landscape as an authentic one in the French Provence, but the description is also, simultaneously, a reprise of the experience of landscape first thematised in block 3 – 'Zwischen dem ausgemachten Ruin / holt mich der Atem schlagartig / legen die Landschaften sich frei im November' (block 12, the third of the 18-line blocks, S 13) – and a particular kind of linguistic construction, opposed to the superficial language associated with the 'Leichtfüßigen': 'Endlich Steinquadrate in Aix. / Tiefgelegener Ruhepunkt *unter den Jargonspitzen* / ungestörter Schlagplatz mitten im kalten Krieg der Wirkwaren' (block 13, p.13, emphasis: GP).[20] This first part of the poem 'Steinschlag' ends (literally comes to rest) in a figure of sleep, always a privileged state in Duden's work:[21] 'die unblutige Tagschlaf-Figur / mit abgewinkeltem Kopf' (S 14). The landscape, nature, situated initially as peripheral to the differing concerns of the everyday, but taking on increasing importance as the poem progresses, is thus posited as the site of release: of the self, of the body, of language itself.[22]

5. The space of poetry

The completion of the first part of the pattern that is the poem reveals the poem's aspiration to integrity, to the point at which it comes to rest: the final word of 'Steinschlag I' is (in a line on its own) 'stillstehen' (S 14). As in T. S. Eliot's 'Burnt Norton', in which 'the detail of the pattern is movement',[23] what is being realised here is the integrity, the final stillness of the poem itself:

> Words move, music moves
> Only in time; but that which is only living
> Can only die. Words, after speech, reach
> Into the silence. Only by the form, the pattern
> Can words or music reach
> The stillness, as a Chinese jar still
> Moves perpetually in its stillness.[24]

The poem provides form and pattern, and, once the composition is finished, has reached a state 'where every word is at home, / Taking its place to support the others / [...] / The complete consort dancing together',[25] it becomes the stillness where still the music reverberates, the meanings and 'die hohen und beweglichen Töne' oscillate (S 7):

> Das Gewölbe, auch das der Sprache, steht, weil alles Feste, alle Materie in einen Rhythmus versetzt worden, in eine sicht- und spürbare Bewegung geraten ist, wo auch der Stillstand noch erkennbar wird als Moment anhaltender Gezeitenreibung [...]. (Z 52)

'Natürlich ALLES ist Ekstase' (S 8): the entirety of the poem is, of course, ecstasy, is the place peripheral or apart; as soon as we enter its space we are ecstatic, beside ourselves, taking a part apart, ourselves made poetic by the poetry. Yet simultaneously, the poem enacts its own positioning in the social topographies it creates and presents to us: it is surely *poetry*, as an excessive and ultimately transgressive form of language, that is 'Eingezwängt in schmalste Zeitritzen', that is the 'Extrakt / eingeklemmt / erkaltet verhärtend in Spalten / Abgründen der Zeit'. That is: it is poetry in a particular tradition. For the poem constantly summons up forebears, summons into renewed life the words of the honoured dead. The prominence of the *Stein* motif is witness to the presence of Celan: some of his formulations are taken up, as with the poem I quoted at the outset as an epigraph,[26] or the 'Steinatem' of a poem from the *Atemwende* collection – 'DAS AUFWÄRTSSTEHENDE LAND, / rissig, / mit der Flugwurzel, der / Steinatem zuwächst'[27] – which reappears in the modulations 'Unterdessen atme ich Steine' (S 11) and 'Steinatem jetzt aus dem Bett der Durance' (S 13). The 'Lebenslänglichen' of block 4, oppressed by 'Raub- und Greifengel[..]', are barred from the space of the ecstatic, but in any case: 'Wer den Ausbruch schaffte / verging an Erschöpfung' – the theme is a reprise of Rilke's in the opening of the 'Duino Elegies': 'Wer, wenn ich schriee, hörte mich denn aus der Engel / Ordnungen? und gesetzt selbst, es nähme / einer mich plötzlich ans Herz: ich verginge von seinem / stärkeren Dasein'.[28] Eliot's concern with the task of the poet 'under conditions / That seem unpropitious'[29] in *Four Quartets* seems to have a bearing on the social world projected in 'Steinschlag I', which is one inimical to poetry. And in 'Steinschlag II', a kind of crisis moment of poetic language – 'heisere Wortspäne zerbröselnde Silben Buchstaben / und die angeschabte Stille / wenn die Notwendigkeiten nicht mehr verfangen' (S 15) – is countered by the explicit summoning up by name of one of the great forebears:

> Hölderlin als Siebzigjähriger
> AUF DEN GASSEN DER GÄRTEN
> starren Auges vornübergebeugt
> immer geradeaus der einwärts geschlagenen Blickrichtung nach
> ohne Weg- und Wendemarke
> eine Schlacke mit geladenem Gedächtnis
> AN ZIMMERN.
> Aufmüpfig der Körperrest
> nachts randalierende Zeitruine
> damit einmal im Gedicht
> im letzten Vers ABER
> DIE LIEBE LIEBT
> allein in der tagsüber geheizten Einöde
> wo die Festen am Hinterkopf nur durch Genickschuß zu sprengen wären.
> (S 15)[30]

Even at the moment of the individual's (the individual poet's) most severe linguistic crisis, or of the surrounding culture's most advanced disregard for – what is it? – the *spiritual* quality that comes to us distilled in the great poems or the great works of art of the past, *this* poem holds fast to the belief in the indestructibility of the cryptic memory that will still go on producing fragments of poem, however fragile the human frame that supports it: 'cryptic' here both in the sense summoned up by Duden's neologism 'Kryptästhesie',[31] referring to a perceptual memory (awareness, knowledge) preserved in the body of the poet and in the dead corpus of words and images that must await their 'Auferstehung in den Text' (Z 32), as also in the sense of the evasiveness of those perceptions, those (poetic) words, those images, once they are thus resurrected, before the would-be penetrating light of quotidian reason.

6. Making a map

So far, this commentary on Duden's poem has focused primarily on the two parts of the first text in the cycle. The opening block of fifteen lines in 'Steinschlag I' was examined as offering a key to the formal aspects of musical composition and spatial relations as these give shape to the poem. This in turn allowed a perception of the body of the poem 'Steinschlag' as a sequence of *Klangräume* that are also thematically defined as contrasting social spheres, in the narrow and overlooked crevices between which are to be found the remembrance of the violated dead and the space of poetry itself. Just as the first block of lines can be taken as a key, as it were a statement of a theme in the opening bars of a musical composition, so the entirety of the first poem in the cycle may be taken as the key to the remainder of the work, where the five subsequent texts represent a passage through an ever more abstract elaboration of themes and motifs from the opening, until the final line releases the completed cycle into the silence 'WO DIE AUGEN ZUGEDECKT', a further citation of the great poetic forebear Hölderlin that ties the end of the cycle to its beginning.[32]

A commentary that looked to do justice to the intricacies of the poem's entire construction might take as its starting-point a map or diagram that marked in the sequences of thematic elaboration from one text to the next, as these add layer upon layer of meaning to the multiplicity already observed, for example in the comments above on the different layers of historical association summoned up by the images of 'Arbeitslager' in block 2 of 'Steinschlag I'. Such a map of the schemata of the poem would also take into account the recurrence of leitmotifs, both in the imagery and in the repetition or near-repetition of words and sounds, all of which conspire to weave the poem into a densely interlaced tracework – or a figure like the tree of Jesse (*Jessebaum*) of which Duden writes in the 'Zungengewahrsam' lectures (Z 40-41).

To engage with the detail of such an imagined map or graphic genealogy goes beyond the compass of what can be achieved in this essay, however, so a briefer survey of the text-scape of the remainder of the poem must, for now, suffice.

The second text in the cycle, 'I Am Your Only Surviving Memory' can be read as a further exploration and elaboration of the contiguity of the social world of human beings and the natural world, a theme already identified in the opening text in the cycle. Here, though, the understanding of 'natural world' is expanded to include the animal nature of human beings themselves, which the construction of the social world, that is, the world of human 'civilisation', aims to suppress or deny (or at least to withhold from public view). The opening two blocks of lines in this text include imagery that calls to mind Duden's contemplation of Piero della Francesca's painting of St. Michael in the text entitled 'Der Auftrag die Liebe' in *Übergang* (1982).[33] Here the 'Rüstungsträger[..] / 'vielleicht zivile[..] Bäcker[..] / vielleicht Innen- oder Außenminister[..]' (S 17) exists in a state of denial of the 'aufgegabelter Zungenwurm [...] gleichgültig abgespreizt vom eigenen Körper' (S 17) that is both his adversary and symbolic of his sex, since the social world, or more precisely: the world of labour, of profession, profit or 'project',[34] demands the suppression of one's animal nature:

> Nichts als ein Traum aus größtmöglicher Ferne
> daß der Berufsschinder aus dem Eisen steigt
> stumpf sein Wasser abschlägt
> weich wird im Liegen [...]. (S 18)

Nature, not just in the form of sexuality or of other bodily functions, but also for example in the form of flowers and plants, is in the world of 'project' habitually confined and domesticated: 'dauernd sollen die Forsythien blühen / auf Moostellern / oder in kleinsten in Zigarrenkisten angelegten Taggärten / zu Ostern' (S 19), imagery that recalls the 'Einheiten in Windeseile hochgezogener / zu hastiger Blüte aufgeputschter Topf-Chrysanthemen / in Gelb Rostrot und Violett' that function as a form of cultural appeasement, a '[v]orbeugende Abwiegelung' in 'Steinschlag I' (S 9-10). It is only those on the extreme margins of the social order that remain in contact with abject animal nature, and these appear as pitiful existences: the 'endgültig Entgeisterten' (S 19), the 'Ausgestoßenen' (S 22), or the 'übriggebliebene[n] Frauen' who feed the birds on the concourses of urban railway stations (S 22).[35]

The poet, figured in the first person 'Ich', is consistently brought into association with these marginalised existences, in that she too is marginalised and under attack in a culture intent on destroying what is not utilisable, what does not serve the 'project': ' Zwischen Von und Nach [wird] alles nicht dem Fortkommen Dienende / zur Strecke gebracht.' (S 23) Her inspiration (or conspirator), nature understood as landscape, is also under attack from the expansion of cultivation, utilisation: 'Gegen Seitenblicke Scheuklappen / aus NATUR Landwirtschaft Zersiedelung. /

Jeder Randflecken bei Bedarf als Kloake vereinnahmt.' (S 23) Her task, the 'project' that will lead beyond the realm of project,[36] is to keep herself concentrated and intent on the marginal spaces while resisting the destruction with which they are everywhere threatened: she (or the poem itself, with which the 'Ich' is here interchangeable) is a 'Traumvergorene Beschaffenheit / hellwach auf des Messers Schneide / mit den sichtbaren Würgmalen der eigenen und anderer Finger' (S 20). And the resurrection (of poetic language) for which she quests is reached in the attentiveness to (abject) corporeality:

> CHRIST IST ERSTANDEN
> HIER ins Dickicht der Eingeweide und Innereien
> ungeschlacht und blakig beleuchtet
> bei großer Frühjahrsmüdigkeit und Mengen von Hundekot. (S 21)

The 'Leichtfüßigen' of the opening text in the cycle are in this second text shifted into a gallery of characters from the social world, the world of 'project' or 'Fortkommen' so inimical to poetry and to animal nature. Here these characters are described in terms which bring them into association with the armoured archangels and saints engaged in eternal battle with the serpents and dragons of multiplicit animal nature which form a consistent focus of Duden's *oeuvre*. Thus the 'Berufsschinder' is simultaneously a 'Rüstungsträger', while the 'Frühreifen ab Mitte Dreißig', '[g]eballte Scharfmacher [...] pausenlos abschmetternd / was unaufgefordert ihren Weg kreuzt', are characterised by their 'eingefressenen mürrisch verfransten Mundbörsen / und *geharnischten* Pupillen' (S 21, emphasis: GP).

The second part of 'I Am Your Only Surviving Memory' (S 25-31), in an extension of the theme of the battle between 'Rüstungsträger' and 'Zungenwurm', enters into an extended contemplation of the figure of the knight or saint as *disarmed* or overwhelmed by nature: the whole of this part of the text can be understood as a *Denkbild*[37] in response to Albrecht Altdorfer's extraordinary painting *Saint George Fighting the Dragon*[38] in which the familiar representation of the battle between saint and dragon occupies a relatively small space in the bottom right-hand corner of the panel, while the remainder of the painting is vast forest of thickly interwoven branches and leaves:

> Er war seinem Auftrag entfallen
> dem Zweck seines Ausritts.
> Der Wald hatte sich über ihn hergemacht
> der vielfache Vogellaut

> das Gedröhn und Gewisper der Luft
> Kälte Wärme Ansteckung
> der Moment
> die Schwäche der Glieder. (S 26)

The relations between the figure of the saint and the figure of the dragon in this part of the poem are much more complex, the boundaries between them become increasingly unclear (does the block 'Er handelte verlangsamt fast bewegungslos' to 'A CAN OF DEAD WORMS', pp.27-8, adopt the perspective of George or of the dragon, for example?), so that the destruction brought by the saint upon the monster acquires an ambivalence, suggesting that the saint brings destruction upon his own nature:

> Die Brennpunkte begannen zu irisieren
> zu schwanken sich zu verschieben:
> sein ungepanzerter Kopf sein Geschlecht in der Schamkapsel
> der rechte Vorderflug der nackt klaffende After des anderen
> die Spitze seines Schwerts. (S 28)[39]

The collapse of the culturally imposed boundaries between self and other, and between self and animal nature in the space of the forest, and the enactment of self-loss (and loss of 'project' or *Auftrag*) are the preconditions for the organic growth of the poem, of which the text's closing lines can be taken as a figure:

> Traumkraut seines Schädels
> dessen Keime heimlich die Fontanelle geöffnet
> wuchernd und ausschlagend den Helm durchstoßen hatten. (S 31)[40]

The third text in the cycle, 'Nacht neben Nacht über Tag', represents in a densely musical text the poet's disposition in a world that is inimical to poetry – the extreme effort of concentration, the isolation, vulnerability, and depression – 'EYE IN THE DOLDRUMS' (S 35) – that afflicts her. This text might be seen as an elaboration of the state addressed briefly in 'Steinschlag II' of *lack* of inspiration 'wenn die Notwendigkeiten nicht mehr verfangen' (S 15), while the image in the earlier text of the poet (or poem) 'an der Unterseite gestoßen und bedrängt' (S 15) is expanded into the scene of the public reading as *Drachenkampf*:

> In Deutschland auf den Rücken geworfen
> wenn's hochkommt auf die Seite gewälzt
> die bleiche Unterseite hingespreizt
> fischblütig lüstern gepfählt
> von streng verkniffenen Recken

Steps towards a reading of Steinschlag

> und der Geilheit und Putzsucht beflissen vorgelegt [...].
> Öffentliche Beschlagnahme
> durch Fahnenpflanzungen ins
> lichtscheue Sonnengeflecht. (S 39)[41]

Yet this text also initiates the movement of the poem away from the exterior topographies of the social sphere and into the interior space of the poet's state of mind, here a state of limbo (S 41) from which, in despite of the desperation and pain experienced, the language of poetry is nevertheless wrung – a 'HARROWING OF HELL' (S 41).[42]

'Rio Terra', the fourth text in the cycle, takes up where the previous text left off, with the extreme difficulty of the poet's pursuit of 'Gegenwelt' (S 36) on the margins of society – 'In die Verneinung / sich aufknüppelnd / den Morgen / abweisend. / Haßerfüllt begeifert und bestiert / von den Rändern der Tretmühle her' (S 43) – but unexpectedly finds the sudden release of a lifting of the cloud, reminiscent of the first experience of landscape ('plötzlich die größte Weite', S 8) in 'Steinschlag I':

> noch beim geflügelten ersten Geleit aus dem Untergetauchten
> riß die schwere Schicht aber auf
> teilte sich
> schloß Blickfetzen im Sichverflüchtigen zusammen
> verwehte leichthin
> und gab in unzulänglicher Tiefe
> einen Atemgrund frei:
> ungerührte Alpenfelder
> sonnenarm eigen
> selbst um die Mittagszeit
> klima- und schlaferhaben. (S 43)

Working with increasingly succinct and dense reprises of earlier images and themes, the poem now gradually moves ever further away from the realm of comprehensible meaning and into the realm of pure linguistic music, as it were building on the ground already established in the earlier texts in order to ascend into the space of air, of breath, of movement:

> Man muß sich nur aufrappeln
> [...]
> und störrisch ergeben
> über dünnste Fadenbrücken ziehen
> Klippen entgegen
> heimlich Luftverschläge aussuchen unterwegs [...]. (S 47)

From here to the end of the cycle, there are ever fewer holds for the commentator seeking to grasp meaning, and indeed, to revert to the image of the map which might give guidance to the poem's reader, such a map would, in the latter reaches of the cycle, surely bear many blank white spaces (perhaps with the traditional legend 'Here Be Monsters') marking incomprehension in the face of the dense polysemy and fragmentation of sense.[43] Here the 'commentator' must be left behind, while the reader goes on alone (like the St. George who loses himself in the forest of 'I Am Your Only Surviving Memory II'), abandoning herself (if she so desires) to the music of the words, to the 'verschlüsselten Noten' ('Mundschluss', S 60), until at last silence is reached.[44]

One more observation before my conclusion and in explanation of my title 'An Easter of Words': in the closing pages of the first of the 'Zungengewahrsam' lectures, Duden writes of the experience of loss – of 'Kindheiten, Potenzen, Intensitäten', both personal and national – which lies at the root of her writing:

> Die Geschichte der Worte setzt ein in der Verlorenheit, sie setzt auf das Verlorene. Auf das Wissen, daß nichts mehr zu gewinnen ist, aber alles dableibt, versteckt, in Worten, in Bildern, die vor allem die einstigen Gefühle, die Empfindungen, die Blicke, die Potenzen der Welt aufbewahren bis zum Tag ihrer Übersetzung, Übersetzung in die *Auferstehung*, in den Text […].(Z 32; emphasis: GP)

This conception of a knowledge of past intensities, as of past devastation (in particular that of the Holocaust), that lies dormant, buried as dead, in words and in images that are yet capable of resurrection, *Auferstehung*, into the life of the text runs like a thread throughout Duden's *oeuvre*. The textual passage of *Das Judasschaf* culminates in the contemplation of Vittore Carpaccio's painting *The Dead Christ* (in German *Grabbereitung Christi*), in which the pale, lifeless figure of Christ laid out on a stone slab in the foreground serves for Duden's narrator as a final focal point and resting place of the agonies of the preceding text: 'Die Welt ist vollständig hier und nicht mehr bloß ein Lebensabschnitt.'(J 129) The (representation of the) dead Christ becomes the embodiment of that preserved and dead (deathly) knowledge. While in the conclusion of her contemplation of the painting, the narrator of *Das Judasschaf* is as it were taken up into an identification with the figure of St. John, a figure of profound mourning turned away from the spectator, in *Steinschlag*, where Duden has liberated herself from the structural necessity for a narrator figure by breaking through into the realm of Orphic voice, it is the *words themselves*, poetic language itself, which trace the passage from burial – 'Eingezwängt in schmalste Zeitritzen' (S 8) and 'erkaltet verhärtend in Spalten / Abgründen der Zeit' (S 9) – to resurrection, the 'Auferstehung in den Text': 'CHRIST IST ERSTANDEN / HIER' (S 21). References to the Christian tradition's Easter sequence form a subtle strand that weaves throughout the fabric of this cycle: from 'Gründonnerstag' (S 19) or 'MAUNDY THURSDAY' (S 44) to Easter Saturday's 'HARROWING OF HELL' (S 41) to resonances of 'Ostern' (S 19) and the resurrection of Christ 'ins Dickicht der Eingeweide und Innereien' (S 21), the text enacts its own Easter sequence, culminating in the reference to the risen Christ's exhortation to Mary Magdalene in the garden, 'NOLI ME TANGERE', in 'Mundschluss', the final text of the cycle (S 60). It would be a misunderstanding, however, to see in this thread of signification an affirmation of religious belief.[45] Unlike the final resting point of Eliot's quest to find the sense in the poet's existence in his citation of Julian of Norwich's serene, because faith-full, 'And all shall be well and / All manner of things shall be well' at the conclusion of *Four Quartets*,[46] Duden's end point is an affirmation of the poet's language: the Easter of *Steinschlag* is a secular Easter of words, of language.

7. *Noli me tangere*: an interim conclusion

To write about Anne Duden's *Steinschlag* is not easy. What has been achieved in this essay can only be considered a beginning, a brief account of a far deeper engagement with the poem's complexity which itself has not yet reached anything like finality: in other words, this is by no means a reading that is finished. It is a tribute to the text that this is so.

What remains, however, as we step once more into the space outside the poem, is the sense of its refusal in so many respects of communication: the words, once resurrected (*auferstanden*) into the text, respond to human approach with the words 'NOLI ME TANGERE': touch me not.[47] This is in contrast to the forebears summoned up by the poem: Eliot's, as suggested above, is ultimately a project in the service of an experience enabled by religion, a social concept that links the individual to community; Hölderlin's poetry, though often the expression of a terrible loneliness, is yet imbued with the presence of the beloved; Celan's *Gedicht* 'ist einsam und unterwegs' and yet there is an *Aber*:

> Aber steht das Gedicht nicht gerade dadurch, also schon hier, in der Begegnung
> – *im Geheimnis der Begegnung*?   Das Gedicht will zu einem
> Andern, es braucht dieses Andere, es braucht ein Gegenüber. Es sucht es auf,

> es spricht sich ihm zu.   Jedes Ding, *jeder Mensch* ist dem Gedicht, das auf das Andere zuhält, eine Gestalt dieses Anderen.[48]

Celan's *Gedicht* is not to be imagined without its 'Du'.

Duden's poem, however, the product of a later cultural moment and a greater disillusionment, continuously addressing its own sense of threat from a social order inimical to it and indeed intent on its destruction, has renounced the 'Du': it is striking that all four occurrences of the second person address in the poem are in the form of voices cited into the text (sometimes apparent quotations): 'Kümmern Sie sich nicht weiter darum', 'Betrachten Sie sie als erledigt' (S 40); 'DAMIT DU DICH NICHT ZUGRUNDE RICHTEST' (S 48); 'WEHE DU VOGEL TÖTEST MICH' (S 55). In the 'ruinous world of Anne Duden's post-*Duino* cycle',[49] the renunciation of communication is a renunciation of a culture focused on utility:

> Solches Schreiben also, nicht Maßnahme, sondern Maßgabe jener "inneren Unermeßlichkeit", immer wieder, anfänglich, Gewalt- und Balanceakt, bildet nicht ab und ahmt nicht nach, es informiert und *kommuniziert nicht*. Überhaupt verweigert es jede Unmittelbarkeit. Es muß sie verweigern, denn die Worte sind nicht da, um gefaßt und in Informationsketten gelegt zu werden. (Z 13, emphasis: GP)

One might see in this gesture of renunciation a poetic praxis corresponding to Adorno's view that, in a culture shaped by the dictates of utilitarianism and commerce, the only way of keeping faith with the human being is, paradoxically, to withdraw from the contact with human beings:

> Daß die europäische Kultur in ihrer Breite, dem, was zum Konsum gelangte und heute von Managern und Psychotechnikern den Bevölkerungen verordnet wird, zur bloßen Ideologie entartete, rührt vom Wechsel ihrer Funktion der materiellen Praxis gegenüber, dem Verzicht auf den Eingriff, her. Dieser Wechsel freilich war kein Sündenfall, sondern historisch erzwungen. Denn nur gebrochen, in der Zurücknahme auf sich selbst geht der bürgerlichen Kultur die Idee der Reinheit von den entstellenden Spuren des zur Totalität über alle Bezirke des Daseins ausgebreiteten Unwesens auf. *Nur soweit sie der zum Gegenteil ihrer Selbst verkommenen Praxis, der immer neuen Herstellung des Immergleichen, dem Dienst am Kunden im Dienst der Verfügenden sich entzieht und damit den Menschen, hält sie den Menschen die Treue.*[50]

But perhaps even to imagine the poem as existing in order to 'keep faith' with the human being is to entrap it once more in a utilitarian purposefulness. Georges Bataille's notion of 'inner experience' could be a more appropriate way of conceiving of the absolute of which Duden's poem is in quest:

> Inner experience not being able to have principles either in a dogma (a moral attitude), or in science (knowledge can be neither its goal nor its origin), or in a search for enriching states (an experimental, aesthetic attitude), *it cannot have any other concern nor other goal than itself.* Opening myself to inner experience, I have placed in it all value and authority. Henceforth I can have no other value, no other authority.[51]

This is a number of radical steps further down the path of culture than Rilke's *Sonnets to Orpheus*, but nevertheless let the poet's voice ring out last here:

> Und die Musik, immer neu, aus den bebendsten Steinen,
> baut im unbrauchbaren Raum ihr vergöttlichtes Haus.[52]

Notes

[1] Paul Celan, 'Steinschlag', from the volume *Schneepart* (1971), in: Celan, *Gedichte in zwei Bänden*, Suhrkamp: Frankfurt a. M., 1975, vol. 2, p.400.

[2] A note on terminology: I have chosen here to regard the entire cycle as a single poem, consisting of six component texts, and use the terms 'poem' and 'text' accordingly.

[3] See, for example, Albert von Schirnding, 'Zusammenbruch eines Immunsystems', *Süddeutsche Zeitung* 31.3.1993; Uwe Schweikert, '"Schlacke mit geladenem Gedächtnis": Die absolute Poesie der Anne Duden', *Frankfurter Rundschau* 24.4.1993; Leonore Schwartz, 'Gesang aus der Tiefe', *Der Tagesspiegel* 23.5.1993; Corina Caduff, '*Steinschlag* von Anne Duden. Schmerzenssprache', *Die Wochenzeitung* 25.6.1993; Anke Westphal, 'Das absolute Gehör des Schmerzes', *Neue Zeit* 21.7.1993. Only Michael Braun, 'Leidensfrau', *Die Woche* 25.3.1993 and 'Letztendlich absolute Poesie?', *Basler Zeitung* 20.5.1993, and Bertram Bock, 'Vom Wortstein erschlagen', *Hessische/Niedersächsische Allgemeine* 10.10.1993, were unwilling to engage with the poem's difficulty, criticising, for example, its 'hermetische Verbissenheit' (Braun).

[4] Most reviewers commented on this obvious aspect while nevertheless engaging with the poem.

⁵ This sequence of poetics lectures was held first in Paderborn during the winter semester 1995-96, then, in revised form, in Zürich during the winter semester 1996-97. The published version is the final 1999 revision.

⁶ Paul Celan, 'Der Meridian', in: Celan, *Ausgewählte Gedichte. Zwei Reden. Nachwort von Beda Allemann*, edition suhrkamp: Frankfurt a. M., 1968, 131-148 (here: p.135).

⁷ Ibid., p.144.

⁸ See Clarise Samuels, *Holocaust Visions. Surrealism and Existentialism in the Poetry of Paul Celan*, Camden House: Columbia, 1993.

⁹ Reviewer Albert von Schirnding [see note 3] found himself reminded by *Steinschlag* of Eliot's *The Waste Land* (1922); in conversation with me, Anne Duden has confirmed the importance of Eliot's poem as an influence on her thinking about form.

¹⁰ See 'Zungengewahrsam' on voice and musicality as opposed to narration, and especially the passage on p.59: 'Hier ist der Treffpunkt, hier kommt es zum Steinschlag im Tonfall. Standort ist nicht mehr, wie bisher und wie im Übergang, der tote Leib, ja es gibt keinen Standort oder -punkt in diesem Sinne mehr, er hebt sich auf und wird aufgehoben durch Stimme und Sprache. Etwas wie Gesang stand an, ein Wechsel zur größten Eigenwilligkeit von Stoff und Ton. Die Person ist der Schrift nicht mehr im Wege, sie ist von ihr eingeholt und wird von ihr beiseite- und zurückgelassen.'

¹¹ See Franziska Frei Gerlach, *Schrift und Geschlecht. Feministische Entwürfe und Lektüren von Marlen Haushofer, Ingeborg Bachmann und Anne Duden*, Erich Schmidt Verlag: Berlin, 1998, 310-401. To be fair, Frei Gerlach does pursue Duden's incorporation of the paintings of Vittore Carpaccio and her reference to the music of Monteverdi in *Das Judasschaf*.

¹² My work on *Steinschlag* was in the first instance the work of reading and re-reading, also in company with others. In 1996-97, *Steinschlag* formed the focus of a reading group in the Department of German Studies at Warwick; the group was a model of mutually stimulating reading, and I thank its members for all that I gained from their insights: Tony Phelan, Roger Thiel, Helmut Schmitz, John Osborne, Petra Whatmore. Thanks in particular to Roger Thiel for subsequent discussions.

¹³ Peter Szondi, 'Durch die Enge geführt. Versuch über die Verständlichkeit des modernen Gedichts', in: Szondi, *Celan-Studien*, Suhrkamp: Frankfurt a.M., 1972, 47-111 (here: p.47).

¹⁴ Helen Gardner, *The Art of T. S. Eliot* [1949], faber and faber: London, 1968, p.1; see also p.57: 'The difficulty or obscurity which many readers feel in *Four Quartets* is

inherent in the subject [...]. Mr Eliot is, in his own words, "occupied with frontiers of consciousness beyond which words fail, though meanings still exist".'

[15] Ibid., p.54.

[16] Kathleen Fraser, 'Things that do not exist without words', in: Fraser, *Translating the Unspeakable. Poetry and the Innovative Necessity*, University of Alabama Press: Tuscaloosa and London, 2000, 7-14 (here: p.7).

[17] See Duden's reference to 'Notenschrift' in 'Zungengewahrsam' (Z 47).

[18] See Gabriele Kachold, 'Mein einzigster innigster Todeswunsch...', a text recollecting her imprisonment in the late 1970s, in: Heinz-Ludwig Arnold and Gerhard Wolf, eds, *Die andere Sprache. Neue DDR-Literatur der 80er Jahre*, edition text + kritik: Munich, 1990, pp.188-190, which opens: 'mein einzigster innigster todeswunsch ich habe ihn gehabt im knast im dreischichtensystem bei esda immer hundert prozent die weißen dederonstrümpfe zusammennähen [...]'.

[19] One notes the use of the word 'Schicht' to denote social class in the case of the *Leichtfüßigen*, whereas it appeared in the sense of '(work) shift' in the context of the *Arbeitslager* (S 7).

[20] The 'Steinquadrate in Aix' here also suggest landscape paintings by Paul Cézanne. See Heike Bartel's essay in this volume on stoney landscapes.

[21] See Duden's commentary on the (deathlike) state of sleep as the privileged state in which the 'Übersetzung' of language into writing is prepared in 'Zungengewahrsam' (Z 37-41).

[22] See the commentary on 'Landschaft, Natur, immer aufs neue Natur des Moments' as 'Erzeugerin eines Überschusses und Überschwanges; Erzeugerin oder auch nur Auslöserin von Intensitäten', in short, on the role of landscape and nature as initiators of the poetic process in 'Zungengewahrsam' (Z 30-31).

[23] T. S. Eliot, 'Burnt Norton', *Four Quartets* [1944], faber and faber; London, 1999, p.8. Compare Duden, 'Zungengewahrsam': 'Die Schrift hat einen Weg eingeschlagen, [...] [n]icht um anzukommen, sondern um aufzubrechen, nicht um Erzählung, Roman oder Buch zu werden, sondern um in Bewegung zu sein und möglichst auch zu bewegen.' (Z 42)

[24] Eliot, 'Burnt Norton', pp.7-8.

[25] Eliot, 'Little Gidding', *Four Quartets*, p.42.

[26] The poem 'Sommerbericht' from the collection *Sprachgitter* (1959) also suggests itself as a source of inspiration for Duden: see especially the final lines 'Wieder

Begegnungen mit / vereinzelten Worten wie: / Steinschlag, Hartgräser, Zeit.' – Celan, *Gedichte* [see note 1], vol. 1, p.192.

[27] Ibid., vol.2, p.70.

[28] Rainer Maria Rilke, *Werke in sechs Bänden*, Insel: Frankfurt a.M., 1980, vol. I.2, p.441.

[29] Eliot, 'East Coker', *Four Quartets*, p.19.

[30] The lines 'ABER DIE LIEBE LIEBT' are an apparent slight misquotation of the final line of the ode 'Vulkan': 'Und immer wohnt der freundlichen Genien / Noch Einer gerne segnend mit ihm, und wenn / Sie zürnten all', die ungelehrgen / Geniuskräfte, doch liebt die Liebe.' – Friedrich Hölderlin, *Gedichte*, ed. Jochen Schmidt, Deutscher Klassiker Verlag: Frankfurt a.M., 1992, vol. 1, p.318.

[31] See Duden, 'Zungengewahrsam' (Z 22); also Frei Gerlach's account of this neologism in *Schrift und Geschlecht* [note 12], pp.312-13.

[32] The line comes from the fragment 'Der Adler': see Hölderlin, *Gedichte*, p.400.

[33] Duden, *Übergang* (Ü 124-128). The painting that provides the imagery of this contemplation was identified by some reviewers not as the Piero, however, but the structurally not dissimilar *St. George* by Albrecht Dürer (left panel of the Paumgartner altarpiece): see Albert von Schirnding, 'Zusammenbruch eines Immunsystems' [note 3].

[34] Georges Bataille's notion of 'project', as a 'narcotic' which opposes the pursuit of 'inner experience' and to which the latter is opposed, seems pertinent here: see Bataille, *Inner Experience*, translated and with an introduction by Leslie Anne Boldt, State University of New York Press: Albany, 1988.

[35] On the abject in Duden's work see Margaret Littler's essay in this volume.

[36] See Bataille, *Inner Experience*, p.46: 'Principle of inner experience: to emerge through project from the realm of project.'

[37] See Sigrid Weigel's account of Walter Benjamin's practice of the written *Denkbild*: 'Here, with the aid of the mimetic faculty, the image, understood as dialectic at a standstill, is transformed into writing, that is, set in motion, in such a way as to reveal the origin of the idea and what has gone into its production: what has preceded it, entered into it, disappeared into it, and, simultaneously with the expression of an idea through the image, become, as its reverse side, invisible and invalidated.' – Weigel, *Body- and Image-Space. Re-reading Walter Benjamin*, translated by Georgina Paul with Rachel McNicholl and Jeremy Gaines, Routledge: London, 1996, p.52.

[38] A number of reviewers noted that the paintings to which Duden makes reference in *Steinschlag* are no longer reproduced in the volume, as they were in *Übergang* and *Das Judasschaf* and saw this as, for example, an indication of the 'Radikalisierung ihrer Schreibweise': Kathrin Reulecke, review in *Rundbrief Frauen in der Literaturwissenschaft* 40 (Februar 1994). Duden herself has made clear that she no longer wished the paintings to be reproduced in the book as an explicit reference point.

[39] This block seems to take inspiration from another painting, perhaps Jost Haller's representation of the George and dragon theme (in the collection of the Museum Unter den Linden in Colmar). Thanks to Barbara Köhler for drawing my attention to this painting.

[40] See Altdorfer's painting, where the plume on St. George's helmet merges into the leaves above his head. On such dissolution of boundaries as a pervasisve theme in Duden's work see Teresa Ludden's essay in this volume.

[41] Acquainted as I am with stories of the extraordinarily aggressive reactions from some (usually male) members of the audience often experienced by Anne Duden at public readings, and indeed having been witness to such myself, I find it difficult not to see in the passage from 'Nacht neben Nacht über Tag' a portrayal, half satirical, half serious, of what it is like to be on the receiving end of such reactions. See also Anne-Kathrin Reulecke's comments on 'affektiv geladene Äußerungen' on the part of commentators in her entry on Duden in the *Kritisches Lexikon zur deutschprachigen Literatur der Gegenwart* (Anne-Kathrin Reulecke, 'Anne Duden', in: *KLG*, Text und Kritik: Berlin, 1995, p.3, entry as at 1.8.2001). But the representation of the poem itself as 'monster' or dragon on account of its polysemy and thus evasion of clear-cut meanings, its corporeality, its resistance to the given social order is also a significant dimension in this passage.

[42] The reference is to William Langland's *Piers Plowman*, passus XVIII, which represents the descent of Christ into hell on Easter Saturday and the resurrection of the dead whom Christ liberates from damnation.

[43] See 'Zungengewahrsam' (Z 49): 'Anfänglich noch eher janusköpfig, später vielgesichtig werdend, rundum mit Augen bestückt und mit Mündern. Noch später dann, und das wäre vielleicht jetzt, immer weiter sich öffnend zugleich, sich aussetzend in alle Richtungen, härter und weicher, immer waghalsiger werdend': this could be read as a description of the genesis of Duden's oeuvre to date, or of the direction of *Steinschlag* itself as the poem unfolds. And, as a description of the later texts in the cycle: 'Gestalt aus Bewegung, die sich an nichts hält als an ihre eigenen Bewegungsgesetze' (Z 55).

[44] See also Uwe Schweikert, '"Schlacke mit geladenem Gedächtnis". Die absolute Poesie der Anne Duden' [note 3]: 'Der Leser muß sich der Sprachgewalt dieser absoluten Poesie, muß sich dem kunstvoll abgestuften rhythmischen Fluß der Alliterationen und Assonanzen überlassen wie der Partitur eines Gesangs.'

[45] On such religious motifs within a Romantic and modernist poetic tradition see Dirk Göttsche's essay in this volume.

[46] Eliot, 'Little Gidding', *Four Quartets*, p.43.

[47] John 20: 17.

[48] Celan, 'Der Meridian', p.144 (emphasis: GP).

[49] Anthony Phelan, review of Roger Paulin and Peter Hutchinson, eds, *Rilke's 'Duino Elegies': Cambridge Readings*, *Austrian Studies* 4 (1998), 244-5 (here: p.245).

[50] Theodor W. Adorno, 'Kulturkritik und Gesellschaft', in: Adorno, *Prismen. Kulturkritik und Gesellschaft*, Suhrkamp: Frankfurt a.M., 1969, 7-31 (here: pp.13-14, emphasis: GP).

[51] Bataille, *Inner Experience*, p.7 (emphasis: GP).

[52] Rilke, 'Die Sonette an Orpheus', II.x, *Werke* [note 32], vol. I.2, p.513.

Claudia Roth

‚Bilder [...] / aus einem Deutschland / das nie existiert hat'
Ein Lektürevorschlag zum Anfang von Anne Dudens ‚Steinschlag'

Published in 1993, shortly after the radical change which overthrew a seemingly fixed political and social structure, Anne Duden's 'Steinschlag' is a poetic text marked by radical departures from fixed linguistic structures. The discourse of the 'Deutsche Wende', and of other moments such as 'Deutschland im Herbst' or the Prague Spring, has left its mark on the text in echoes of meteorological metaphors and other modes of speech which have pervaded the discourse of revolution from the French Revolution on. The following reading traces the shifts of perspective that the poem performs in highlighting meteorological metaphors and then, in the closing word of the striking opening section, leaving behind these features of current discourse in a self-referential shift towards poetic discourse.

In einer Besprechung, die 1993 in einer Tageszeitung erschien, schreibt eine Rezensentin zum im selben Jahr publizierten Buch *Steinschlag* von Anne Duden: ‚Gleich zu Beginn des ersten Teils, „Steinschlag", macht man eine vom Gedichtelesen her vertraute Erfahrung, man versteht nicht: „Der Tonfall ein Dauerregen / gleichmäßig geschnürt Litaneien des Verhangenen / in denen die Bilder ertrinken / aus einem Deutschland / das nie existiert hat"'.[1] Die Rezensentin greift zwar auf eine ihr nicht neue Rezeptionsweise einer bestimmten literarischen Gattung zurück — der Lyrik. Doch ist dieses Vertraute zugleich das Unbekannte und weist auf einen Mangel, nämlich auf das Fehlen des Verstehens. Andere Rezensierende werden gerade von dem auf den ersten Blick Unverstandenen angezogen und formulieren beispielsweise: ‚Ich verstand kein Wort — und las weiter, gierig nach dieser Fremdheit',[2] oder: ‚Der Schritt in diese Lyrik macht bewußtlos — man versteht nichts und glaubt alles zu erahnen'.[3] Während diese beiden das Unverständnis den Ebenen un-vernünftiger Persönlichkeitsschichten parallel setzen — es ist von ‚Gier' und ‚Ahnung' die Rede, die die Lektüre zu bestimmen vermögen, also von einer der Vernunft entzogenen Faszination —, will die zuerst zitierte Rezensentin den Mangel am Text selbst festmachen. Sie schreibt weiter: ‚Unklar, wovon hier die Rede ist. Der Satz ist nicht nach bekannten Regeln gebaut, die Leserin befindet sich in der deutschen und doch in einer „anderen" Sprache'.

Die nicht nur ungenaue, sondern falsche Behauptung, der Anfangssatz von ‚Steinschlag' sei nicht nach bekannten Regeln gebaut, bietet einen Ausgangspunkt für die folgenden Überlegungen. Mag dieser Fehler Reflex einer bestimmten Sprachpraxis der Massenkommunikation sein, in welcher es kaum noch möglich scheint, komplexerer Literatur die ihr gebührende Aufmerksamkeit und Genauigkeit zu schenken, soll der hier zur Verfügung stehende Raum in solchem Sinn genutzt werden. Das Verstehen, Ver-stehen, setzt sozusagen bei dem in ihm enthaltenen ‚stehen' ein: stehen, das heißt auch ‚nicht weitergehen, innehalten'; es geht dabei ebenso von einem Mangel aus, wie es auch von einer Faszination vorwärts getrieben wird und eine vielschichtige Sprache in ihrem zeitgeschichtlichen Kontext erfahrbar machen möchte.

> Der Tonfall ein Dauerregen
> gleichmäßig geschnürt Litaneien des Verhangenen
> in denen die Bilder ertrinken
> aus einem Deutschland
> das nie existiert hat.
> Unter vorgezogenem Dach und niedriger Decke
> Antizyklone
> lichtscheu und kalkig bestäubt
> auf engstem Raum beieinander
> während wenige Meter weiter
> grellweiß vor geschuppten Stämmen
> eine steilaufgerichtete Helle steht
> in der nur die hohen und beweglichen Töne
> angeschlagen werden.
> Witterungsunabhängig. (S 7)

Während der Text mit einer Ellipse einsetzt, ‚Der Tonfall ein Dauerregen', lassen sich im Verlaufe der ersten beiden durch Punkte abgeschlossenen Sätze auch Teile isolieren, die durch syntaktische Verflechtungen miteinander verbunden sind. Es sind die Teile ‚Litaneien des Verhangenen / in denen die Bilder ertrinken / aus einem Deutschland / das nie existiert hat' und ‚während wenige Meter weiter / [...] / eine steilaufgerichtete Helle steht / in der nur die hohen und beweglichen Töne / angeschlagen werden'. Diese beiden Teile weisen eine parallele syntaktische Struktur auf, und sie werden auch phonetisch miteinander verknüpft.

Beide verorten ein Geschehen in einem näher bestimmten Substantiv: ‚Litaneien', ‚in denen die Bilder ertrinken', und eine ‚Helle', ‚in der' ‚Töne angeschlagen werden'. Beiden Substantiven ist eine mit einer g-Alliteration verbundene Wortgruppe vorangestellt: ‚gleichmäßig geschnürt Litaneien des Verhangenen' und ‚grellweiß vor geschuppten Stämmen / eine steilaufgerichtete Helle steht'.

In den ersten Textzeilen erscheinen akustische und visuelle Aspekte in der Poetik gewisser Wetterphänomene ineinander verschränkt: ‚Der Tonfall ein Dauerregen / gleichmäßig geschnürt Litaneien des Verhangenen'. ‚[G]leichmäßig geschnürt' kann als bildliche Vorstellung eines ‚Dauerregen[s]' verstanden werden, wie sie auch im Ausdruck ‚Schnürlregen', und — innerhalb derselben Isotopieebene wie ‚geschnürt', Schnur und Faden — in der Redeweise ‚es regnet Bindfäden' evoziert wird. Wenn dabei das Gleichmaß, die Unterschiedslosigkeit hervorgehoben wird, fällt bei der ‚Litanei' ebendiese Bedeutungskomponente ins Gewicht, und sie wird zugleich ins Akustische übertragen. ‚Litanei', ein aus dem Griechischen kommendes Lehnwort, das ‚einen tief in der rel[igiösen] Überl[ieferung] der Menschheit verankerten Gebetstyp bez[eichnet]', bei dem ‚nach jedem Ruf eine *gleichbleibende* Antwort des Volkes folgt',[4] wird umgangssprachlich für ‚eintöniges Gerede'[5] sowie für ‚das schon oft Gesagte'[6] verwendet, also für monotones, sich wiederholendes Sprachgeschehen. Mit dem Genitivattribut, ‚Litaneien *des Verhangenen*', wird der akustische wieder mit einem visuellen Eindruck zusammengefügt. An diesem wird die undurchsichtige oder unklare Qualität hervorgehoben.

Das ‚grellweiß vor geschuppten Stämmen' ist im Vergleich zu ‚gleichmäßig geschnürt' um eine relative Standortbestimmung erweitert, ‚*vor* geschuppt*en* Stämme*n*'; ‚eine steilaufgerichtete Helle' wird dadurch genauer verortet, während ‚Litaneien des Verhangenen' bezüglich der Situierung im Raum unbestimmt bleibt. Auch durch das finite Verb wird die ‚Helle' weiter präzisiert. Sie ‚steht'. ‚Stehen' ist mit ‚Stamm' verwandt, die ‚Stämme[...]' bilden ein gleichsam körperliches Echo zur ‚steilaufgerichtete[n] Helle'. Die Orientierung im Raum ist mit dem zusammengesetzten Adjektiv, ‚steil-aufgerichtet', zusätzlich gewichtet. Auch ihre optische Qualität erscheint in ‚grellweiß' vorweggenommen und verdoppelt. Im Unterschied zu den Anfangszeilen, in denen Eindrücke sozusagen fließend ineinandergehen, sind hier klar voneinander getrennte Intensitäten präsentiert: eine Fülle von Licht und eine scharf konturierte räumliche Ausrichtung.

Wie erwähnt, loten beide syntaktisch ausgeformten Teile jeweils den Bedeutungsraum des Substantivs mit einem darin stattfindenden Geschehen aus: ‚Litaneien', ‚in denen die Bilder ertrinken' und ‚eine'

‚Helle', ‚in der nur die hohen und beweglichen Töne / angeschlagen werden'.

Im ersten syntaktisch ausgeformten Teil ist eine Abwärtsbewegung in einer sprachlich gefaßten Monotonie verortet: ‚Litaneien [...] / in denen die Bilder ertrinken / aus einem Deutschland / das nie existiert hat'. In dieser Abwärtsbewegung werden ‚Bilder' nichtig, die durch ihre Herkunft genauer präzisiert sind. Sie entstammen einem Raum, der zwar mit einem Namen aus der politischen Geographie, ‚Deutschland', belegt wird, der aber so, in diesen Bildern ‚nie existiert hat'. Das Wort ‚Deutschland' tritt überdies in seiner Eigenschaft, als Eigenname Objekt und Sachverhalt ‚im Kontext eindeutig' zu ‚identifizieren',[7] in ein Spannungsverhältnis zum meteorologischen Terminus am Beginn des zweiten Satzes: ‚Antizyklone'. Syntaktisch zwar nicht eingebunden, wird dieser Begriff im Text jedoch mehrfach verankert und motiviert, sowohl durch die Wiederaufnahme eines thematischen Aspektes aus dem ersten Satz als auch durch die Bildlichkeit der ihn umgebenden Wortgruppen. Diese Überdetermination des einen auf eine genau definierte Realität verweisenden Begriffs — ‚Antizyklone'— läßt die Leerstelle umso deutlicher hervortreten, die sich beim andern — ‚Deutschland'— im Verweis auf eine negierte Existenz öffnet.

Der zweite syntaktisch ausgeformte Teil geht von einem optischen Eindruck aus: ‚eine steilaufgerichtete Helle steht / in der nur die hohen und beweglichen Töne / angeschlagen werden'. In einem durch Intensitäten ausgezeichneten Raum geht es um die Erzeugung von Tönen und um die besondere und ausschließliche Qualität dieser Töne. Wie schon im ersten Satz gerade bei den akustisch-sprachlichen Geschehen sind auch hier sowohl die wörtlich genommenen als auch die übertragenen oder verfestigten Bedeutungen mitzulesen. ‚Der Ton*fall*' des Textanfangs benennt ganz wörtlich genommen ein ‚Fallen', eine Abwärtsbewegung von Tönen, wie schon ‚ein Dauerregen' an eine Abwärtsbewegung *des* Wassers und das Ertrinken der Bilder an eine Abwärtsbewegung *im* Wasser denken lassen. Als im Sprachgebrauch verfestigter Ausdruck meint der ‚Tonfall' eine bestimmte ‚Art der Betonung'.[8] So kann auch die gegen den Schluß des Absatzes stehende Fügung ‚einen Ton anschlagen' verstanden werden; als idiomatische Wendung genommen heißt es ‚sich auf bestimmte Weise äußern'.[9]

Im Verb ‚anschlagen', ‚durch Schlag erzeugen', ist zudem eine kurze Heftigkeit, somit eine Kraft und Intensität inbegriffen, die in den die ‚Töne' noch ausschließlicher bezeichnenden Adjektiven ‚hoch' und

‚beweglich' ebenfalls aufgenommen wird. Die Qualität der Töne steht in mindestens doppelter Weise in Opposition zur Abwärtsbewegung: einerseits durch ihre Erhebung in eine extreme Stimmlage, andererseits auch durch die Prägnanz und Schärfe der *einzelnen* Elemente, wohingegen beim ‚Tonfall' wie auch bei einer ‚Litanei' ein akustisch-sprachlicher *Gesamt*eindruck maßgebend ist.

Durch den Vergleich, der von den strukturell ähnlichen und syntaktisch ausgeformten Satzschlüssen ausgegangen ist, können also signifikante Unterschiede festgehalten werden: Läßt der erste in der Poetik gewisser Wetterphänomene prägnante Raum in einer Abwärts-Bewegung und einem Vorgang der Auflösung eine immer schon vorhandene Leerstelle —‚Deutschland' — hervortreten, wird die Ordnung des zweiten Raumes durch einen wörtlich genommenen Auf-Stand, das heißt: ein aktives, in der Vertikalen orientiertes Stehen geprägt. Dieser Raum begründet sich ebenso durch eine Intensität der Licht- und Sichtverhältnisse, wie in ihm eine Intensität der Äußerungsweise maßgebend wird.

Der dritte, letzte und kürzeste Satz des ersten Abschnittes, ‚[w]itterungsunabhängig', fällt in mehrfacher Hinsicht auf. Er bildet den Schluß einer größeren Texteinheit, auf die anschließend eine Zäsur in Form einer Leerzeile folgt. Dadurch, daß das einzelne Wort eine Zeile bestimmt, ergibt sich ein Bogen zur siebten Zeile, zu ‚Antizyklone'. ‚Witterungsunabhängig' ist eine Lossage von genau dem Bereich, der am spezifischsten durch jenen fachsprachlichen Terminus vertreten ist. Durch seine ganz andere Struktur wird dieser dritte Satz sozusagen zu einer Bilanz und einem Kommentar der beiden vorhergehenden, grammatikalisch-strukturell vergleichbaren, jedoch inhaltlich unterschiedlichen Sätze. Dieses Schluß-Wort, ‚[w]itterungsunabhängig', bildet auf der untersten sprachlichen Ebene, das heißt der lautlichen, genauer gesagt durch seine w-Anlautung noch eine Klammer zu der Zeile, die den Wechsel von der einen Raum-Ordnung in die andere ebenso markiert wie vollzieht: ‚während wenige Meter weiter'. Damit wird gewissermaßen der Raum eingerahmt und hervorgehoben, in dem die qualitative Art der Äußerung Ereignis wird, die sich genau in dem vom ersten Raum unterscheidet, wovon sich ‚[w]itterungsunabhängig' lossagt und freimacht.

Der Textanfang und insbesondere die Leerstelle ‚Deutschland' sowie das Thema der Äußerungsweise und auch die Unabhängigkeitserklärung des dritten Satzes sollen im Folgenden in einen größeren Zusammenhang, nämlich in denjenigen der Zeitgeschichte situiert werden. 1989, also vier Jahre vor der Veröffentlichung von Dudens Text, wird jene

‚friedliche Revolution' angesetzt, die zur sogenannten ‚Wiedervereinigung' Deutschlands führte. Im öffentlichen Diskurs von 1993, sei es in den Massenmedien, sei es in der ‚Fülle von Publikationen, in denen die vielfältigen Aspekte der welt- und deutschlandpolitischen Veränderungen erörtert werden',[10] zirkulieren das Schlagwort der ‚Vereinigung' und Redeweisen aus dem Bedeutungsfeld von ‚Einheit'. Ein Beispiel soll hier noch näher betrachtet werden. Im Nachwort einer ‚thematisch gebundene[n]'[11] Anthologie mit dem Titel *Von einem Land und vom andern. Gedichte zur deutschen Wende* beleuchtet der Herausgeber kritisch die verschiedenen Begriffe, die das bezeichnen, ‚[w]as 1989/1990 in Deutschland geschah'.[12] Nicht nur die Begriffsbildung und deren Implikationen, sondern auch *der Modus der Erinnerung* kommt zur Sprache, wenn es beispielsweise heißt, nur ein ‚sentimentaler Rückblick, von Melancholie verhangen', könne die Vorstellung einer deutschen Einheit noch erreichen.[13] Ebenso wird bei der Frage nach dem ‚Sinn der neuen deutschen Einheit' *die Art und Weise des Sprechens* problematisiert: ‚Vaterländischer Singsang' — eine Reminiszenz an Hölderlins ‚Vaterländische Gesänge' und vielleicht auch an deren enge Beziehung zur Französischen Revolution[14] — ‚Vaterländischer Singsang zur Weihe der Einheit, gleich welcher Tonart, ist nicht gefragt'.[15]

Mit der Reminiszenz an die ‚Vaterländischen Gesänge' wird die verborgene Verbindung deutlich, die die Rede vom ‚Vaterländischen Singsang' konstruiert zwischen der Französischen Revolution von 1789 und der — in Analogie dazu so genannten — ‚friedlichen Revolution' von 1989. Erscheint der Ausdruck ‚Singsang' gerade auch im Vergleich mit ‚Gesang' als negativ, weist dies auf die ganz verschiedenen historischen Orte der Ereignisse, die im selben Adjektiv, ‚vaterländisch', so gegensätzliche Konnotationen hervorzurufen vermögen.

Wenn nun die vorher zitierte Äußerungsweise im Hinblick auf die bisherige Lektüre von ‚Steinschlag' gelesen wird, ergeben sich verblüffende Überschneidungen und Parallelen. Wie zu zeigen versucht, sind im Anfang von ‚Steinschlag' zwei gleichzeitig vorhandene, qualitativ sehr verschiedene Gegebenheiten formuliert, in denen jeweils ein Geschehen verortet ist. In der einen, sprachlichen Gegebenheit werden in einer Abwärtsbewegung Vorstellungen und Bilder aufgelöst ‚aus einem Deutschland / das nie existiert hat'. Das zeitgeschichtliche Thema der deutschen Einheit könnte eine verführen, den unbestimmten Artikel hier als Zahlwort zu betonen: ‚aus *einem* Deutschland / das nie existiert hat'. Ist die sprachliche Gegebenheit in Dudens Textanfang als ‚Tonfall' und

,Litaneien' gefaßt, erscheint im Vergleich dazu der negierte ,Vaterländische[...] Singsang zur Weihe der Einheit, gleich welcher Tonart' wie eine Paraphrase zu sein. Die gemeinsamen Bedeutungselemente von monotoner Sprechweise und einem aus dem kultischen Bereich stammenden Vokabular in Verbindung einerseits mit den vereindeutigenden Worten ,vaterländisch' und ,Einheit', andererseits mit dem Wort ,Deutschland' erinnern daran, daß nach Benedict Anderson ,nationale Vorstellungen' ,eine starke Affinität zu religiösen Vorstellungen'[16] aufweisen. Das Nachwort der weiter oben erwähnten Anthologie fordert in diskursiver Manier anstelle des ,Schwall[s] von Polit-Rhetorik' ,das *vielfältige* Erbe' ,zu sichten'.[17] Die poetischen Formulierungen Dudens hingegen zeigen die in der Wahrnehmung dieses Sprachgeschehens liegende Möglichkeit des dialektischen Umschlags und der Änderung. In der Darstellung der Monotonie und der unendlichen Repetition des Gesagten entsteht eine Gegenbewegung: ,Bilder ertrinken'; eine Leere tut sich auf; Vorstellungs-Raum wird frei.

In der anderen räumlich ausgerichteten und durch Intensitäten hervorgehobenen Gegebenheit geht es um das Erzeugen von Tönen. Setzte der Text ein in ein vorgängiges Sprachgeschehen, rückt nun das im Beginnen und Entstehen Begriffene, das ,[A]ngeschlagen werden' der ,Töne' selbst ins Blickfeld. Insofern wird dieser Teil autoreferentiell und somit poetologisch bedeutsam. Auffällig ist dabei das Prinzip der Sonderung, ,*nur* die hohen und beweglichen Töne' werden angeschlagen. Das folgende ,[w]itterungs*un*abhängig' betont die Sonderung weiter, indem es sich ausdrücklich von einem Zusammenhang lossagt. Jener meteorologische Zusammenhang ist im ersten Teil mit dem Sprachgeschehen verknüpft.

Aus diesem Blickwinkel und auf den zeitgenössischen politisch-öffentlichen Diskurs übertragen, beginnt in diesem die verbreitete naturalisierende Metaphorik aufzufallen. Der Herausgeber der besagten Anthologie verortet die im Nachwort zu besprechenden Ereignisse zuerst jahreszeitlich, ,im Herbst des Jahres 1989',[18] und setzt sie seiner Schreib-Zeit, ,jetzt im Frühjahr 1993',[19] entgegen. Ohne offensichtlich im Text motiviert zu sein, wird weiter unten die eine Formulierung spezifiert zum ,deutschen Herbst des Jahres 89'. Wenn sowohl diese Textbewegung als auch die erweiterte Formulierung als Erinnerungs-Cluster gelesen werden, sind darin zwei weitere historische Zäsuren verdichtet: Zum einen bezeichnet der ,„Deutsche Herbst", zum stehenden Begriff geworden', ,eine Kumulation von Ereignissen im September und Oktober 1977', ,den

Höhepunkt der Auseinandersetzung zwischen staatlicher und terroristischer Gewalt'[20] und den ‚massive[n] Rückfall der jungen Republik in eine autoritäre Staatsverfassung'.[21] Zum andern aktualisiert die Entgegensetzung Herbst-Frühling den sogenannten ‚Prager Frühling'. Die Wochenzeitschrift *Der Spiegel* veröffentlicht im März 1993 unter der Rubrik ‚Zeitgeschichte' ‚vorab Auszüge aus den Memoiren'[22] Alexander Dubceks. Die erste der beiden Folgen ‚über die entscheidenden Phasen des Prager Frühlings' geht vom Datum ‚der sowjetischen Invasion' aus und beginnt folgendermaßen: ‚Der 20. August 1968, ein Dienstag, war ein typischer Spätsommertag, warm, die Sonne dunstverschleiert'.[23] Werden beim zuletzt Zitierten die politischen Ereignisse unmittelbar in einen meteorologischen Zusammenhang gestellt, scheint das ‚bekannteste[...] Plakat der Studentenbewegung'[24] mit seinem Spruch gerade auf diesen Modus der Bedeutungskonstitution zu reagieren und sich davon abzusetzen: ‚Alle reden vom Wetter. Wir nicht'.

In den Anfangszeilen von *Steinschlag* sind weder eine Handlung in Form einer story noch personale Identitäten als durchgehende Handlungsträger auszumachen. Die Verweigerung ‚[w]itterungsunabhängig' wird somit auch nicht innerhalb einer personalen Konstellation als Veranschaulichung gesellschaftlicher Ordnungen dargestellt. Sondern sie ist unvermittelt in der Sprache selbst angesetzt und nimmt Bezug auf eine Ordnung des Diskurses. Die Lossage folgt dabei gerade auf die poetologisch bedeutsame Passage und hebt diese durch die lautliche Verflechtung mit den w-Alliterationen des Übergangssatzes noch weiter hervor.

Der Textanfang schreibt sich in ein Sprachgeschehen, eine sprachliche Gewohnheit, also in eine Tradition ein. Die Funktion der meteorologischen Bildebene kann dahingehend verstanden werden, daß sie — so steht es in einer Untersuchung zu Hölderlins seinerseits naturalisierenden Metaphorisierung der Französischen Revolution — ‚die historischen „Ereignisse" zu solchen Naturvorgängen' umstilisiert, ‚die dem menschlichen Zugriff am gründlichsten entzogen sind' und dadurch ‚von Geschichte' ‚entlasten'.[25] Insofern ist die Lossage des Schluß-Worts am Anfang eines Textes — der nota bene an seinem nach acht Seiten folgenden Ende und übrigens wieder mit w- und g- Alliterationen auf den nun aber schon ‚gescheiterten' und ‚umnachteten' Hölderlin weist — zugleich eine Aufforderung, das ‚man made desaster' als solches ins Blickfeld und in die Sprache zu rücken: ‚Hölderlin als Siebzigjähriger', ‚ohne Weg- und Wendemarke / eine Schlacke mit geladenem Gedächtnis'.

Anmerkungen

[1] Christa Kaufmann, ‚Anne Dudens *Steinschlag*. Ein anderes Leben aus dem Getöteten', *Luzerner Neuste Nachrichten*, 4.11.1993.

[2] Uta Runge, ‚Mennigrot in kleinsten Portionen. Zum *Steinschlag* von Anne Duden', *die tageszeitung*, 22.4.1993.

[3] Corina Caduff, ‚*Steinschlag* von Anne Duden. Schmerzenssprache', *Die WochenZeitung*, 25.6.1993.

[4] Walter Kasper et al., Hgg., *Lexikon für Theologie und Kirche*, Herder: Freiburg i.Br., Basel, Rom, Wien, 3., völlig neubearb. Aufl., 1993 ff.; Bd. 6, S. 954; Hervorhebung: CR.

[5] Gerhard Wahrig, *Deutsches Wörterbuch*, Bertelsmann Lexikon Verlag: Gütersloh, München, Jubiläumsausgabe, 1986/1991, S. 840.

[6] Günther Drosdowski und Werner Scholze-Stubenrecht, Hgg., *Duden. Redewendungen und sprichwörtliche Redensarten. Wörterbuch der deutschen Idiomatik*, Dudenverlag: Mannheim, Leipzig, Wien, Zürich, 1992 (Der Duden in 12 Bänden; Bd. 11), S. 459.

[7] Hadumod Bußmann, *Lexikon der Sprachwissenschaft*, Kröner: Stuttgart, 2., völlig neubearb. Aufl., 1990 (Kröners Taschenausgabe, Bd. 452), S. 204.

[8] Wahrig, *Deutsches Wörterbuch*, S. 840.

[9] Drosdowski, *Duden. Redewendungen und sprichwörtliche Redensarten*, S. 728.

[10] Karl Otto Conrady, Hg., *Von einem Land und vom andern. Gedichte zur deutschen Wende*, Suhrkamp: Frankfurt a. M., 1993, S. 174.

[11] Ebd., S. 175.

[12] Ebd., S. 206.

[13] Ebd., S. 174.

[14] Freundlicher Hinweis Y. Elsaghes vom 8. Mai 2001.

[15] Conrady, *Von einem Land und vom andern*, S. 218.

[16] Benedict Anderson, *Die Erfindung der Nation. Zur Karriere eines folgenreichen Konzepts*, Campus: Frankfurt a. M., New York, ^{2}1993 (Reihe Campus, Band 1018), S. 18.

[17] Conrady, *Von einem Land und vom andern*, S. 218; Hervorhebung: CR.

[18] Ebd., S. 173.

[19] Ebd., S. 174.

[20] Petra Kraus et al., *Deutschland im Herbst. Terrorismus im Film*, Münchner Filmzentrum: München, 1997, S. 6. Das Kollektiv der Regisseure, das den Film ‚Deutschland im Herbst' gedreht hat, benennt die Ereignisse unter anderem durch die Namensfolge ‚Schleyer, Mogadischu, die Toten von Stammheim' (ebd., S. 80).

[21] Gertrud Koch, ‚Film', in: Klaus Briegleb, Sigrid Weigel, Hgg., *Gegenwartsliteratur seit 1968*, München, Wien, 1992 (Hansers Sozialgeschichte der deutschen Literatur, Band 12) S. 557-85, hier S. 573.

[22] *Der Spiegel*, 9 (1993), S. 5 (Inhaltsverzeichnis).

[23] *Der Spiegel*, 9 (1993), S. 180.

[24] Silvia Bovenschen, ‚Die Generation der Achtundsechziger bewacht das Ereignis. Ein kritischer Rückblick', *Frankfurter Allgemeine Zeitung*, 3.10.1988.

[25] Yahya Elsaghe, *Untersuchungen zur Funktion des Mythos in Hölderlins Feiertagshymne*, Francke: Tübingen 1998, S. 20.

Heike Bartel

‚Steinatem'
Zur Metaphorik des Atmens in Anne Dudens ‚Steinschlag'

The sign 'Steinschlag' warns of things threatening to break out of their normal setting unexpectedly, often dangerously. This essay on Anne Duden's 'Steinschlag' explores the disruptive force in her poetic style. The innovative metaphors in 'Steinschlag' break away from conventional expression, interrupt the continuity of 'normal' language and lay open an unfamiliar linguistic terrain. Particular focus is placed on metaphors like 'Steinatem' and the tense fusion they create between diametrically opposed elements: breathing and dead stony matter; (female) voicing and (male) silencing; sanctuary and threat. The motif of breathing is explored within the context of poetic writing. Historical references are followed up and the question of poetry after Auschwitz is touched upon.

Unter dem Stichwort ‚Steinschlag' läßt sich im *Duden, Deutsches Universalwörterbuch* nachlesen: ‚(Fachspr.): **1.** das Herabstürzen von durch Verwitterung losgelösten Steinen (im Bereich von Felsen und Felsformationen). **2.** [o. Pl.]: (seltener) Schotter'.[1] Steinschlag, das sind Geröllbrocken, die sich lösen und so den Wandernden, der in unserer heutigen Zeit ja doch meist ein Autofahrer ist, bedroht, wenn er/sie meint, sich auf sicherem, wenn auch engem Weg durch ein Gebirge oder eine Felslandschaft zu befinden. Beim Steinschlag lösen sich unverhofft Felsstücke, die eine/n schlimmstenfalls erschlagen können oder, wenn man/frau[2] glimpflich davonkommt, plötzlich daran erinnern, daß der gewählte Pfad unsicher, die umgebende Landschaft zerfurcht, porös, instabil und voller Geröll ist, bei dem man nicht weiß, wie lange es sich noch hält und wann es ins Rutschen kommt.

Dem Weg durch ein solches Gebiet mit Steinschlag ähnelt das Lesen des gleichnamigen Textes von Anne Duden. Ein glattes Durchkommen ist für den Lesenden schwierig, denn die Bilder, Begriffe, Wendungen und Sätze sind oft keine, die der Norm unseres herkömmlichen Sprachgebrauchs entsprechen. Vielmehr kommt hier Sprache ins Rutschen, löst sich aus der durch ihren tradierten Gebrauch gefestigten Umgebung. Wozu Duden häufig so findet, ist eine neue Form des poetischen Sprechens; neu insofern als sie mit innovativen Metaphern und neuen Wort- und Sinnkombinationen alte, leere Worthülsen abzuwerfen vermag. ‚Neu' ist diese Sprache auch insofern zu nennen, als die Zusammenfügung von Worten in Dudens Texten dem Lesenden abverlangt, sich einen eigenen Zugang zu den so entstehenden Bedeutungsveränderungen zu schaffen, zu diesem unerwarteten Aufeinandertreffen von Wortelementen in Wendungen wie ‚Steinatem'.

Es gehört jedoch vor allem zur Eigenart dieser Sprache, daß sie öfter als einen neuen Zusammenhang zu stiften und zu einer Synthese zu führen, Brüche, Spannungen und Gegensätze aufzeigt. Der 'Steinschlag' von Dudens Sprache erlaubt keinen leichten Zugang zum Text und kein sicheres Vorankommen bei seinem Lesen. Vielmehr weist der Text so viele in- und gegeneinandergefügte Elemente auf, daß die Orientierung oft schwer fällt und man Gefahr läuft, sich in den vielfältigen Schichten und verschachtelten Ebenen zu verlaufen. In dem noch recht unerkundeten Gelände von Dudens Text ‚Steinschlag' im gleichnamigen Band besteht gar die Gefahr, von den monumentalen Brocken dieser Sprache erschlagen zu werden oder sich mindestens an ihren Ecken und Kanten zu stoßen. Steinschlag, das Herausbrechen von Elementen aus ihrem festen Zusammenhang, und Verletzungsgefahr gehen Hand in Hand. Die Topographie des Textes verweist auf Landschaften, in der ein solcher Steinschlag droht; sie evoziert – und ich greife hier auf Landmarken zurück, die der Text selbst angibt, – steinige Gebirge und Wüsten (S 12), ‚aufgerissene[…] Straßendecken' (S 13) oder das ‚Bett der Durance' (S 13), jenen Zufluß der Rhone in den französischen Alpen, dessen Flußbett durch seine große Unebenheit, die unter anderem von Felsbrocken herrührt, eine sehr unregelmäßige und reißende Wasserführung verursacht. Die Topographie des Textes führt auch zu jenen ‚Steinquadrate[n] in Aix' (S 13), bei denen es sich vielleicht um die bizarr übereinandergetürmten Felsblöcke handeln könnte, die Paul Cézanne im verlassenen Steinbruch von Bibémus bei Aix zu einem seiner dramatischsten Werke inspirierten.[3]

Der erste Teil dieses Essays wird versuchen, einige motivische Leitlininien durch den Text aufzuzeigen. Im darauffolgenden wird anhand einiger Wortkompositionen im Text näher auf Anne Dudens ‚dichterische Verfahrensweise' eingegangen – um es mit einer Wendung Friedrich Hölderlins zu sagen. Der Schwerpunkt wird dabei auf der Dynamik von Dudens Metaphern liegen, insbesonders auf jenen, in denen Brüche, Risse und Verletzungen thematisiert werden: die ‚klaffende[n] Schluchten' (S 9) dieses Textes, die ‚Zeitritzen', ‚Haarrisse', ‚Sichtkeile[e]' und ‚Platzwunden' bis hin zum den Hinterkopf sprengenden ‚Genickschuß' (S 8, 14, 15). Anhand dieser Themenbereiche soll die große Nähe von Sprachlichkeit und Körperlichkeit bei Duden beleuchtet werden, um im letzten Teil zu dem Moment zu kommen, an dem die Ineinsführung der

beiden Ebenen – Körperlichkeit und Sprachlichkeit – gezeigt werden soll: ‚Steinatem' (S 13).
Dudens Texte mit literaturwissenschaftlichen Begriffen fassen zu wollen, bedeutet immer auch, (Neu)Definitionen mitzuliefern. So ist es auch schwierig, für ‚Steinschlag' eine passende Gattungsbezeichnung zu finden, überhaupt gängige Definitionen auf ihn anzuwenden, denn obwohl der Text sich auf Begriffe aus der literarischen Rhetorik bezieht, wie ‚Metaphern' (S 11), oder auf Dichter wie Friedrich Hölderlin und Paul Celan verweist, die Dichtungstradition entscheidend geprägt haben, entzieht er sich eindeutigen Kategorisierungen. Ich werde im folgenden auf eine Festlegung des Textes als einer bestimmten Gattungsart zugehörig verzichten und einfach von ‚Text' sprechen.

I
Leitlinien

Verschiedene Bilder und Referenzpunkte verdichten sich in ‚Steinschlag' zu etwas, das sich am ehesten mit dem Begriff ‚Texteindruck' fassen läßt: dem Lesenden präsentiert sich der Text als Gefüge von Bildern und Verweisen, die rückwirkend und vorausweisend wechselseitig aufeinander wirken. Mit aller gebotenen Vorsicht wird dieses Kapitel versuchen, einige motivische Leitlinien im Text nachzuzeichnen, um ihn für das Arbeiten zugänglicher zu machen. Das anschließende Kapitel, in dem es um Dudens ‚dichterische Verfahrensweise' geht, ist bemüht, eventuelle Vereinfachungen dieser groben Leitlinien zurückzunehmen und die Vielfalt und Komplexität von ‚Steinschlag' zu beleuchten.

Die ersten Substantive des Textes, die uns einen Referenzpunkt bieten, indem sie eine zeitliche und räumliche Zuordnung des Beschriebenen zu erlauben scheinen, sind die Worte ‚Deutschland'[4] in der vierten und ‚Arbeitslager' in der 16ten Zeile (S 7). Vom Wort ‚Arbeitslager' ausgehend lassen sich die unmittelbar umgebenden Zeilen als Beschreibung der Situation in den Lagern Nazi-Deutschlands lesen. Vom Wort ‚Arbeitslager' her gelesen lassen sich die in ersten 15 Zeilen entworfenen Bilder rückwirkend auch als Evokation der Duschräume der KZs lesen, in denen ‚[u]nter vorgezogenem Dach und niedriger Decke', ‚auf engstem Raum beieinander' (S 7) aus den Duschköpfen statt des erwarteten gleichmäßig geschnürten Wassers das Giftgas entströmt, das den Namen Zyklon B trägt. Die ‚steilaufgerichtete Helle' ‚vor geschuppten Stämmen' mag die hohen Kamine der Brennöfen ins Gedächtnis rufen, die ‚hohen und beweglichen Töne' die Sirenen einer

Fabrik oder die heulenden Warnsignale, die einen Bombenangriff ankündigen.

Die Evokation des Bildes vom Vernichtungslager wird durch vielfältige direkte und indirekte Verweise auf Texte Paul Celans bestärkt.[5] Celans Werk – hier mag man insbesonders an ‚Todesfuge' und ‚Engführung' denken – läßt sich in Dudens Text als Referenzpunkt lesen für Gedichte nach Auschwitz, oder – mit Peter Szondis Anwort auf Adornos These zur (Un)Möglichkeit von Gedichten nach Auschwitz - für Gedichte ‚auf Grund von Auschwitz'.[6]

Die Vielfalt des Textes verlangt jedoch danach, neben einer Lesart – wie der oben anskizzierten - zugleich verschiedene andere mitzulesen. Dudens Bilder fordern kein einfaches Parameter, nach dem sie verstanden werden können, sondern verlangen vom Lesenden, verschiedene Bedeutungen miteinander zu kombinieren. So verweisen Begriffe wie ‚Dauerregen', ‚verhangen', ‚Antizyklone' und ‚[w]itterungsunabhängig' (S 7) auch deutlich auf einen meteorologischen Zusammenhang, der mit dem Wort ‚witterungs*unabhängig*' (Hervorhebung: HB) aber zugleich auch wieder zurückgenommen wird.[7] Ein Begriff wie ‚Antizyklone' bietet dabei trotz seiner scheinbaren Fixierung als Fachausdruck, der in der Meteorologie ein Wetter Hoch ankündigt, verschiedene Lesarten an. Damit entzieht er sich im weiteren Kontext einer eindeutigen Festlegung und läßt sich gleichsam ‚witterungsunabhängig' auch als das tödliche Giftgas Zyklon B lesen. Der vielschichtige Text führt verschiedene Zeiten, Themen, Bilder und Diskurse zusammen. So gibt es neben der Leitlinie, die uns in die Periode Nazi-Deutschlands führt, andere, die uns später im Text zeitlich zurück zu den Lebensdaten Friedrich Hölderlins leiten, aber auch auf Jüngstvergangenes wird verwiesen mit der ‚[s]eit zwei Jahren tote[n] Cathy' (S 10). Ein Wort wie ‚Strumpfhosenproduktion' (S 7) wirkt hier passend und irritierend zugleich, weil es einerseits im Kontext eines Lebens im (Arbeits)Lager gelesen werden kann, andererseits aber auch aus ihm herausfällt und Bilder der modernen Industrie- und Konsumgesellschaft mitevoziert.[8] Auf diesen Bereich verweist der Text später mit Schlagwörtern aus der Business-Sprache und mit aktuellen Werbeslogans (S 14-15).

Während die Zeilen 16 bis 32 die oben beschriebenen historischen Zusammenhänge in Deutschland zur Zeit des Dritten Reiches auf den Plan rufen, verwendet der deutlich abgesetzte erste Textteil Vokabeln, die in einen ganz anderen Bereich hineinführen: den der Sinneswahrnehmung durch Auge und vor allem Ohr. Neben ‚optischen' Signalen –

insbesonders Hell-Dunkel Kontrasten – spielt der Bedeutungsbereich des Musikalisch-Akustischen eine wichtige Rolle. In diesen gehört das erste Substantiv, ‚Tonfall' (S 7), das gleichsam den Auftakt zum Text gibt; dazu zählen des weiteren die ‚hohen und beweglichen Töne', aber auch die ‚Litaneien' (S 7). Im weiteren fügen sich nicht-musikalische Äußerungen wie ‚Aufschluchzen' (S 8) und später das Schreien und Wimmern des Ich (S 12) in diesen akustischen Themenbereich ein. Wie in vielen anderen Texten Dudens ist diese Ebene des Musikalisch-Akustischen eine wichtige Spur durch den Text.[9] Duden verwendet häufig noch vor der Sprache angesiedelte Elemente wie Tonfall und Stimme. Im Gegensatz zur vom Körper abgelösten Schrift wird die Stimme dabei als ein Ausdrucksmittel lesbar, das – ebenso wie der ‚Steinatem', von dem später noch ausführlicher die Rede sein wird – Sprache und Körperlichkeit ineinsführt.

In diesem vielschichtigen Text entziehen sich einzelne Wendungen einer eindeutigen Lesart. Das trifft insbesondere auf die Zeilen vier und fünf zu, die von einem ‚Deutschland' handeln, das ‚nie existiert hat' (S 7). Die Auseinandersetzung mit diesem ‚Deutschland' kann zwar bei Daten und Orten aus der deutschen Vergangenheit ansetzen, die zum Beispiel mit dem Wort ‚Arbeitslager' evoziert werden, zugleich findet im Text jedoch keineswegs historische Rückschau statt. Vielmehr wird die wesentlich komplexere Frage nach dem Zusammenhang von Kunst und Gedächtnis aufgeworfen. Winfried Menninghaus erklärt diesen Zusammenhang in seiner Studie zu Paul Celan mit Verweis auf die Frühromantiker und das 116. Athenäumsfragment. Auch auf Anne Dudens Werk läßt sich dieses Prinzip des Umgangs mit Geschichte anwenden, das nicht nur ein ‚rückläufiges Einholen [des] Anfangs, sondern buchstäblich seine, mit Schlegels Charakteristik der romantischen Kunst(-Kritik) zu reden, „potenzierende Reflexion" ist, Abfolge einer virtuell „endlosen Reihe von Spiegeln".'[10] Anne Dudens Werk zeigt deutliche Anknüpfungspunkte an die Frühromantik,[11] und in ihren Texten erfahren die Inhalte nach dem Muster der Frühromantiker eine ständige ‚potenzierende Reflexion'. Die Reflexion auf das Thema ‚Deutschland' erfährt in ‚Steinschlag' - teilweise durch die Biographie der Autorin beeinflußte - vielfältige und weitläufige Spiegelungen und Brechungen wie zum Beispiel im Verweis auf den ‚kalten Krieg', der mit dem Zusatz ‚der Wirkwaren' (S 13) gleichzeitig sowohl ironische Brechung erfährt als auch einen Bezug zur ‚Strumpfhosenproduktion' (S 7) erhält. Der Blick auf die deutsche Vergangenheit erfolgt mit kritischem Seitenblick auf die hochindustrialisierte Gesellschaft im späten 20ten Jahrhundert oder in Auseinandersetzung mit dem Thema ‚Vergangenheitsbewältigung', das der Text mißtrauisch und ironisch zugleich in einem Terminus wie ‚Heimwiederaufbereitungsanlagen' (S 11) aufgreift. Gleichzeitig gebrochen und gespiegelt wird diese Reflexion auf Vergangenes auch im Sprung von den Toten des Holocaust zu den (weiblichen) Opfern der Gegenwart eines zeitgenössischen (englischen?) Lebensraumes, die der Text mit der [s]eit zwei Jahren tote[n] Cathy' (S 10) macht. ‚Cathy' ist eine Stellvertreterin der Opfer, die im historischen oder Geschlechterdiskurs mundtot gemacht wurden, deren Mäuler durch brutale Soldatengewalt, Unterdrückung oder politische Repression gestopft wurden und denen das Ich im Text das Wort gibt und eine Stimme verleiht. Der Text erinnert an die toten Opfer und geht den von ihnen hinterlassenen Spuren nach, er ruft Bilder ins Gedächtnis, die zu verschwinden, zu ‚ertrinken' (S 7) drohen. Diese vom Untergehen bedrohten Bilder dienen als letzte Belege für die Existenz von Menschen oder Ereignissen, sie sind Gedächtnisstütze, Erinnerung und Versicherung. Sie liefern eine ‚verbliebene Anschaulichkeit' (S 11), von der der Text später sagt, daß sie bedroht sei und ‚[l]aut Gesetz' ‚ausgehändigt' werden müsse (S 11). Der Verlust solcher Bilder birgt die Gefahr, daß Menschen und Ereignisse ‚von der Gegenwartsliste gestrichen' werden (S 10) und ihre Existenz verdrängt wird. Wie die Worte ‚sich nach innen [krümmen]/ und [...] gebückt in den Verstorbenen stecken' (S 7), so stecken auch die Bilder, die das ‚kulturelle Gedächtnis'[12] aktivieren könnten, in den Toten. Franziska Frei Gerlach spricht von solchen Bildern als ‚Aufbewahrungsorte eines anderen Gedächtnisses, respektive des Gedächtnisses des Anderen, in unserer Kultur Ausgeschlossenen, Verdrängten, zum Schweigen gebrachten, Ermordeten.'[13] Zu diesen zum Schweigen Gebrachten lassen sich in ‚Steinschlag' die Opfer des Naziterrors, aber auch ‚Cathy' zählen. Zu diesen Ausgeschlossenen und Anderen gehört jedoch ebenso ‚Hölderlin als Siebzigjähriger' (S 15), der in der Zeit von 1806 bis 1843 entmündigt und für unheilbar verrückt erklärt seine letzten Jahre im Turm zubringt und seine Briefe mit Scardanelli, Buonarotti oder Salvator Rosa unterzeichnet.

Der Text beschreibt eine Hierarchie, in der Figuren leitmotivisch in Über- oder zwangsweise Untergeordnete unterteilt sind. Zu letzteren zählen die ‚Verstorbenen' (S 7), ‚Cathy' und der alte Hölderlin, ‚Körperrest' und ‚Zeitruine' (S 15). Zu den Übergeordneten gehört neben den ‚Soldaten auf dem Weg zwischen Schlag und Schlacht' (S 8) die

Gruppe der ‚Raub- und Greifengel[...]', zu der sich auch der Beute machende 'braunkohlenfarbene Engel' rechnen läßt (S 8). Zu diesen Dominierenden zählt auch der Vater Cathys, der jagt, steckt und festtritt (S 10). Zu den Übergeordneten, Privilegierten gehören aber vor allem die ‚Leichtfüßigen', die ‚Vertreter der leisure class' (S 9, 10). Diesen privilegierten ‚Gipfelhocker[n]' (S 11) ist ein Leben gegönnt, das ‚sich grundsätzlich von der erstbesten Zerstreuung beim Schopf packen läßt' (S 12). ‚Sie brauchen sich keine Gedanken zu machen' (S 11) und evozieren diejenigen, denen die Gnade ihrer späten Geburt die Unschuld und Energie liefert, ein unbefangenes Leben in ihrer Heimat Deutschland zu führen. In dieser Hierarchie untergeordnet sind die Erkalteten, Nackten, Blutleeren, Toten (S 9), denen das (weibliche?) Ich im Text eine Stimme verleiht.

Ein Begriff aus dem Wortfeld des Musikalisch-Akustischen liefert einen Verweis darauf, wie der Text zu dieser Stimme findet: Es ist das Wort ‚Litaneien' (S 7). Eine Litanei bezeichnet in der katholischen Liturgie ein zwischen Vorbeter und Gemeinde wechselndes Bittgebet. Im nicht spezifisch religiösen Sprachgebrauch meint es eine langatmige, monotone Aufzeichnung. Des weiteren jedoch benennt eine Litanei eine immer wieder hervorgebrachte Klage. Diese Form der Klage läßt sich in Beziehung setzen zur Form der Auseinandersetzung mit der deutschen Vergangenheit, die die Form eines Klageliedes annimmt. Sigrid Weigel bezieht sich in ihrem Vorwort zu Suzanne Greuners Studie *Schmerzton* auf den Mythos, daß Athene die Flötenkunst erfunden habe, um die klagenden Töne der Gorgonen nachzuahmen. Diese nachahmende Klage – so Weigel mit Verweis auf Pindar – ist dabei jedoch nicht lediglich Imitation, sondern ‚ein echter „Mimus" [...], ein gespieltes „in die Haut des anderen Schlüpfen"': ‚wer die klagende Gorgo nachahmt, der läuft Gefahr, sich in sie zu verwandeln'.[14] Das erste Auftreten des Ich im Text mit den Zeilen ‚Unterdessen atme ich Steine' (S 11) weist darauf hin, daß wir es hier mit einer in diesem Sinne mimetischen Klage zu tun haben, die nicht besingt, sondern selbst wie ein Opfer schreit, wimmert und ausschlägt. Das Klagelied artikuliert ein Gedächtnis, das sich nicht in hohlen Ritualen zum Jahrgedächtnis oder dem Schmücken der Gräber mit ‚aufgeputschte[n] Topf-Chrysanthemen' zeigt (S 9), sondern sich ganz dem Verletzten, Verstoßenen und Toten anheimgibt. ‚Unterdessen atme ich Steine' (S 11) ist in diesem Zusammenhang lesbar als die Erfahrung elementarer körperlicher Gewalt und Todesgefahr, die zugleich Anlaß für und Inhalt dessen ist, was artikuliert werden soll ‚im verschwimmenden

Mund' mit ‚aufgeriebene[r] taube[r] Zunge' (S 14). Im Ein und Aus des Atemprozeßes reflektiert sich auf körperlicher Ebene der Sprachprozeß selbst. Vor dem Hintergrund des ‚Steinatems', des Steins, der aus dem Mund austritt, der aber auch knebeln und den Erstickungstod hervorrufen kann, erfährt dieser Sprachprozeß noch eine zusätzliche Dynamik, auf die der letzte Teil dieses Essays weiter eingehen wird.

Trotz aller Anstrengung scheint es dem Ich gegen Ende des mit römisch I markierten Textteiles möglich, einen Moment des Ruhens zu finden, auf den Vokabeln aus dem Wortfeld der Ruhe, der Erleichterung, des Lösens und sich Fallenlassens hinweisen. Dieser Fall endet jedoch nicht weich, sondern mit Verletzung, bei der Blut ‚erleichtert' aus den Platzwunden quillt (S 14). Das Ich kommt trotz seines Fallens jedoch auf keinem Grund an, sondern bleibt in der Schwebe ‚sich einpendelnd in der Waagerechten' (S 14), gleichsam aufgespannt zwischen den Neonlichtern der Gegenwart und den Gasflammen der Vergangenheit. Der Eindruck von zeitlicher Linearität, den der Text mit Ausdrücken wie ‚Unterdessen' (S 11), ‚Gleich danach' (S 12), ‚jetzt' (S 13) und ‚Endlich' (S 13) erweckt, wird mit diesem Schwebezustand wieder zurückgenommen. Gesetze der zeitlichen Abfolge wie auch der Physik greifen hier nicht: Auf den Fall folgt kein Aufprall, sondern ein traumartiges Sich-Einpendeln über dem ‚Steinspiegel' (S 14), das dennoch die Platzwunde verursacht. Die Erwähnung der ‚Kanäle zu Füßen zu Köpfen' (S 12) unterstützt diesen Zustand, denn sie deuten auf Wasser und den fast schwerelosen Zustand des Dahintreibens im Liquiden. Die ‚Kanäle [...] in Berlin vor allem' lassen sich dabei jedoch auch als einen der Verweise auf Rosa Luxemburg in Dudens Werk lesen: eine weitere mundtot gemachte weibliche Stimme, deren Leichnam im Berliner Landwehrkanal treibend gefunden wurde.[15]

Im mit römisch zwei gekennzeichneten, deutlich kürzeren letzten Teil von ‚Steinschlag' wird das Ich nicht mehr explizit genannt, und der Name Hölderlin liefert einen Referenzpunkt. Doch dieser Name und die mit ihm verknüpften intertextuellen Elemente fixieren den Text keineswegs, sondern eröffnen vielmehr neue Ausblicke und Anknüpfungspunkte.

II
Dudens ‚dichterische Verfahrensweise'
Metaphern des Textes

Die oben grob als Leitlinien im Text angedeuteten verschiedenen Diskurse prallen im Text aufeinander. Unterschiedliche Bedeutungsebenen lagern sich schichtartig über-, unter- und nebeneinander: deutsche NS Geschichte und die Erinnerung an sie; Verweise auf Alltags- und Webesprache; die Auseinandersetzung mit anderen Autoren wie Hölderlin oder Celan; das Motiv von Körperwahrnehmung und der Artikulation von Sprache durch den weiblichen Körper; die Reflexion auf Sprache selbst mit ihren konventionellen Metaphern und Jargons sowie die Möglichkeit des individuellen poetischen Schreibens; der Geschlechterdiskurs, der durch Ausdrücke wie ‚Frischvulven' (S 12) oder auch ‚Adamsäpfel' (S 14) angedeutet wird und im Bild der ‚vom Vater in die Erde gejagt[en]' (S 10) Cathy deutlichere Formen annimmt.

Der Vielfalt dieser Diskurse folgend fordert Dudens Text kein bestimmtes Parameter, nach dem er gelesen werden muß, sondern vielmehr einen Zugang, der gleichsam ‚symphilosophisch' den Verknüpfungen so vielfältiger Bereiche wie Geologie und Anatomie, Akustik und Optik, Theologie und Philosophie – um nur einige zu nennen – folgt. ‚Steinschlag' weist keine homogene Sprache auf, sondern kombiniert meteorologische, geologische, medizinische, botanische oder musiktheoretische Fachausdrücke; Begriffe aus dem theologischen, poetologischen oder politischen Zusammenhang; Zitate – vom Werbeslogan ‚VORSPRUNG DURCH TECHNIK ' (S 14) bis hin zum Hölderlinschen Gedichtzitat ‚AN ZIMMERN' (S 15), die als intertextuelle Elemente eingefügt werden, sowie Englisches – ‚in all fairness and if I may say so' (S 15). Oft wird die Bedeutungstiefe von Einzelbegriffen erst durch die Arbeit mit dem etymologischen oder fachsprachlichen Wörterbuch deutlich, die dem Lesenden vor aller Theorie zum wichtigen Hilfsmittel bei der Arbeit an Anne Dudens Texten wird. In manchen Wörtern, die beim ersten Lesen Fachausdrücke zu sein scheinen, entdeckt der Lesende Schöpfungen der Autorin. So finden sich zwar nach langem Suchen die ‚Ringmuskeln' (S 9) – es sind die Muskeln, welche Hohlorgane wie den Mund verschließen – aber nicht die ‚Rauten- und Riemenmuskeln' (S 14). Es findet sich der Meeres- nicht aber der ‚Steinspiegel' (S 14), das Substantiv ‚Irrigation' nicht aber die Verbform ‚irrigiert' (S 11). Es gibt den Hölderlinschen Gedichttitel ‚An Zimmern', nicht aber wortwörtlich das Zitat ‚ABER / DIE LIEBE LIEBT' (S 15).[16] Wir bewegen uns auf einem schwierigen Wort- und Bedeutungsfeld, auf dem kein Tritt sicher ist und auf dem der dominante Sprachgebrauch unterlaufen und die Orientierung an typischen Sprachfiguren vom Erstaunen über neugeformte abgelöst wird.

Eine zentrale Stellung in diesem Sprachprozeß nehmen Wortschöpfungen ein, die ich im folgenden - trotz der Schwierigkeit, ‚Steinschlag' mit Hilfe literaturwissenschaftlicher Gattungskonventionen und tradierter Termini einzuordnen - als Metaphern bezeichnen werde. Die Dynamik, die bereits im Terminus ‚Metapher' angelegt ist, offenbart sich hier als ein wichtiges Grundprinzip zum Verständnis von Dudens Text. Die wörtliche Bedeutung von *meta-pherein* ‚anderswohin tragen, übertragen, herüberbringen' wirkt als das am Anfang dieses Essay beschriebene Prinzip des ‚Steinschlags': Einzelne Worte oder Wortelemente werden aus ihrem konventionellen sprachlichen Zusammenhang gelöst und in einen neuen überführt, in dem sie innovativ wirken und eine große Dynamik entfalten. Metaphern wie ‚Heimwiederaufbereitungsanlagen' (S 11) und ‚Frischvulven' (S 12) verdeutlichen, daß im Text der neue Bedeutungszusammenhang, den die Wortelemente bilden, sowohl auf den dominanten typischen Gebrauch – ‚Wiederaufbereitungsanlage', ‚Frischfleisch' – verweist als ihn auch erweitert oder sogar mit ihm bricht. So entwickelt die innovative Wortzusammensetzungen ‚Heimwiederaufbereitungsanlage[...]' im Kontext von ‚Steinschlag' eine starke Dynamik: Deutsche Vergangenheitsbewältigung – die Wiederherstellung des Heimes ‚Deutschland'– und die gefährliche und umweltpolitisch umstrittene Entsorgung abgebrannter radioaktiver Brennelemente in Wiederaufbereitungsanlagen stehen in einem komplexen Spannungsverhältnis zueinander. Integraler Bestandteil dieser Dynamik ist das Aufeinandertreffen konventioneller Metaphern, die längst zur Alltagssprache zählen, und der innovativen Metaphorik der Autorin. Der Text reflektiert darauf, daß Sprache in einem Begriff wie ‚Wiederaufbereitungsanlage' dazu dient, im Interesse herrschender Industrien über seinen gefährlichen Inhalt hinwegzutäuschen. Hier ist es die Sorge um radioaktiven Müll, die mit positiven Assoziationen von neuer Nutzung und Wiederverwertung ent-sorgt werden soll. Einer solchen verschleiernden Metaphorik, die ganz gezielt ein bestimmtes politisches Interesse verfolgt, stehen Dudens Metaphern jedoch deutlich entgegen.[17] Ihre Begriffe wirken im Gegensatz zu konventionalisierten Metaphern nicht als Beschönigung oder Rationalisierung, um beim Beispiel der politischen Sprache zu bleiben, sondern weisen auf die problematische Beziehung zwischen Wortform und -inhalt hin. In ‚Heimwiederaufbereitungslage[...]' wird an die Grundbedeutung der Entsorgung von Abgebranntem angeknüpft. Die Metapher verweist auf das Problem des Umgehens mit der deutschen Vergangenheit vor dem historischen Hintergrund der Vernichtungsanlagen und Brennöfen des Holocaust.

Das Wort ‚Bedarfsmehrung' (S 14) ist ein weiteres Beispiel dafür, wie der Text Kritik an herkömmlicher Sprache und postmoderner Wohlstandsgesellschaft übt. ‚Bedarfsmehrung' stößt beim ersten Lesen wahrscheinlich nicht als ungewöhnlich auf, man liest das bekannte ‚Bedarfsdeckung' mit. Das Wort ist jedoch in sich widersprüchlich. Die beiden Wortkomponenten ‚Bedarf' und ‚Mehrung' passen nicht zusammen wie bei ‚Bedarfsdeckung', sondern erzeugen gemeinsam eine Dynamik, die zugleich ein kritisches Licht auf unsere Konsumgesellschaft wirft: Statt Bedarf an etwas zu decken, wird dieser erzeugt, weiter angefacht, was oft auf Kosten anderer, schwächerer Nationen und deren Ressourcen geschieht. Aus Gründen der ‚Bedarfsmehrung' muß gesucht werden nach ‚global organisiertem Nachschub / über Gegenden hinweg / denen Deutschland / die Landschaft abnötigte' (S 14). Die Passage endet mit dem Werbeslogan der Automarke Audi 'VORSPRUNG DURCH TECHNIK'. Im Kontext von Umweltpolitik und Konsumkritik sowie des Gefälles von der Ersten zur Dritten Welt erhält dieser jedoch eine ganz andere Wendung. Der ‚Vorsprung' Deutschlands basiert auf der Ausbeutung anderer, und der Ruf von hervorragender ‚Technik', den der ‚Meister aus Deutschland' (Celans ‚Todesfuge') hat, mahnt an die gut geölte Vernichtungsmaschinerie des Dritten Reiches.

‚Steinschlag' erhält seine Komplexität und Vielfalt durch die starke Dynamik von Metaphern, die zwar die konventionelle Bedeutung einzelner Worte aufgreifen, die jedoch nicht auf dieser scheinbar sicheren und festgefügten Ebene von Sprache verharren, sondern ihr mißtrauen, sie kritisieren und unterlaufen. In dieser sprachkritischen Auseinandersetzung unternimmt Duden zugleich das Aufbrechen von und den Ausbruch aus konventioneller Sprache.

Die Wortneuschöpfung ‚angebotene Frischvulven' (S 12) ist ein Beispiel, das uns in den Geschlechterdiskurs führt. Hier stiftet der Text neue Sinnzusammenhänge, indem er Fleischwaren evoziert, die in Auslagen des Metzgers oder Supermarktes zum Kauf angeboten werden. Die Assoziation von angebotenem Frischfleisch wird kombiniert mit dem medizinischen Terminus für die äußeren weiblichen Geschlechtsorgane: ‚Vulva' für Schamlippen und Klitoris. In Zusammenhang mit dem Adjektiv ‚angeboten' hat der Lesende hier Bilder von der Vermarktung des Weiblichen in der Sexindustrie vor Augen: explizite Fotos in Pornomagazinen, Slogans wie ‚Eat Pussy' oder gar extreme Fälle von kosmetischer Chirurgie, die Frauen zur ‚Designer Vagina' zurechtschneiden. Die ‚vorgeschobene[n] Sekundärmerkmale' (S 12) weisen einerseits auf weitere Geschlechtsmerkmale hin, die von der Industrie in ‚Push-Up' BHs und Stilettos hervorgehoben und vermarktet werden. Andererseits entlarvt diese Metapher zugleich auch das Oberflächliche, Sekundäre und Degradierende dieses Prinzips.

Der Text findet zu einer neuen Sprache jedoch nicht nur mit Wortneuschöpfungen, sondern auch indem er einen oft in Vergessenheit geratenen sprach- oder kulturgeschichtlichen Hintergrund wiederbelebt und ihn in den Bedeutungszusammenhang einzelner Worte integriert. Dies trifft besonders auf den kulturgeschichtlichen Hintergrund bestimmter Pflanzen zu, wie zum Beispiel der Bezug zur Grabgestaltung beim ‚Ilex' oder den ‚Chrysanthemen',[18] und auch auf den ‚Kaiserling[...]' (S 11). Beim ‚Kaiserling' folgt Duden einem Prinzip, das Rolf Zuberbühler mit Bezug auf Hölderlin als ‚Phänomen der etymologischen Spracherneuerung' beschreibt: Begriffe erfahren aufgrund der gedanklichen Verbindungen, die durch den Rückbezug auf seine sprachgeschichtlichen Hintergründe entstehen, eine neue Bedeutung.[19] Dudens Verfahren erinnert hier an Hölderlin, der insbesonders in seinen sehr späten Texten oft Wurzelwörter in den Zusammenhang integriert oder sprachgeschichtliche Herleitungen eines Wortes miteinbezieht. So vereinbart der ‚Kaiserling', ein eßbarer Blätterpilz, der jedoch in seinem Aussehen dem hochgiftigen Fliegenpilz sehr ähnelt, durch seine Etymologie das Nahrhafte und das Vergiftende miteinander, denn er verdankt seinen Namen Kaiser Claudius, der an Gift starb, das man seiner Leibspeise aus eben diesen Pilzen beimischte.[20] Die Tiefe des Begriffs zeigt sich – wie so oft bei Duden – erst durch das akribische Nachspüren der im Text ausgelegten Spuren. Daneben nutzt der Text auch andere Konnotationen wie die Superiorität, die in ‚*Kaiser*ling' (Hervorhebung: HB) steckt im Gegensatz zur Inferiorität des zum Tode Verurteilten, der die ‚Henkersmahlzeit' erhält (S 11).

Stellen die Metaphern, die Alltagssprache oder Fachausdrücke bearbeiten, schon Ansprüche an den Lesenden, so sind jene noch schwerer zu analysieren, die einen unvergleichbar weiteren Bedeutungshintergrund aufweisen. In ‚Steinschlag' sind es insbesondere Worte aus dem christlich-religiösen Bedeutungsfeld wie ‚Ekstase' (S 8) und ‚Auferstehung' (S 7), letzteres soll hier kurz und ohne Anspruch auf Abgeschlossenheit kontextualisiert werden. Indem der Text das Verb ‚auferstehen' in Zusammenhang mit dem Verb ‚aufstehen' bringt - ‚in die Auferstehung getrieben/ [...]/ obwohl sie unbedingt liegen müßten' (S 7) - führt er die christlich-religiöse übertragene Bedeutung und die nichtmetaphorische triviale zusammen. Zusätzliche Spannung entsteht dadurch, daß in ‚Steinschlag' Auf(er)stehen zudem deutlich negativ konnotiert wird mit Bildern aus dem Kontext der Arbeits- und Vernichtungslager, des gewaltsamen Weckens und Antreibens derer, die ‚sich nichts wünschen als nie wieder aufstehen zu müssen' (S 9). Metaphorische und nicht-metaphorische Bedeutung werden gekoppelt und wirken simultan aufeinander, um eine neue Metapher zu erzeugen. Das Auf(er)stehen ist nicht der End- und Erlösungspunkt des Opfertodes, sondern im Gegenteil sein Anfang, auf den nicht wie in der christlichen Mythologie die Erlösung folgt. Das christliche Erlösungs- und Auferstehungsmotiv wird hier konfrontiert mit Bildern aus der deutschen Nazi Vergangenheit, die mit Vokabeln wie ‚gewaltsam', ‚getrieben', ‚sich krümmen', ‚Abtritt' und ‚schwere[...] Eisentore[...]' (S 7) ohne jegliche Poetisierung anschaulich gemacht werden. Im starken Kontrast zur christlichen Heilslehre ist der Tod hier nicht die Versöhnungstat, die Sünde und Tod überwindet, sondern Endpunkt aller Hoffnung.

Dudens Metaphern brechen mit den konventionellen Regeln des Wortgebrauchs, selbst wenn dieses Wort - wie zum Beispiel bei ‚Abtreibung' - selbst schon Metapher ist wie die meisten Wörter, mit denen wir uns sprachlich verständigen.[21] Duden führt uns jedoch hinaus aus dem typischen Gebrauch, an dem wir uns orientieren, und hinein in Bedeutungsfelder, die vom Lesenden Neuorientierung angesichts der innovativen und teilweise radikalen Bedeutungsveränderungen und -erweiterungen verlangen. Das Unverständnis, das ein Text wie ‚Steinschlag' auslösen kann,[22] basiert unter anderem auf diesem innovativen und kritischen Gebrauch von Sprache außerhalb der Sprachpraxis von Massenkommunikation. Anne Dudens Metaphern sind keine sanft-poetischen Übertragungen (um beim Wortsinn von *metapherein* zu bleiben), sondern radikal-poetische ‚Steinschläge': das Herausbrechen von Elementen aus ihrer normalen Umgebung, aus der sie mit mehr oder weniger Wucht herabstürzen und dann daliegen auf neuem ungewohntem Grund. In diesem Sinne läßt sich ihr Text ‚Steinschlag' in Verbindung setzen mit Adornos Bemerkung zu hermetischer Dichtung, bei der er jedoch betont, daß die Abgeschlossenheit solcher Dichtung nicht ‚eins mit Unverständlichkeit' ist:

> Künstlerisch zu erreichen sind die Menschen überhaupt nur noch durch den
> Schock, der dem einen Schlag erteilt, was die pseudowissenschaftliche
> Ideologie Kommunikation nennt.[23]

Schon hier soll auf das verwiesen werden, was später noch genauer angesprochen werden wird: daß ‚Steinatem' – das Wort, das der Titel dieses Essays zitiert – in diesem Zusammenhang als das Dichterwort zu lesen ist und als das Produzieren und Lösen dieser schlagenden Steine.

Brüche und Risse

Der Text kombiniert einzelne Bild- und Bedeutungsbereiche derart, daß keine neuen abgeschlossenen Sinneinheiten entstehen. Vielmehr wirkt er gerade dadurch, daß seine Metaphern typische Bedeutungen aufbrechen und aus dem bekannten Kontext lösen, ohne sie jedoch in einen neuen einzufügen. Vor dem Hintergrund einer Vielfalt an Diskursen erweckt der Text so den Eindruck, nicht ‚ganz' zu sein, sondern sprunghaft, fragmentiert und zerrissen. Ein Zugang zu ihm erfordert ständige Neu- und Umorientierung vom Lesenden. Diese Charakteristika korrespondieren mit bestimmten Motivbereichen in ‚Steinschlag'. Es überwiegen Motive aus dem Wortfeld von Spaltung und Zerrissenheit. Die Topographie, die der Text beschreibt, ist zerfurcht und rissig. Auch auf anderen Ebenen läßt sich die Thematik des Zerteilten, Nicht-Ganzen nachvollziehen. Sie wird lesbar auf der Ebene des Schreibens, das nicht in ganzen, sondern in ‚Flattersätzen' vonstatten geht (S 12). Sie zeigt sich auf der Ebene der Sprache, die von Heiserkeit bedroht ist und deren Elemente wie loses Gestein zerbröckeln: ‚heisere Wortspäne zerbröselnde Silben Buchstaben' (S 15). Und sie wird deutlich auf der Ebene des konkret Körperlichen mit Verletzungen und ‚Platzwunden' (S 14). Eine Wunde ist es ja auch, die Anne Duden für das Titelbild des Bandes ausgewählt hat: die Wunde am Leibe Jesu, ein Ausschnitt aus dem Bild ‚Christus als Schmerzensmann' vom unbekannten Meister des Bartholomäus-Altares.[24] Besonders dieser Verweis auf den ‚Schmerzensmann' macht deutlich, daß die Motive des Spaltenden, Offenlegenden und Disparaten nicht nur Schmerzhaftes, sondern auch Erlösendes beinhalten. Die Wunde weist hier sowohl auf tödliche Verletzung als auch auf Hoffnung und Auferstehung; die Verletzung ist zugleich Spaltung und Versöhnungstat. In Dudens Text schafft dann auch eine Wunde Erleichterung und (wenigstens zeitweilig) Ruhe - das Blut quillt ‚*erleichtert* [...] aus den Platzwunden' (S 14, Hervorhebung: HB). Radikalisiert wird dieses paradoxe Bild der Wunde als Heilerin oder wenigstens Erleichterung Spendenden noch in der letzten

Zeile des Textes, ‚wo die Festen am Hinterkopf nur durch Genickschuß zu sprengen wären' (S 15). Der Schuß aus allernächster Nähe ins Genick eines Wehrlosen evoziert Hinrichtungen und Erschießungen von Häftlingen. Zugleich sprengt dieser Schuß jedoch auch die ‚Festen'. Dieses Wort führt uns in den Bereich von Versteinerung und Verhärtung; ‚Festen' können steinerne, befestigte Orte sein. Das Durchbrechen von fester Materie und massiven Versteinerungen ist im Text deutlich positiv konnotiert, denn Versteinerung geht mit dem, was der Text ‚Gedächtnisabtrieb' (S 12) nennt, Hand in Hand. Zu diesen Verhärtungen zählt insbesonders das ‚Zentralmassiv' (S 11), das aufgebaut von den ‚Leichtfüßigen' (S 10) massiv und erdrückend emporragt. Hierzu gehören auch die ‚Marmorplatten' (S 10), die Grabplatten auf der Erde, in die Cathy ‚vom Vater [...] gejagt gesteckt festgetreten' (S 10) wurde. ‚Betäubung', ‚Dämmerzustand', ‚Lähmung', ‚Einlullen' und ‚Tiefschlaf der Killer'(S 10) sind die Vokabeln, mit denen der Text diese Grabstätte, die vielmehr ein Wegstecken, Festtreten und ‚Gedächtnisabtrieb' ist, in Verbindung setzt.

Die Metapher ‚Gedächtnisabtrieb' ist auf das Problem deutscher Vergangenheitsbewältigung beziehbar. Die Wendung beschreibt jedoch auch das Problem eines kulturellen Gedächtnisses und damit verbunden den kritischen Blick auf das oberflächliche Leben der Wohlstandsgesellschaft, das sich ‚hinterhältig verwöhnt und feige verstohlen umsehend/ in die entgegengesetzte Richtung davonmacht' (S 12). Diese ‚entgegengesetzte Richtung' führt fort von dem, nach dem sich nur verstohlen umgesehen wird, und dies ist mehr als nur die deutsche Vergangenheit: es ist das Verdrängte, Totgeschwiegene schlechthin. Suzanne Greuner sieht, das eine – wenn sich solches sagen ließe – gegen das ‚im Grunde jeder der Texte Anne Dudens' anschreibt als das ‚ungeschriebene[...], aber alles beherrschende[...] Gesetz', das in Dudens *Judasschaf* im Satz formuliert ist: ‚Der Tod muß so schnell wie möglich unsichtbar werden.'[25] Greifen wir diese These auf und führen sie weiter, so wird deutlich, daß es bei diesem Tod nicht nur um die im Text angesprochenen Toten geht, die Opfer der Nazivernichtung oder ‚Cathy', die für so viele andere, besonders weibliche Opfer unserer Zeit steht. Vielmehr läßt ‚Tod' sich hier auf vieles beziehen, das verschwiegen oder mit nichtssagenden Phrasen totgeredet wird. Zu diesem weiteren Bereich gehört die Sprache selbst, die zum Beispiel in Werbeslogans oder mit dem ‚sprudelnde[n] Wortschatz' (S 10) der Leichtfüßigen, mundtot gemacht wird. Dieser so von der Sprachlosigkeit des Todes bedrohten Sprache wird

‚jede verbliebene Anschaulichkeit abgegraben [...]/ zwecks Ausdünnung bis Beseitigung der Metapher' (S 11). Gerade gegen diese Ausdünnung der Sprache, die letztlich zu ihrem Tod im Werbeslogan oder sprudelnden Small Talk führt, schreibt der Text an mit seinen innovativen und radikalen Metaphern. Die Ebene des Todes und der körperlichen Schmerzerfahrung und die Ebene des sprachlichen oder akustischen Ausdrucks sind dabei eng verwoben. Der Text betont diese Verknüpfung, indem sie den Körper selbst zum sprachlichen Zeichen werden läßt: ‚in der Form eines Fragezeichens die Wirbelsäule' (S 14). Die ‚zäh[en] und biegsam[en] Gerüstknöchelchen' (S 14) sind hier nicht als bloße Metonymie für das Satzzeichen zu lesen, sondern haben Anteil an beidem, dem Körperlichen und dem Sprachlichen.

Im Text sind es zwei Referenzpunkte, bei denen sich körperlicher Zerfall und Verletzung sowie der Mundtod der Sprache, das Erlöschen der Stimme miteinander verbinden. Den einen bildet das Ich im Text, auf den wir im letzten Teil dieses Essays zurückkommen werden, der andere ist Hölderlin, genauer gesagt ‚Hölderlin als Siebzigjähriger' (S 15). Das ist der Hölderlin, dem als 37jähriger von den Ärzten nur noch drei Jahre Lebenszeit gegeben werden, der aber in Tübingen im Turm am Neckar, umsorgt vom Schreinermeister Zimmer noch bis zu seinem 73. Lebensjahr lebt. Der Name Hölderlin evoziert hier einerseits den bekannten Dichter, aber andererseits auch den fragilen, alternden Menschen, als der er oft in seiner Turmzeit beschrieben wird. Der Text verweist nicht nur auf das Idealbild des göttlich begabten Poeten, sondern ruft auch den alten Dichter am Rande der Sprachlosigkeit und in einem ‚Körperrest' (S 15), der vom Verfall bedroht ist, vor Augen. Diesem 'anderen' Hölderlin gelingen in seiner Turmzeit zwar noch kleinere Texte, manchmal nur Textfetzen, von großer Anmut und Tiefe bei gleichzeitiger Klarheit, er kann aber nicht mehr die nervöse Spannung und den großen Schwung halten, die seine früheren Text prägen. Das Hölderlin-Bild ist gleichsam zwischen zwei Porträts aufgespannt: das eine ist das bekannte Pastell Hiemers (Württembergische Landesbibliothek), das den Dichter als etwa 22jährigen in zarten Farben und schön wie einen idealtypischen Apollo abbildet. Das andere zeigt ihn ein Jahr vor seinem Tod ‚starren Auges vornübergebeugt' (S 15). Dudens Beschreibung des Siebzigjährigen ruft dieses späte Bild vor Augen, das an die Bleistiftzeichnung Louise Kellers erinnert (Schiller Nationalmuseum). In ihrem Bild wird besonders der körperliche Zerfall des Dichters, welcher einhergeht mit dem Zerfall seiner Sprache, anschaulich gemacht. Es ist ein wichtiges Merkmal, daß Duden hier das

‚Gesetz' durchbricht, das sie als Diktum der ‚Leichtfüßigen' einführt und laut dem ‚jede verbliebene Anschaulichkeit abgegraben' (S 11) werden muß. Das letzte Aufbegehren dieses siebzigjährigen Körpers, der gebeutelt von den persönlichen Umständen und politischen Erfahrungen seiner Zeit und letztendlich zusammengebrochen im Turm am Neckar dahinlebt, wird in direkten kausalen Zusammenhang gesetzt mit einem letzten Aufflackern seiner früheren sprachlichen Fertigkeit: ‚nachts randalierende Zeitruine/ *damit* einmal im Gedicht im letzten Vers ABER / DIE LIEBE LIEBT' (S 15, Hervorhebung: HB).

III
‚Steinatem'

Neben Hölderlin ist der andere Referenzpunkt, an dem Körperlichkeit und Sprachlichkeit zusammenlaufen, wie so oft bei Duden, das Ich im Text. Während Hölderlin, der andere Dichter, in der mit römisch II gekennzeichneten kurzen zweiten Texthälfte im Zentrum steht, führt der lange erste Teil ein Ich an relativ später Stelle in Zeile 80 ein: ‚Unterdessen atme ich Steine' (S 11). Dieses Ich im Text steht von Anfang an in Bezug zum ‚Steinatem', und das Motiv wird in regelmäßigen Abständen je zu Anfang neuer Strophenzeilen weitergeführt: ‚atemraubend' (S 12), ‚Steinatem jetzt aus dem Bett der Durance' (S 13) und ‚Endlich Steinquadrate in Aix' (S 13).

Die beiden mit I und II gekennzeichneten Texthälften verbindet, daß sie Atem- und Sprachverlust nicht bloß beschreiben, sondern als körperliche Bedrohung nachvollziehen. Das ‚geladene[...] Gedächtnis' Hölderlins (S 15) kann sich nur im tödlichen ‚Genickschuß' und nicht mehr im Gedicht entladen; das Ich im Text wehrt sich ‚schreiend wimmernd und ausschlagend' (S 12) körperlich und stimmhaft seines Lebens. Körperlichkeit und Sprachlichkeit werden ineinsgeführt in dem Akt, der grundlegend ist sowohl für die Produktion von Sprache und akustischen Äußerungen als auch für das Leben überhaupt: dem Atmen, dem die Metapher ‚Steinatem' (S 13) eine besondere Dynamik verleiht.

Atmen können und dürfen ist existentielle Voraussetzung für Leben und zugleich elementarer Bestandteil und Medium des Artikulierens vom ersten Schrei des Säuglings bis zum letzten Atemzug. Die Topoi Artikulation und Körperlichkeit sind mit dem Atmen elementar verknüpft. In den semantischen Konnotationsbereich von Atem gehört die theologische Vorstellung von Pneuma aber auch das Gegenteil von Atmen, Maßnahmen, die mit Folter und Mord verbunden sind: knebeln und das

Maul stopfen, erdrosseln, ersticken und vergasen sind alles Methoden, um Opfer durch Entzug der Atemluft für immer stumm und mundtot zu machen. Viele solcher Verweise lassen sich in Dudens weiterem Werk finden. Ein prominentes Beispiel ist der zertrümmerte und zugedrahtete Mund in *Übergang*.

Atmen wird in ‚Steinschlag' jedoch auch als Vorgang deutlich, dem das Ich nicht entkommen kann – wenigstens nicht so lange es lebt. Dem Ich gelingt es nicht, ‚gestisch anmutig' Luft zu holen (S 10) wie die ‚Leichtfüßigen', die in der Kombination der Wendungen ‚sich etwas holen' und ‚Luft holen' ihren Besitzanspruch auf Luft verdeutlichen: ‚die Leichtfüßigen [...] holen sich Luft/ gestisch anmutig' (S 10). Im Falle des Ich ist es vielmehr umgekehrt der Atem, der sich die Person holt. In Anlehnung an die Phrase ‚den holt sich der Tod' (oder auch der Teufel) heißt es vom Ich: es ‚holt mich der Atem schlagartig' (S 13). Von Ruhe ist einige Zeilen vorher nur die Rede in Zusammenhang mit der Abwesenheit vom stetigen Ein und Aus des Atmens, das den Tod antizipiert, im Wort ‚atemraubend' (S 12). Atmen ist Notwendigkeit, zugleich aber auch Anstrengung, wenigstens bei jenen, die sich im Gegensatz zu den ‚Leichtfüßigen' ‚Gedanken [...] machen' (S 11).

Neben den Verweisen auf den Atem finden wir auch viele Verweise auf die andere Wortkomponente in ‚Steinatem', den Stein. Oben wurde bereits auf die zentrale Metaphorik von ‚Steinschlag' hingewiesen sowohl als sprachliche Vorgehensweise des Herauslösens von Elementen aus ihrem Kontext als auch als Motivbereich. Das Wortfeld ‚Stein' nimmt einen weiten Bedeutungsraum im Text ein. Einerseits umfaßt es massive Versteinerungen wie das ‚Zentralmassiv' (S 11) und das Erdrückende marmorner Grabplatten; beides steht in Zusammenhang mit dem Verdrängen der Vergangenheit und ihrem Zum-verstummen-Bringen, gegen das der Text angeht. Andererseits liegt im ‚Stein*schlag*' (Hervorhebung: HB), im Aufschlagen von kleineren Steinen auf solche versteinerten Flächen, die Möglichkeit, diese zu durchbrechen. Diese durchschlagende Wirkkraft des Steins ist jedoch im Text immer eng mit schmerzhaften körperlichen Erfahrungen verbunden: Das ‚Aufmerken' (S 8) der versteinerten Fläche der Autobahn ist ein ‚Aufschluchzen' (S 8). ‚[A]uf die Härte des Pflasters zu' (S 11) fällt nicht der Stein, sondern das Ich, dessen Körper dabei zu zerschmettern droht.

‚Steinatem' evoziert das Bild vom Stein im Mund und davon, mit diesem geknebelt zu werden, und in diesem Zusammenhang versinnbildlicht es die Gefahr nicht atmen und sprechen zu können und den

Erstickungstod. ‚Steinatem' kann als gewaltsames Eintreten von Steinen durch den Mund in den Körper gelesen werden. Es läßt sich verbinden mit der ‚täglichen Portion[...] Henkersmahlzeit/ aus Fliegenpilz Schotter und geschrotetem Schwermetall' (S 11). Das Einatmen von Steinen deutet hin auf das schmerzhafte Nach-innen-Nehmen von etwas, das den Atmenden beschwert, zu Fall bringt und von den ‚Leichtfüßigen' unterscheidet. Dem Prozeß des Atmens folgend kann ‚Steinatem' jedoch auch als Ausatmen von Steinen gelesen werden, als ihr Austreten aus dem Mund, das auch als das Hervorbringen des Wortes gelesen werden kann. Hier könnte der Stein im Mund auch für das Schulen des Sprechens stehen, wie bei dem antiken Sänger und Rhetoriker Demosthenes, der mit einem Stein im Mund gegen die Brandung anbrüllte, um so sein Stottern zu überwinden und seine Artikulation zu schulen. Dieses Sprechen ist im Text jedoch nicht ‚sprudelnde[r] Wortschatz' (S 10), sondern das unter Schmerzen hervorgebrachte Klagewort.[26]

Steine und steinerne Materie sind wichtige Topoi bei vielen AutorInnen jüngerer Dichtung. Monika Schmitz-Emans liefert in ihrer Studie *Poesie als Dialog*, in der sie neben Jean Paul auf Ernst Jandl und besonders auf Paul Celan eingeht, ein Beispiel für die Analyse dieses Themas.[27] Sie verweist auf Otto Pöggelers Wort, daß der Dichter nach Auschwitz ‚Steine spucken' müsse:

> Das Gedicht kann seinem Autor vom Herzen fallen wie ein Stein. Es sind für Celan vor allem [...] der Holocaust und seine Folgen, welche zu einer Versteinerung von Entsetzen führten und nun als Steine auf dem Herzen liegen. Solche Steine durch (poetische) Artikulation loszuwerden, wäre Ausdruck einer Befreiung.[28]

Diese Deutung des Steine-Spuckens in Zusammenhang mit einer wenn nicht Überwindung, dann doch wenigstens Artikulation des versteinerten Schmerzes über die jüngere deutsche Geschichte, paßt in den bereits angesprochenen Kontext des Klage-Liedes bei Anne Duden. Das Speien von Steinen kann dabei jedoch auch ein Zeichen von Wehrhaftigkeit sein, das Steinespucken ein Anspucken, die Klage eine Anklage.

Des weiteren betont Schmitz-Emans die ‚tiefe Ambivalenz' von Steinen als Metaphern mit sowohl positiven als auch negativen Konnotationen.

> Den mit ihnen als harter, kalter und lebloser Materie verbundenen negativen Konnotationen steht als Positivum ihre [...] Dauerhaftigkeit gegenüber. Steine sind ein ‚Grund', auf dem man stehen oder liegen kann, aber ein harter und kalter Grund. [...] Aus Steinen werden Häuser aber auch Grabstätten gebaut.

[...] Man kann jemanden steinigen, ihm aber auch mittels steinerner Anker einen Halt in seiner Bodenlosigkeit zu verschaffen suchen.[29]

Eine solche Ambivalenz, die sich durch Verweise auf Volksglauben und Märchen noch weiter fortsetzen ließe, liegt auch im Zentrum von Dudens ‚Steinatem'. Die Gefahr der Versteinerung von Wirklichkeit und die Möglichkeit ihrer sprachlichen Lösung stecken in dieser Metapher und der mit ihr korrespondierenden Wendung ‚Steinschlag'. In ‚Steinatem' liegen Verweise auf Gebirge aber auch auf den 'langen Atem', ‚unter den Gebirgen' aufzustehen (S 11). Es gibt das Versprechen von Ruhe, die der ‚Steinatem [...] aus dem *Bett* der Durance' verheißt (S 13, Hervorhebung: HB), zugleich aber auch das Reißende und Gefährliche der Wasserführung dieses Stroms. Der 'Stein' kann die Möglichkeit des Überlebens und Zuhauseseins versprechens in Häusern, die als ‚Steinquadrate in Aix' (S 13) lesbar werden; zugleich lassen sich letztere aber auch als viereckige Steinsärge und Grabkammern lesen.

Stagnieren und Randalieren, beides steckt im Stein, und dieses Gegensatzpaar führt uns zum anderen Dichter im Text, zu Hölderlin, mit dem der Text abschließt. Das ‚starre[...] Auge[...]' Hölderlins verweist auf die Gefahr des körperlichen und geistigen Stagnierens, des Verstummens und Versteinerns. Die ‚einwärts geschlagene[...] Blickrichtung' (S 15) korrespondiert mit den Worten, die ‚sich nach innen [krümmen]/ und [...] gebückt in den Verstorbenen [stecken]' (S 7). Sie deutet auf die Gefahr hin, daß nichts mehr von innen nach außen gelangt. Die ‚Schlacke mit geladenem Gedächtnis' (S 15) kann sich nicht entladen und droht zu erkalten und zu verhärten, so wie zu Anfang des Textes das Ekstatische ‚erkaltet verhärte[t]' (S 9). Mit dem Wort ‚Schlacke' führt der Hölderlin-Schluß zurück zum Anfang. Schlacke[30] kann die harte, poröse und steinartige Masse bezeichnen, die ein Verbrennungsprozeß (insbesonders von Steinkohle) hinterläßt. Einerseits verweist ‚Schlacke mit geladenem Gedächtnis' auf den ‚ausgebrannten' Hölderlin in der Isolation im Turm am Neckar, andererseits deutet dieser Verbrennungsrückstand auch auf die Brennöfen der Vernichtungslager hin und den ‚braunkohlenfarbene[n] Engel' des Textanfangs (S 8). Das Wort Schlacke führt auch zur Motivkette der Versteinerungen zurück: zu Cathys marmorner Grabplatte und dem von den ‚Leichtfüßigen' errichteten Zentralmassiv, zum Bereich des Verdrängten, Vergessenen, Versteinerten.

In seiner *Ästhetischen Theorie* greift Adorno den Topos des Steins auf in seinen Bemerkungen zur Lyrik Paul Celans:

[Die] Gedichte wollen das äußerste Entsetzen durch Verschweigen sagen [...] Sie ahmen eine Sprache unterhalb der hilflosen der Menschen, ja aller organischen nach, die des Toten von Stein und Stern. Beseitigt werden die letzten Rudimente des Organischen.[31]

Anne Dudens ‚Steinschlag' zeigt vergleichbare Übergänge ins Anorganische, Versteinerte, Verhärtete, dem jedoch das Organische als schmerzlich Körperhaftes entgegen- und ausgesetzt ist: im Bild der gewaltsam ‚aus dem steinernen Karree mit den schweren Eisentoren' Getriebenen (S 7), im Bild des unter Marmorplatten begrabenen weiblichen Körpers (S 10), des auf den ‚Steinspiegel' auftreffenden Leibes (S 11) und im Bild des Genickschusses, der zugleich die steinernen Festen und den menschlichen Hinterkopf sprengt (S 15).

Anmerkungen

[1] *Duden. Deutsches Universalwörterbuch A-Z.* Hg. und bearbeitet vom Wissenschaftlichen Rat und den Mitarbeitern der Dudenredaktion unter der Leitung von G. Drosdowski. Dudenverlag: Mannheim, Wien, Zürich, 1989², S. 1461.

[2] Ich bitte im folgenden bei der Verwendung der männlichen grammatikalischen Form, immer die weibliche mitzulesen.

[3] Paul Cézanne: ‚Der Steinbruch Bibémus', 1898-1900. Öl auf Leinwand, 65 x 81 cm. Essen, Museum Folkwang.

[4] Vergl. Claudia Roths Interpretation dieses ‚Namen[s] aus der politischen Geographie' in ihrem Beitrag zu diesem Band.

[5] Neben der thematischen Evokation von ‚Engführung' und ‚Todesfuge' lassen sich andere mögliche Verweise auf Paul Celan im Text finden, zum Beispiel in den Wendungen ‚Steinschlag' und ‚Steinatem', die auch in Celans späten Zyklen ‚Schneepart' und ‚Atemwende' auftauchen. (Paul Celan, Gedichte in zwei Bänden, Suhrkamp: Frankfurt a.M., 1987, Bd. II, S. 400, S. 70.) Diese Wendungen, die auf Celan mitverweisen können – nicht müssen – sind, im Gegensatz zu den Hölderlinzitaten, jedoch nicht im Text als Zitate oder intertextuelle Elemente ausgewiesen. Im Rahmen dieses Essays wird auf Celan-Spuren in ‚Steinschlag' nicht weiter eingegangen. Dieses Thema würde jedoch viel Material zu einer umfassenden Studie liefern, zu der Georgina Pauls Beitrag in diesem Band bereits grundlegende Ideen liefert.

⁶ Peter Szondi, *Celan-Studien*, Suhrkamp: Frankfurt a.M., 1972, S. 102-103: ‚Nach Auschwitz ist kein Gedicht mehr möglich, es sei denn auf Grund von Auschwitz.' Zur weiteren Diskussion der These Adornos in der jüngsten Forschung siehe Günter Bonheim, *Versuch zu zeigen, dass Adorno mit seiner Behauptung , nach Auschwitz lasse sich kein Gedicht mehr schreiben, recht hatte*. Königshausen & Neumann: Würzburg, 2002.

⁷ Vergl. Claudia Roths Lesart des Wortes als ‚Verweigerung' in diesem Band.

⁸ Vergl. Georgina Paul, die in ihrem Beitrag zu diesem Band das Wort ‚Strumpfhosenproduktion' (S 7) als Verweis auf (Frauen-)Gefängnisse der DDR liest und diese als ein Eckdatum in den historischen Entwicklungsprozeß moderner Industriegesellschaft zwischen ‚Arbeitslager' und moderner Produktion stellt.

⁹ Es sei hier auf Suzanne Greuners Studie *Schmerzton: Musik in der Schreibweise von Ingeborg Bachmann und Anne Duden*, Argument: Hamburg, 1990, verwiesen, in deren Zentrum die Bedeutung von Musik in Werken beider Autorinnen steht.

¹⁰ Winfried Menninghaus, *Paul Celan: Magie der Form*, Suhrkamp: Frankfurt a.M, 1980, S. 18.

¹¹ Vergl. Dirk Göttsches Beitrag in diesem Band.

¹² Der Begriff ‚kulturelles Gedächtnis' im Zusammenhang von Dudens Texten entstammt Franziska Frei Gerlachs Studie *Schrift und Geschlecht: feministische Entwürfe und Lektüren von Marlen Haushofer, Ingeborg Bachmann und Anne Duden*, Erich Schmidt: Berlin, 1998, S. 310.

¹³ Ebd., S. 312.

¹⁴ Sigrid Weigel, ‚Vorwort', in: *Suzanne Studie Schmerzton: Musik in der Schreibweise von Ingeborg Bachmann und Anne Duden*, Argument: Hamburg, 1990, 4-6 (hier: S. 4).

¹⁵ Deutlichere Verweise auf Rosa Luxemburg und ihren Tod macht Duden beispielsweise in *Übergang* ($Ü^2$ 42).

¹⁶ In einem kürzeren Gedicht Hölderlins mit dem Titel ‚Vulkan', geschrieben im Winter 1803/1804 nach dem Tod Susette Gontards und seiner Rückreise aus Bordeaux, die ihn völlig erschöpft ins heimatliche Nürtingen zurückführte, lauten die letzten Zeilen: ‚Und immer wohnt der freundlichen Genien/ Noch Einer gerne seegnend mit ihm, und wenn/ Sie zürnten all', die ungelehrgen/ Geniuskräfte, doch liebt die Liebe.' Friedrich Hölderlin, *Sämtliche Werke*, 8 Bde, hg. v. Friedrich Beissner und Adolf Beck, Kohlhammer: Stuttgart, 1946-1985, Bd 2.1, S. 61. Unter dem Titel ‚An Zimmern' finden sich zwei Texte in Hölderlins Spätwerk: ‚Die Linien des Lebens [...]' (Bd. 2.1, S. 268) und ‚Von einem Menschen sag ich [...]' (Bd. 2.1., S. 271).

[17] Eine solche Verschleierungstaktik findet sich auch bei Ausdrücken der Nazipropaganda wie beim Euphemismus Arbeits- für Vernichtungslager.

[18] Vergleich Juliet Wigmores Beitrag in diesem Band und ihre Analyse der Pflanzen im Text ‚Wildwuchs' in *Zungengewahrsam*.

[19] Rolf Zuberbühler, ‚Etymologie bei Goethe und Hölderlin', in: *Hölderlin ohne Mythos,* Ingrid Riedel, Hg., Vandenhoeck & Ruprecht: Göttingen, 1973, S. 44.

[20] *Kluge. Etymologisches Wörterbuch*, de Gruyter: Berlin, [16]1960, S. 339.

[21] Diese Ausführungen zur Metapher sind weder neu noch allein auf Anne Duden zu beziehen. Vergl. Gerhard Kurz, *Metapher Allegorie, Symbol*, Vandenhoeck & Ruprecht: Göttingen, [2]1988. Heinrich Lausberg, *Elemente der literarischen Rhetorik*, Max Hueber: Ismaning, [10]1990.

[22] Siehe die Beiträge von Claudia Roth und Georgina Paul, die sich mit Kritiken zu ‚Steinschlag' auseinandersetzen.

[23] Theodor W. Adorno, *Ästhetische Theorie*, Suhrkamp: Frankfurt a.M., 1970, S. 476.

[24] Wiebke Sievers weist in ihrem Beitrag zu diesem Band auf die Verbindung von dieser Wunde zum ‚Trümmermund' in *Übergang* hin, für dessen Umschlag in der englischen Fassung Duden dasselbe Bild gewählt hat.

[25] Suzanne Greuner, *Schmerzton: Musik in der Schreibweise von Ingeborg Bachmann und Anne Duden*, S. 119.

[26] In einem Text, in dem ‚auferstehen' eine wichtige Vokabel ist, kann der Stein in der Mundhöhle auch als Stein vor der Grabkammer Christi gelesen werden, den die beiden Marien als Zeichen der Auferstehung Christi fortgerollt finden, einer Auferstehung jedoch, die über Leiden und Schmerz erfolgt.

[27] Monika Schmitz-Emans, *Poesie als Dialog. Vergleichende Studien zu Paul Celan und seinem literarischen Umfeld*, Winter: Heidelberg, 1993, S. 18 ff.

[28] Ebd., S. 24.

[29] Ebd., S. 18.

[30] Bei Hölderlin selbst kommt die ‚Schlacke' in seinem Gedicht ‚Der gefesselte Strom' vor als Metapher für den Stromgeist / Dichter, der sich aus Stagnation zu neuem Leben zu befreien sucht.

[31] Theodor W. Adorno, *Ästhetische Theorie*, S. 477.

Bibliography

Texts by Anne Duden discussed in this volume

Übergang, Rotbuch: Hamburg, 1982, second edition 1996.

Das Judasschaf, Rotbuch: Hamburg, 1985, second edition 1997.

Steinschlag, Kiepenheuer & Witsch: Cologne, 1993.

Der wunde Punkt im Alphabet, Rotbuch: Hamburg, 1995, second edition 1996.

Wimpertier, Kiepenheuer & Witsch: Köln, 1995, second edition 1997.

Zungengewahrsam. Kleine Schriften zur Poetik und zur Kunst, Kiepenheuer & Witsch: Cologne, 1999.

'Vom Versprechen des Schreibens und vom Schreiben des Versprechens', in: Heinz Ludwig Arnold, ed., Robert Gernhardt, Peter Waterhouse, Anne Duden, *Lobreden auf den poetischen Satz,* Wallstein: Göttingen, (Göttinger Sudelblätter), 1998, 37-45.

Hingegend. Gedichte. Zu Klampen: Lüneburg, 1999, second edition 2001.

'Ausgehend von Liegenden', in: Wolfgang Kemp et al, eds, *Vorträge aus dem Warburg-Haus,* Band 4, Akademie Verlag: Berlin, 2000, 37-64.

'A mon seul desir', in: Heinz Ludwig Arnold, ed., Lutz Seiler, Anne Duden, Farhad Showgi, *Heimaten,* Wallstein: Göttingen, (Göttinger Sudelblätter), 2001, 29-37.

Interviews

Anne Duden, Claudia Kramatschek, 'In den Faltungen der Sprache', *Neue deutsche Literatur 48* (2, 2000), 32-44.

Anne Duden in Translation

Anne Duden, *Opening of the Mouth,* übers. von Della Couling, Pluto Press: London, Leichhardt, 1985.

Anne Duden, *Traversée*, übers. von Pierre Furlan und Dominique Jallamion, Alinéa: Aix-en-Provence, 1987.

Secondary Texts on Anne Duden's works

Leslie Adelson, 'Anne Duden's *Übergang*. Racism and Feminist Aesthetics. A Provocation', in: Leslie Adelson, *Making Bodies, Making History. Feminism and German Identity*, University of Nebraska Press: Lincoln, London, 1993, 37-55.

Stephanie Bird, 'Desire and Complicity in Anne Duden's *Das Judasschaf*, *Modern Language Review*, 93 (3/1998), 741-53.

Joanna Bossinade, 'Original Differentiation. The Poetics of Anne Duden', in: Chris Weedon, ed., *Post-war Women's Writing in German: Feminist Critical Approaches*, Berghahn: Providence, R.I. and Oxford, 1997, 131-55.

Margret Brügmann, 'Das gläserne Ich. Überlegungen zum Verhältnis von Frauenliteratur und Postmoderne am Beispiel von Anne Dudens *Das Judasschaf*, in: Mona Knapp, Gerd Labroisse, eds, *Frauen-Fragen in der deutschsprachigen Literatur seit 1945 (Amsterdamer Beiträge zur Neueren Germanistik 29)*, Rodopi: Amsterdam, Atlanta, 1989, 253-272.

Elsbeth Dangel, 'Übergang und Ankunft. Positionen neuerer Frauenliteratur. Zu Anne Dudens *Übergang* und Verena Stefans *Wortgetreu ich träume*', *Jahrbuch für Internationale Germanistik*, 22 (2/1990), 80-94.

Franziska Frei Gerlach, *Schrift und Geschlecht. Feministische Entwürfe und Lektüren von Marlen Haushofer, Ingeborg Bachmann und Anne Duden*, Erich Schmidt: Berlin, 1998.

Andrea Geier, 'Unterminierte Apokalypse. *Michel, sag ich* von Ulla Berkéwicz und *Übergang* von Anne Duden', in: Verena Lobsien, Maria Moog-Grünewald, eds, *Apokalypse. Der Anfang im Ende*, Heidelberg, forthcoming.

Suzanne Greuner, *Schmerzton. Musik in der Schreibweise von Ingeborg Bachmann und Anne Duden (Argument-Sonderband 179)*, Argument: Hamburg, 1990.

Brigid Haines and Margaret Littler, *Contemporary Women's Writing in German. Feminist Perspectives*, Oxford University Press: Oxford, forthcoming

Margaret Littler, 'Diverging trends in feminine aesthetics: Anne Duden and Brigitte Kronauer', in: Arthur Williams, Stuart Parkes and Julian Preece, eds, *Contemporary German Writers, their Aesthetics and their Language*, Peter Lang: Berne, 1996, 161-180.

Annette Meusinger, 'The Wired Mouth: On the Positionality of Perception in Anne Duden's *Opening of the Mouth* and *Das Judasschaf*', *Women in German Yearbook*, 13 (1997), 189-203.

Georgina Paul, '"Life-writing": Reading the Work of Anne Duden Through Virginia Woolf's "A Sketch of the Past"', in: Mererid Puw Davies, Beth Linklater, eds, *Autobiography by Women in German*, Peter Lang: Oxford, Berne, Berlin, Bruxelles, Frankfurt a.M., New York, Vienna, 2000, 291-305.

Anne-Kathrin Reulecke, 'Anne Duden', in: *Kritisches Lexikon zur deutschprachigen Literatur der Gegenwart,* Text und Kritik: Berlin, 1995.

Ricarda Schmidt, 'Arbeit an weiblicher Subjektivität. Erzählende Prosa der siebziger und achtziger Jahre', in: Gisela Brinker-Gabler, ed., *Deutsche Literatur von Frauen, 2, 19. und 20. Jahrhundert*, Beck: Munich, 1988, 459-477.

Sigrid Weigel, *Die Stimme der Medusa. Schreibweisen in der Gegenwartsliteratur von Frauen,* tende: Dülmen-Hiddingsel, 1987.

Newspaper reviews of *Steinschlag*

Corina Caduff, 'Schmerzenssprache', *Die Wochenzeitung,* 25.6.1993.

Bertram Bock, 'Vom Wortstein erschlagen', *Hessische/Niedersächsische Allgemeine*, 10.10.1993.

Michael Braun, 'Leidensfrau', *Die Woche,* 25.3.1993.

Michael Braun, 'Letztendlich absolute Poesie?', *Basler Zeitung,* 20.5.1993.

Christa Kaufmann, 'Anne Dudens *Steinschlag*. Ein anderes Leben aus dem Getöteten', *Luzerner Neuste Nachrichten,* 4.11.1993.

Kathrin Reulecke, 'review', *Rundbrief Frauen in der Literaturwissenschaft 40,* Februar 1994.

Uta Runge, 'Mennigrot in kleinsten Portionen. Zum *Steinschlag* von Anne Duden', *die tageszeitung,* 22.4.1993.

Albert von Schirnding, 'Zusammenbruch eines Immunsystems', *Süddeutsche Zeitung,* 31.3.1993.

Leonore Schwartz, 'Gesang aus der Tiefe', *Der Tagesspiegel,* 23.5.1993.

Uwe Schweikert, '"Schlacke mit geladenem Gedächtnis": Die absolute Poesie der Anne Duden', *Frankfurter Rundschau*, 24.4.1993.

Anke Westphal, 'Das absolute Gehör des Schmerzes', *Neue Zeit*, 21.7.1993.

Index

Adelson, Leslie, 58, 95, 120
Adorno, Theodor W., 6, 19, 32, 34-6, 36, 73, 77, 142, 171-2, 178-9, 180
Agatha, 15
Albertus Magnus, 99
Altdorfer, Albrecht, 3, 96f., 98, 99, 137
Anderson, Benedict, 155
Arnim, Achim von, 21, 23
Artaud, Antonin, 46, 51f., 53, 60
Baader, Andreas 2
Bach, Johann Sebastian, 110
Bachelard, Gaston, 9
Bachmann, Ingeborg, 22, 28, 39, 124
Baldwin, Claire, 93
Barthes, Roland 6, 7
Bartolomäus-Altares, Meister des, 172
Bataille, Georges, 46
Battersby, Christine, 50, 52, 57, 60, 77, 86
Baudelaire, Charles, 9, 17
Benjamin, Walter, 19, 20, 34, 102, 124, 146
Bird, Stephanie, 43, 57f., 60
Blanckenburg, Christian Friedrich von, 33
Bloch, Ernst, 34
Bonheim, Günter, 180
Bossinade, Joanna, 86
Bovenschen, Silvia, 156
Buback, Siegfried 2
Caduff, Corinna, 149
Carpaccio, Vittore 3, 10, 140, 144
Caruth, Cathy, 58
Catherine of Sienna 5
Celan, Paul, 7, 123, 124, 125, 133, 141-2, 145, 161, 162, 163, 167, 169, 177, 178-9
Cézanne, Paul 4, 55, 145, 160
Chvatík, Krestoslav, 22
Cixous, Hélène, 21
Conrady, Karl Otto, 154, 155
Couling, Della, 104
Dangel, Elsbeth, 57

Dauthendey, Max, 23
Deleuze, Gilles, 80f., 87
Demosthenes, 177
Derrida, Jacques, 21, 86, 102, 120, 122
Droste-Hülshoff, Annette von, 13
Dubcek, Alexander, 156

Duden, Anne:
  'A mon seul désir' 4, 7, **8-10**
  'Ausgehend von Liegenden' 3
  Das Judasschaf 3, 5, 6, 10, 19, 23, 34, 60f., 62, 64, 70, **73-80**, 93, 104, 124, 140, 173
  Der wunde Punkt im Alphabet 3, 28, 58
    'Das schöne Leben', 29; 'Der wunde Punkt im Alphabet'; 'Gegenstrebige Fügung', 112, 121; 'Im verlorenen Ton', 24f.; 'I wish you well', 38f.; 'Paläontographie', 28f.; 'Umwege', 38f.
  Hingegend 4, 5, **8-18**, 48
  Steinschlag 3, 4, 5, 6, 8, 24, 48, 51, 108, **123-48**, **149-58**, **159-81**
  Übergang 2, 3, 5, 7, 34, **43-9**, 51, 62, 63, 70, 73, 74, 95, 103, **104-9**, 117, 176
    'Das Landhaus', 65, 68, 82, **88-93**, 95, 106, 129-30; 'Der Auftrag der Liebe', 63, 186; 'Die Kunst zu ertrinken', 106; 'Herz und Mund', 63f., 72, 73, 103, 105, **109-16**, 117; 'On Holiday', 64, **81-3**; 'Tag und Nacht', 63, 74f.; 'Übergang', 8, **44-9**, 50, 53, 54, 62, 106f.
  'Vom Versprechen des Schreibens und vom Schreiben des Versprechens', 4, **6-8**, 9, 10
  Wimpertier 3, 5, 24, 44, 48, 62
    'Arbeitsgänge', **52-6**, 65; 'Arbeitsplätze'; 'Chemische Reaktion', 62, 63, 65, 68, 69; 'Die Jagd nach schönen

Gefühlen', 68; 'Fancy Calling It Good Friday', 33, 69; 'Fassungskraft mit Herzweh'; ''Fleischlaß', 64, 68, 69; 'Krebsgang', **31-3**; 'Wimpertier', **27f.**, 31, 64, 65, 69
Zungengewahrsam, 4, 8, 20, 35, 73, 88, 93, 96, 100, 129, 147
'Die Dinge sind dem Raum geneigt', **37f.**; 'Unter einem Dach', **36f.**, **94f**, 96, 99.; 'Vergittert im Gefilde', 38, **83-5**; 'Wildwuchs', **96-100**; 'Zungengewahrsam. Erkundigungen einer Schreibexistenz', 1, **19-23**, 44, **49-53**, 66, 69f., 123-4, 144

Dürer, Albrecht, 146
Eliot, T. S., 7, 124, 125-6, 133, 141
Elsaghe, Yahya, 156
Ensslin, Gudrun 2
Eyck, Jan van, 16
Fallaize, Elizabeth, 119
Felman, Shoshana, 44
Fernie, Eric, 100
Fink, Bruce, 60
Foucault, Michel, 29
Fouché, Pascal, 119
Fraser, Kathleen, 126
Frei Gerlach, Franziska, 40, 121, 124, 144, 164
Freud, Sigmund, 51, 58, 86
Fried, Erich, 2, 65, 66, 70
Fritz, Walter Helmut, 23
Fülleborn, Ulrich, 40
Furlans, Pierre, 104
Gardner, Helen, 125-6
Geier, Andrea, 120
Goethe, Johann Wolfgang von 4, 13, 14, 17, 23, 94
Gogh, Vincent van, 108
Goya, Francesco de, 32
Graf, Marion, 118
Greuner, Suzanne, 40, 118, 165, 173
Grosz, Elizabeth, 46

Haller, Jost, 147
Haushofer, Marlen
Heine, Heinrich, 17
Hölderlin, Friedrich, 7, 22, 124, 130, 134, 141, 154, 156, 160, 161, 162, 164, 166, 167, 170, 174-5, 178, 180
Horkheimer, Max, 32, 73, 77
Irigaray, Luce, 74, 77
Jallamions, Dominique, 104
Jandl, Ernst, 177
Janzen, Reinhild, 99
Julian of Norwich, 141
Kachold, Gabriele, 145
Kafka, Franz, 6, 24, 27, 28
Kant, Immanuel, 66, 86
Kaschnitz, Marie Luise, 24, 28, 29f., 31
Kaufmann, Christa, 149
Keller, Louise, 174
Kramatschek, Claudia, 60, 61, 87, 118
Kraus, Petra, 155-6
Kristeva, Julia, 21, 44, 46-8, 50, 52, 57, 59
Lacan, Jacques, 29, 43, 58
Lang, Fritz, 91
Langland, William, 147
Lessing, Gotthold Ephraim, 21
Lévi Strauss, Claude, 100
Levinas, Emmanuel, 6, 49, 50, 66f., 68f.
Littler, Margaret, 59
Luther, Martin, 110
Luxemburg, Rosa, 111, 112, 166
Mallarmé, Stéphane
McGonigall, William, 14, 17
Menninghaus, Winfried, 163
Merleau-Ponty, Maurice, 37, 103
Meschonnic, Henri, 121
Mitcherlich, Alexander and Margaret, 29
Mörike, Eduard, 13
Müller, Filip, 55f., 60
Musil, Robert, 19, 20, 34
Novalis, 21, 23
Paracelsus, 99
Paul, Georgina, 119
Phelan, Anthony, 148

Index

Pindar, 165
Poethen, Johannes, 23
Pöggeler, Otto, 177
Ponto, Jürgen, 2
Raselius, Andreas, 96
Raspe, Jan-Carl 2
Reulecke, Anne-Kathrin, 100, 146-7
Richter, Jean Paul, 177
Rilke, Rainer Maria, 124, 134, 142, 143
Robinson, Douglas, 122
Runge, Uta, 149, 157
Samuels, Clarise, 144
Schama, Simon, 101
Schelkle, Karl Hermann, 121
Schiebinger, Lorna, 100
Schirnding, Albert von, 143, 144, 146
Schlegel, Friedrich, 163
Schleyer, Hanns Martin 2
Schmidt, Ricarda, 57
Schmitz-Emans, Monika, 177-8

Schweikert, Uwe, 81, 83, 87, 121, 143, 147
Steinbach, Erwin von, 94
Stevens, Wallace, 126
Strauß, Botho, 30
Szondi, Peter, 125, 162, 180
Tacitus, 96
Tallis, Thomas, 129
Trakl, Georg, 23, 28
Venuti, Lawrence, 118
Walburga, 15, 18
Waldenfels, Bernhard, 103, 118
Wallis, Clea 4, 38, 83
Walser, Robert, 19, 20, 34
Weigel, Sigrid, 57, 120, 146, 165
Weiss, Peter, 129
Wieland, Cristoph Martin, 23
Winkel, Hubert, 120
Wittgenstein, Ludwig, 66, 70f.
Wood, Christopher, 97
Zuberbühler, Rolf, 17

Notes on Contributors

Heike Bartel is lecturer in German at the University of Nottingham. She studied German and Philosophy at the Universities of Bonn and Oxford and was a DAAD-Lektorin at the University of Bristol. She has worked and published on Friedrich Hölderlin, Goethe, Mythology and Paul Celan. Her monograph on Hölderlin was published in 2000 (Würzburg: Königshausen & Neumann).

Stephanie Bird is lecturer in German at University College London. Her research interests include narrative fiction, the interaction of history and fiction, female and national identity and narrative ethics. Her first book *Recasting Historical Women. Female Identity in German Biographical Fiction* was published by Berg in 1998, and her forthcoming book, *Women Writers and National Identity: Ingeborg Bachmann, Anne Duden, Emine Özdamar* will be published by CUP in 2003.

Elizabeth Boa is Emeritus Professor of German at the University of Nottingham. She has published books on Wedekind and Kafka, as well as a study of Heimat discourse between 1890-1990 (co-author Rachel Palfreyman) and numerous articles on German literature from the eighteenth century to the present. She was co-editor (with Janet Wharton) of *Women and the Wende* (German Monitor 31, Amsterdam, Rodopi, 1994).

Dirk Göttsche is Reader in German at the University of Nottingham. He has published books on the 'language crisis' in modern prose, on the Social Novel (Zeitroman) and on Wilhelm Raabe and numerous articles on German literature from the eighteenth century to the present. He is co-editor (with Monika Albrecht) of the critical edition of Ingeborg Bachmann's *Todesarten* (Munich: Piper 1995) and of the *Bachmann-Handbuch* (Stuttgart: Metzler 2002).

Margaret Littler is Senior Lecturer in German at the University of Manchester. She is editor of *Gendering German Studies* (Blackwell 1997) and has published mainly on post-1945 women's writing. Her current research interests include German literature by writers of Turkish origin.

Notes on Contributors

Teresa Ludden lectures part-time in German language and literature at the University of Warwick. She has just completed a doctoral thesis on Anne Duden entitled 'Kulturkritik and the Representation of Difference in the Work of Anne Duden'.

Georgina Paul is Lecturer in German Studies at the University of Warwick. She has published on a range of aspects of contemporary German literature, including articles on Christa Wolf and on gender issues. She is co-editor (with Helmut Schmitz) of *Entgegenkommen: Dialogues with Barbara Köhler* (German Monitor 48, Amsterdam: Rodopi, 2000).

Claudia Roth is based at the Institut für Germanistik at the University of Berne, Schwitzerland where she is writing on a doctoral thesis on the work of Anne Duden.

Wiebke Sievers works in the Department of Modern English at the Heinrich Heine University, Düsseldorf, where she studied literary translation. After her studies, she spent four years as DAAD-Lektorin at the University of Nottingham and is currently working on a doctoral thesis for the University of Warwick on the translation of contemporary German prose into English and French. Her publications include translations from and into English and a reader of materials for teaching translation.

Juliet Wigmore is Senior Lecturer in German at the University of Salford. Her research focuses mainly on women's writing in German since 1970 and contemporary Austrian literature. She has published on Elfriede Jelinek, Elisabeth Reichart, Ingeborg Bachmann and Peter Handke.

www.ingramcontent.com/pod-product-compliance
Lightning Source LLC
Chambersburg PA
CBHW020649300426
44112CB00007B/307